Talking with African Writers

INTERVIEWS WITH AFRICAN POETS PLAYWRIGHTS & NOVELISTS

Edited by

JANE WILKINSON

University of Rome
'La Sapienza'

JAMES CURREY • LONDON
HEINEMANN • PORTSMOUTH (N.H.)

James Currey Ltd
54b Thornhill Square, Islington
London N1 1BE

Heinemann Educational Books Inc
361 Hanover Street
Portsmouth, New Hampshire 03801

Published by James Currey in a limited edition with
Bagatto Libri Soc. Coop a.r.1. Roma 1990
First published in this edition 1992

92 93 94 95 96 5 4 3 2 1

British Library Cataloguing in Publication Data

Talking with African writers : interviews with
African poets, playwrights & novelists.
I. Wilkinson, Jane
896

ISBN 0-85255-529-6 pbk

Library of Congress Cataloging-in-Publication Data
Talking with African writers: interviews with African poets,
playwrights & novelists/edited by Jane Wilkinson.
p. cm.—(Studies in African literature. New series)
Includes bibliographical references.
ISBN 0-435-08065-2
1. African literature (English)—History and criticism.
2. Authors. African—20th century—Interviews.   I. Wilkinson, Jane.
II. Series.
PR9340, T35   1992
829.9′896—dc20   91-32506
CIP

Typeset by
Colset Private Ltd, Singapore
in 9/10 pt Paladium
Printed by
Villiers Publications Ltd.,
London N6

Contents

Acknowledgements

My first thanks are due to the authors themselves for agreeing to the interviews and good-naturedly allowing them to last way beyond the time agreed upon, but also for patiently revising the initial transcripts and answering further questions. The person whose information and advice enabled me to get started was Alastair Niven. Others who helped me contact authors in the early and therefore most difficult stages were Maggie Butcher, Martin Banham and Olutolu Onijala. Several of the interviews were held in offices or private flats that were made available for this purpose. I am grateful to the staff of Heinemann Educational Books, the Africa Centre and the School of Oriental and African Studies, as well as to Rex Collings, James Currey, Ros de Lanerolle, Liz Gunner and Vicky Unwin. Bibliographical research was carried out at the Libraries of the SOAS in London and the Istituto Italo Africano in Rome: I am particularly indebted to Carla Ghezzi for her assistance. I also wish to thank Ben Okri and Jonathan Cape for allowing me to read the proofs of *The Famished Road*. Several of the interviews have already appeared in journals and newspapers and I am grateful to the editors for allowing me to include them in this collection. Finally, I would like to express my thanks to Lynn Taylor for her help in preparing this volume for publication.

Acknowledgements for Photographs

Kofi Anyidoho photographed by Kodjo Walter Griffin (reproduced with the kind permission of Heinemann International)

Kofi Awoonor photographed by Sandra Gatten (reproduced with the kind permission of Heinemann International)

Mohammed ben Abdallah (reproduced with the kind permission of Woeli Publishing Services)

Chinua Achebe photographed by George Hallett

Odia Ofeimun photographed by Giovanni Giovanneti

Ben Okri photographed by Douglas Brothers (reproduced with the kind permission of Jonathan Cape)

Wole Soyinka photographed by George Hallett

Ngũgĩ wa Thiòng'o photographed by Carrie Craig

Mazisi Kunene (reproduced with the kind permission of Heinemann International)

Essop Patel (reproduced with the kind permission of Skotaville Publishers)

Mongane Wally Serote photographed by Tessa Colvin

Tsitsi Dangarembga photographed by Ilo the Pirate (reproduced with the kind permission of The Women's Press)

For

Jack Mapanje

Detained without trial in Malawi
25 September 1987
Released
10 May 1991

Introduction

A series of interviews in which African writers would talk about writing; their own, writing in general, the writing of others: such was the initial idea from which this book developed. But talking is a digressive occupation, opening unforeseen passageways and corners – particularly, perhaps, when the talking is about writing. And talking with African writers, the heirs both to a rich and lively tradition of creative talking and to an art set firmly within the life of the community, is obviously no exception.

Writing itself is seen, constantly, within a wider context. Several of the authors interviewed appear more willing to speak about the traditions they find significant for their work than about the work itself. Thus talking about writing means going into their relationships to the written and oral literature that has already been produced within their countries, or in countries with which, for historical, political and cultural reasons, they in some way feel connected. It means discussing the official paradigms of Writing, Literature, Culture and perhaps even Civilization they were presented with at school: the writing of Shakespeare, Dickens, Wordsworth, Keats, Hardy and Lawrence, but also – thanks to the colonial educators' search for a not altogether appropriate 'relevance' – of Conrad, Kipling, Cary, Forster and Greene. But it also means talking about the other kinds of writing they eventually discovered: that of other Africans, of Afro-Americans and Caribbeans and of Third World authors in general; and sometimes about their later rediscovery and transgressive reappropriation or 'twisting' – to use Wole Soyinka's expression – of Western myths and models, woven, together with those of their own lands, into an original, unexpected synthesis.

Among the topics that are raised is the difficulty of creating written literature in countries where writing itself is a relatively recent phenomenon. Compared with the literary production of Europe, or of much of Asia, written literature in Sub-Saharan Africa is of course still at its beginnings, even if, as Kofi Awoonor points out for the case of Ghana, a significant and varied history of writing can be traced, reaching back to the middle of the last century. Talking with African writers consequently entails discussing the literary institutions and structures (little magazines, book pages or supplements in local or national newspapers, writers' groups, drama societies, literary associations, publishing houses) in which the authors themselves are often directly involved. Instead of providing literature with much-needed practical support, they are often insufficient, forced as they are to grapple with financial and organizational problems or with various forms of censorship.

Inevitably, it seems, talk about African writing must lead to the question of the languages in which the writing is produced and the issues the choice of language brings to light. Here a shift in emphasis has taken place since the fifties and sixties, even among authors who do not embrace Ngũgĩ wa Thiong'o's policy of limiting 'African literature' to writing in the *African* languages. The issues that now seem worthiest of discussion are not the discrepancy between form and matter, or between 'African speech and English words', but the public(s) to which the chosen language may give access or, more frequently, that it may exclude. Changes, too, are apparent in the position of the South African writers. Both Ndebele and Serote are attentive not only to problems of national unity and to contrasting the governmental policy of 'separate development' applied to the field of languages, as in the past, but to promoting new and more progressive writing within the languages of the black population. On the other hand, as has emerged not only in some of the interviews but during informal conversations with other African authors, many writers feel that the principle of artistic freedom is of paramount importance and the author's choice of language needs no further justification.

Behind and alongside the *writing* of the authors who are talking is the *oral* (or 'talking') culture of their people. A tradition that goes back deep into the past, it continues also into the present, in a constant, metamorphic process of adjustment and adaptation in which all of the authors interviewed in this book are in some way implicated. Several have in fact made direct contributions to research into the oral tradition, studying, collecting, transcribing and translating the compositions of the poet-cantors and storytellers, and even, at times, incorporating passages within their own work, giving them new, written – or rather printed – channels of diffusion and facilitating their access to new and different kinds of audience. But the relationship with the tradition can be seen also and perhaps more significantly in the attempt by many of the authors to open their (written) texts to oral/aural fruition through the medium of performance, whether in the form of poetry reading or of theatre.

The 'talking' in these interviews is thus about a writing that is itself both a 'writing about talking', or a writing that incorporates talking, and a writing that aims at becoming, once again, a kind of talking. For it is the direct, dynamic, reciprocal relation orality permits between the participants in an oral event for which the authors seem to feel the need. Obvious examples include the constant and indeed growing interest in theatre of writers like Ngũgĩ wa Thiong'o; or, to an even greater extent, the *oral* destination of his Gĩkũyũ novels *Caitaani Mũtharaba-inĩ* (*Devil on the Cross*) and *Matigari ma Njirũũngi*; or again the popularity of street theatre and poetry readings in situations of political repression (as in the South Africa of Mongane Wally

Serote or Essop Patel, or the Nigeria of Wole Soyinka's shot-gun sketches). But, even in less oppressive circumstances and in less obviously committed forms of expression, the 'talking' and acting element may be assigned such absolute predominance that no publication other than performance is envisaged, as was the case until quite recently with the theatre of Mohammed ben Abdallah.

The interplay between orality and writing that is such a constant feature of African literature carries over into the interview itself, considered as a literary form in its own right. Appearing variously in the authors' bibliographies as a kind of appendage to primary sources of the author's work or as an awkwardly unclassifiable ingredient of the secondary bibliography, the interview has a hybrid, indeterminate status. Neither critical essay nor autobiographical statement, but overlapping into both, it is a compromise between monologue and dialogue and between orality and writing. Through the vehicle of the interview, the *writer* is made to express himself/herself through a different, *oral* medium, and it is in the apparently spontaneous, conversational, 'oral' flavour that remains in the printed text, even after it has been subjected to several stages of editing, that the interview's main attraction surely lies.

The interviews included in this volume were carried out over a fairly extensive period of time and in a variety of circumstances and settings. Editing by the interviewer has been kept, purposely, to a minimum, although a certain amount of cutting has been necessary due to space limitations, and no great effort has been made to fit the interviews into a homogeneous pattern. The intention throughout has been to respect the individual authors' style and personality. Some of the interviews, therefore, read virtually as monologues, the interviewer's questions appearing as occasional and probably dispensable interruptions in the flow. In some, the focus is on the work of the writer himself/herself, in others on the literary production of his/her country. Some were carried out in different sittings, some at a distance in time of months or even of a year or more. Others were the outcome of a single, all too brief encounter. In several cases, additional questions were responded to or further remarks were made by letter or in the margin of the typescript submitted for the author's approval. Finally, it seemed appropriate in editing the interview with Ngũgĩ to combine the dialogic logic of the 'inter-view', carried to its extreme consequences, with the writer's own increasing interest in collective forms of authorship, in writing as the 'work of many hands and tongues' as he puts it, speaking of the novel, in *Detained* (p. 8). Thus the printed text is actually a collage of three of my own interviews with the author, of a discussion that took place in the University of Rome between Ngũgĩ and teachers and students of the English Department, and of the author's remarks on the final typescript.

The writers interviewed come from different countries and have adopted a variety of genres. Ghana is represented by Kofi Anyidoho and Kofi Awoonor (poets who have also broached the fields of theatre and, in the case of Awoonor, of literary history and of the poetic novel) and by the playwright – or rather, at the time the interview was held, play-*maker* – Mohammed ben Abdallah. Nigerian authors included are Chinua Achebe, novelist, short-story writer, poet and essayist; Odia Ofeimun, poet and would-be biographer; Ben Okri, novelist and short-story writer; and finally Wole Soyinka: playwright, poet, novelist, short-story writer, autobiographer, biographer, essayist and even film-maker and record producer. From Kenya come both Mĩcere Gĩthae Mũgo (poet and playwright) and Ngũgĩ wa Thiong'o, whose production covers just about all the fields of writing with the exception of poetry. They are also co-authors of the play *The Trial of Dedan Kimathi*. South African authors interviewed are Mazisi Kunene, the exiled Zulu poet; Njabulo Ndebele, poet and short-story writer, at present in Lesotho*; Essop Patel, poet and editor of anthologies of poetry and prose; Mongane Wally Serote, in exile from South Africa*, principally a poet, but also the author of a few short stories and of a novel. Zimbabwe is represented by Tsitsi Dangarembga, novelist and playwright, and Musaemura Bonas Zimunya, poet, critic and literary historian. Most of the writers are also literary critics and several have specifically written for children. Two – at least – have published English translations of work by other African authors.

Although it is hoped that the collection will offer a fair representation of the very considerable variety of outlook, intention and achievement characteristic of the African authors of today, gaps, absences and imbalances are evident. The disproportion between male and female writers is fortunately no longer a true reflection of the general situation of African writing as more and more women are both writing and – perhaps less often – finding outlets for their work. One of the absences that is regrettably still representative of a more general reality, albeit not limited to Africa, is that of an interview with a writer – Jack Mapanje from Malawi – who was detained before he was able to see the transcript and authorize its publication. Five of the authors whose interviews are included in this collection (Awoonor, Ngũgĩ, Serote, Soyinka and Zimunya) have been subjected to periods of imprisonment, and it seems unhappily significant that each should come from a different country. The absence of Jack Mapanje's interview may thus be taken as a reminder of the many voices in Africa that have been and continue to be unable to find expression, the many authors prevented both from writing and from 'talking about writing'.

*Both Ndebele and Serote have now returned to South Africa.

Kofi Anyidoho

Taking 'from Earth her gifts of Songs' and from the 'bleeding anger of her wounds' the 'volcanic ash' which becomes 'the hope / that gives rebirth to abundance of seedtimes'. Kofi Anyidoho's poetry is rooted in the culture and traditions of his people, the Ewe of Eastern Ghana, and in the political and social vicissitudes of his country. Born in 1947 at Wheta, on the Keta lagoon, to a family of poets and cantors (which includes Kofi Awoonor, to whom several of his writings are addressed), Anyidoho's first poems appeared in the Creative Writing Programme's *Talent For Tomorrow* anthologies (Tema: Ghana Publishing Corporation, vols. VI and VII, 1972, 1973). He taught in the Brong-Ahafo region and later at Achimota Secondary School before going to university and obtaining an Honours degree in English and Linguistics from the University of Ghana, Legon, a Master's in Folklore from Indiana University and a PhD in Comparative Literature from the University of Texas at Austin (with a dissertation on 'Oral poetics and traditions of verbal art in Africa').

Voted Poet of the Year in 1984 by the Entertainment Critics and Reviewers' Association of Ghana, Anyidoho has won a number of literary prizes, including the BBC 'Arts and Africa' Poetry Award. He is the author of three volumes of poetry and of a number of articles and essays. He is also co-editor (with Avorgbedor, Domowitz and Giray-Saul) of *Cross Rhythms: Papers in African Folklore* (Bloomington: Trickster Press, Indiana University Folklore Department, 1983), with Abioseh M. Porter, Daniel Racine and Janice Spleth of *Interdisciplinary Dimensions of African Literature* (Washington, DC: Three Continents Press, 1985), and with Musaemura Zimunya and Peter Porter of *The Fate of the Vultures: New Poetry of Africa* (Oxford: Heinemann International, 1989). He now teaches at the University of Ghana, Legon.

1

Kofi Anyidoho

This interview was held in London during the 'New Directions in African Literature' conference in November 1984. Further questions were answered in writing on 25 March 1987.

Tell me about your early life and education and how you came to write poetry.
I was born in a small town in the Volta region of Ghana, Wheta. My mother moved out of the town very early, some ten months after my birth, and stayed in the northern part of the Volta region for a while, which is where I finally started school. I became a bit of a truant; not basically because I didn't want to go to school, but there were some problems and I stayed out of school for a year or two. Later on, my uncle, Kodzovi Anyidoho, sent for me – this was about 1955 – so I left my mother and went back home. I was brought up by this uncle: he sent me to school, based on a kind of 'instalmental' education – I was in for a while, out for a year or two and back in there.

I finished primary school finally around '64, went to the Accra Teacher Training College for four years and then started teaching in the Brong-Ahafo region of Ghana, first primary school and then middle school. I then went back to school for two years, to the Advanced Teacher Training College at a town 40 miles or so from Accra called Winneba, for a specialist diploma in English. After that I taught for two years at Achimota Secondary School, mainly English language and literature and some Ewe. Then I again went back to school, this time to the University of Ghana, Legon, where I did an Honours degree in English and Linguistics. I taught for a year after that before going on to the United States on a government scholarship and starting work for my Master's at Indiana University; I was there for two years. I left in 1980 to go to the University of Texas at Austin, where I finally finished my PhD in May 1983. That's as far as my education goes. Since January, I have been back in Ghana as a lecturer at the University of Ghana, Legon.

I started writing around 1965, when I was a student at the Accra Teacher Training College. That was actually the beginning of a programme of the Creative Writers' Association, the Creative Writing Programme, originally started by Mrs Ellen Geer Sangster, an American lady who was teaching in Ghana at the time and was very impressed with the potential for creative writing that she saw in some of the students. So it started very modestly from one training college in Aburi, but later on it was adopted by the Ministry of Education and someone was seconded from the Ministry to help her set up a small secretariat.

The way it operated was that there were writers' clubs for students in the various colleges which were affiliated to the national programme. Each club in each school had its patron. You had your meetings and whatever you wrote you submitted for general discussion by the group. At the local level, some schools had their own little literary magazines, which published some of these things. Then from the school level you'd submit your scripts to the programme office and they had consultants based at the Institute of African Studies: Efua Sutherland, Jawa Apronti, Ofori Akyea, later on Kofi Agovi. Most of these people were themselves writers or well known critics and we had comments on the scripts we had submitted and of course the comments of the people who were running the programme – Ellen Geer Sangster helped later on by Kwabena Asiedu. All of them would take a look at your scripts and often these were returned to you with comments for improvement, or, say, 'Yes this one we really can't do anything about, but if you could work next time along *these* lines things might work better.' Then there were usually seminars organized at the district level, then at the regional level and finally every year we had a national conference with delegates from various schools across the country, training colleges, secondary schools. It first started with the teacher training colleges, but later on it was extended to the secondary schools. Then from '65 they would select the best scripts submitted during the year for an anthology which ran for a few years under the title of *Talent for Tomorrow*.

It was really through this that I began, and I became increasingly involved in this programme. I was also helped partly in that one of the very first things I wrote got accepted and published in *Talent for Tomorrow* and that was a tremendous encouragement. Later on, especially when I started teaching in Accra, I became involved with other programmes, first through the Ghana Association of Writers and then through the National Association of Writers of which I became the organizing secretary at one point. Once I was out of school, of course I couldn't submit anything for the *Talent for Tomorrow* series, but by then I think I'd improved sufficiently for me to be able to place my poems in other things. But that was really the beginning.

What poems and literary conventions and forms have most interested you and perhaps influenced you?
I would say the primary source of influence and interest for me has been the Ewe oral tradition. Partly because I believe that by the time I formally got started on these things I had had a fairly intensive exposure over all my life as a child to various forms of Ewe oral poetry. I come from a family background where you do have a lot of composers. My uncle, who looked after me when I was growing up, was a very keen drummer and composer himself. One of the first things I remember, for instance, was my grandfather, Abotsi Korbli Anyidoho, who lived in the northern part of the Volta region. Usually when

anything happened – it was often funerals – each time he came home every-body knew that it was an occasion for songs, because he came, literally, with lots of songs, new songs flowing from him. That is the nature of poetry, not all, but a great deal, in the tradition: it's part of a whole performance that involves music and dancing. We are now interested in it as a poem, in the words, but in the tradition you don't really often separate the words from the performance.

Your uncle was a creator of poetry then; he didn't merely repeat traditional verse?
No, no! Well, we have two types of singer in Ewe tradition. There is the poet proper, what we call in Ewe *heno*. It's an interesting situation in which some people can perform but they may not be able to compose: in this particular case they will then borrow somebody else's composition and will perform it. Then there are some people who are very good composers but they do not have either the voice or the kind of personality: if you are shy you just can't do it, or if your voice is not good enough to be effective in a public performance. In that case other members of the group will – that's why there is a slight difference between the cantor, the person who simply performs the composition, and the person who actually composes it originally, but in most cases it's the same person who is able to compose who will actually perform it. But usually you are dealing with a group of people: sometimes you will never know who composes a particular song. In fact in the tradition they could make it a particular point not to reveal the person's name. Then there are other cases of an individual who founds a group which is clearly identified with him and everybody knows that he is singing most of the songs that he himself has composed.

After some time my mother also moved back home and then she also took it up and at least on a local level she made quite a reputation for herself by the time of her death. She didn't live long enough to become well known in the region, but in the immediate surrounding area everybody got to know her because she became a leader of the dirge group in the town. These were tremendous influences on me. But of course I did go to school and become very interested in literature, which for us at that point was mostly British. So it's obvious that some influence will be coming in from that tradition as well.

In the *form* of your poetry are you using any particular conventions?
The form varies. Some of my poems are very closely modelled on the Ewe traditional poetry, particularly on the dirge tradition. Partly because my mother and the immediate people around me were very much involved in the dirge tradition and I used to listen to their songs, so that quite a bit of that comes through my poetry. In terms of the impulse, the dirge impulse for the Ewes goes beyond the fact of death as the end to everything: there is always a certain projection beyond death, that's why there is that combination of a real sadness with a touch of optimism, the ability to look beyond the present circumstances of sorrow.

What basic concepts would you say are at the heart of Ewe culture? What image does the Ewe tradition give of man and of his role in society? Would you say that the traditional concepts and way of life are able to survive in present-day Ghana?
I'll start with the last question. I believe that every society goes through change.

9

But it's also in the nature of human beings and of societies to survive; and the way to survive is quite often through adaptation, transformations, so a change is inevitable. But change does not necessarily have to mean the death or the end to older ways. There will be specific beliefs, practices that will no longer work, but I think that is because they are not necessary any more, there is no longer any need of them. However, we have to make a distinction between the natural course of transformation that goes on in a society and the kind of change that will come as a result of violence from, say, in this particular case, outside sources: an outside force comes in and puts a stop to something against the natural laws of the society's evolution. That has happened with some aspects of the tradition; other changes that have taken place would have taken place anyway, regardless of whether anyone comes in from outside. So the colonial experience did succeed and has succeeded in completely cutting these off. But when you get into other areas, belief systems, the tradition of poetry or of music, these are very difficult to kill. They are intangible in a way – one has to play a very intensive psychological game to be able to kill them. They also happen to be those aspects of the individual and the society's life that are very difficult to get hold of and kill, so that's another way of surviving.

With the storytelling tradition, for instance, the situation may be such that you do not have people gathering in the evening to tell stories, but one of the most important agents for keeping this tradition alive today is the school. When I went to school you had to be prepared for the fact that you could be called upon any time in the afternoon to tell a story to the class. Now you no longer generally tell stories in the evening. The situation has changed; the child is in school, he's not on the farm or in the market or anywhere helping his parents, he's in school, and if the school has decided to take up the function of educating the children then of course some of these things have to be carried on. So the storytelling tradition survives, no longer through the evening story-telling sessions but through the classroom, and a child who does not know any story to tell will make sure when he or she goes home to press his parents or older sisters and brothers into telling him stories, so that next time he's called upon he can tell a story himself, and so the tradition survives.

Those are the aspects that are surviving. There have obviously been adaptations and changes, but since we are particularly interested in the tradition of poetry and literature in general, I believe that very basic changes have taken place but they haven't reached that point where they would make a strong enough impact to put a stop to these traditions. In fact if you go to Accra, every week there are performances by traditional groups that are carrying on the tradition even in the middle of the city. You don't have to go back to the village to experience traditional poetry. I have a friend, Daniel Avorgbedor, who was with me at Indiana University and who is in ethnomusicology. He is in the process of completing his dissertation on the continuities of the Ewe musical poetic tradition in the cities and was there in the summer for his research: he was amazed at the sheer number of the groups. Almost every major and in some cases small Ewe town is represented in Accra by its own group and they regularly meet and carry on. Some of these people haven't been to school. They're the basic working-class people. It doesn't matter who you are, there is a certain obligation on you to belong to these groups and take part in their activities.

To go on to Ewe culture, there is the world of the living and the world of the ancestors and the world of the yet to be born, and there isn't any real break, there isn't a gulf between any two of them that you couldn't cross. A human being's life at any one of these stages is connected with life on other planes. It's not just human beings; it's a belief that the force that animates human beings is essentially the same force that animates other things that share the environ- ment, animals, plants . . . There is a fundamental respect for life here that goes beyond the sense that makes everyone accountable for any action you may take in destroying a poetic tradition or a musical tradition. The poet will not start a performance without invoking the ancestral voice. It is the ancestors who have passed on the inheritance of poetry to you: you are following in their line and you have a duty to carry the line on to the point where your children can take it up; you have to pass it on. When I give a poetry reading I sometimes begin with a song, a song of invocation from the Ewe tradition, which briefly states: 'This song of ours we shall sing and sing until they throw us into jail. Our ancestors fought for this land and left it for us.' It's a question of dedication to your calling. You recognize that you don't just happen to be a poet, but that you are part of a tradition and nothing can stop you from carrying it through, even though political powers, whatever, will try to intervene, you have a duty to carry it through. And that is part of the concept of human beings and their place in the universe that will come directly into the poetic tradition.

There is a belief not just in the presence of the ancestors in your own life but also it's believed that song or poetry is a gift from the gods. We talk of a god of song, you are more or less a spokesperson, you pass on certain messages. Although you do have to be prepared to make yourself a medium for these things, that doesn't necessarily mean that you as an individual have nothing to contribute, but there is that conception which imposes a certain sense of the sacred on the tradition of poetic talent or ability: it has to be conceived of in these terms that border on the sacred. You have a sacred duty.

Your first published collections of poetry were *Elegy for the Revolution* (1978) and *A Harvest of Our Dreams* (1984), which incorporates the earlier work. Would you discuss their titles?

Elegy for the Revolution was written in a particular context of national politics – and by politics here I mean everything from the economy to social life, education, everything. It was a particular period of the national life in Ghana where we had a military regime coming into power. They had just come in to displace a civilian government that for most of us had lost its bearing – if it had ever really had any bearing – so that it would seem to be a welcome change. I was a student at the time. The Government came into power before I entered the University of Ghana. It became apparent after about two years that we were heading for trouble. The interesting thing was the long time it took the population at large to come to this realization. It's a peculiar situation in which students find themselves in a lot of developing countries; in Ghana we have now reached the position where students are almost always directly involved in national politics, sometimes in a supportive role, at other times in a confron- tational role with the established administration. With this particular Govern- ment students played a very supportive role for about a year or two until they realized that there wasn't sufficient sincerity in the Government's declared plans, so instead of demonstrating in support of the Government they began demonstrating against it.

It's at that point that I begin to celebrate the *Elegy for the Revolution*: the book is dedicated to the revolution that went astray and beyond that to those who refused to die. It was part of the revolutionary failure, a negation of the revolutionary process, that the political power would bring its political machinery to bear to kill the spirit and in a few cases the body of those who seek to speak up and protest against the brutalities and callousness or whatever it is. So you might say that it is a song of sorrow in a way; but just like the Ewe funeral dirge you will see that I'm also interested in looking beyond that and that's why it is in part dedicated to those who refuse to die. You have this particular poem, 'The Last Testament', in which one hero has obviously fallen, he's been cut down, and the person who is left has to rededicate himself to the struggle. I tried to capture that in a particular image:

Whatever befalls the panther in the desert / The leopard would not forget the jungle war.

Most of the first poems in *A Harvest of Our Dreams* were written I would say towards the end of that military regime. The very first one, 'Mythmaker', for instance, was written immediately after one of the many student confrontations with the Government in which some students lost their lives: this was 1 June 1977:

The children are away / The children are away / The children / These children are away.

Other moments in the poem capture certain details of things that happened to cause the confrontation, or during the confrontation, but again the moment of hope comes in:

Though our memory of life now boils / into vapours, the old melody of hope / still clings to tenderness of hearts / locked in caves of stubborn minds.

The children may be away, but by the end of the poem:

'The children will be home / The children will be home / The children / Those children will / be home / Some Day'.

'Seedtime': again, April 1979 – by this time I was in the US – the Government was still in power but although there is some talk of prophecy for the poet, I don't think that you had to be specially blessed by the gods to predict what I foresaw. The situation was such that just looking at it logically you could see that it could not continue for ever. It seems to me it was not prophecy but just a logical deduction from the way things were going that all this would have to come to an end sooner or later.

'A Harvest of Our Dreams', 'Seedtime', all these were written between February and April and of course about two months later the Government was out of power. As usual that becomes another occasion for hope and that is where I hope that this time we will be able to reap the harvest of our dreams – our dreams of fruitfulness, of success – in life, economic recovery and all that. The title poem itself is in a curious situation of starting from a very personal experience. It was actually when I had to struggle to write, when I had to deal directly with my mother's death. She died just when I was getting ready to go off to the US. It's a specially painful thing to know that a parent takes care of you only up to that point where it would seem that you should also be in a position to help. So my departure for the US to do graduate work was a very positive development in my life, but the sense of joy was held back by the fact that those that you would like to have around you to share this joy are no longer there. That's why it opens with the line:

There is a ghost / on guard / at Memory's door.

But that personal thing undergoes a transformation into the larger national situation: what is personal success without the general success of the society? One would want to hope to believe that you can only be completely happy if the society as a whole is prospering, otherwise your individual joy will always have that ghost on guard at Memory's door. In the middle of a feast something can come up in your mind and you can feel very nervous even about what you are eating – it may be stolen food or, for instance, how about those who cooked the food, where are they?

There are other pieces in here which I wrote after the first few months of the military take-over, in the enthusiasm that goes with it, and later on, because they quickly handed over to a civilian government, one watched with a certain sense of apprehension, because of experiences of the past. So you have poems like 'From Christiansborg to UssherFort', because suddenly you find that people who were political leaders a year or two ago are now going to become political prisoners. Christiansborg is the seat of government, Ussher Fort is the Central Prison in which most of our political prisoners are kept. But I also have a sub-title: 'From Ussher Fort to Christiansborg'. While some people are moving from Government House to the Prison House, others are on their way from the Prison House to the Government House. So there is some apprehension in some of the poems: 'Yes, it's good, this new set-up, but will they work it out?'

In some of the poems this comes through in a different kind of language, almost as if you were turning from the dirge song to the song of abuse.
Yes, there is that, that comes through. I've written a few pieces modelled on the traditional songs of abuse. Sometimes it only comes in briefly as a part of a longer piece. That is of course another very major aspect of Ewe tradition that I find extremely exciting. Poetry is used very much to pull the reins in on the stupidity of individuals in their private or public life.

Another noticeable feature is the careful structuring of the collection itself. The poems in *A Harvest of Our Dreams* do not strictly follow the order of composition, but you have gathered them together into five parts.
Yes. The very first ones, in 'Part One – Seedtime', are poems in which I try to wrestle with that state of uncertainty and of hope and I tend to wrestle with certain situations. 'The Diviner's Curse', for instance, is a look at the poet in the middle of a very despairing situation:

Your prayers my people / are doing a dance of ghosts / upon the courtyard of my song / and I wake to meet / my voice running naked / across our house of storms

. . . so that threatens to shut you up, there is a storm raging in the house, so what do you do? We may find that we are just as much to blame as the people we choose to blame for this now and we will in fact be blamed if we choose silence. If we choose silence in the face of the storm then one day:

The children will come pointing questions at / Us.

So that's the main point of that first part. But they are also, almost all of them, poems that were written within a certain period.

Part Two is a long poem, entitled 'Akofa'. Akofa is the name of my daughter, but this poem was written before she was born. The name itself translates as 'solace'. The poem as a whole tries to deal with the situation of a woman whose man has left her, not abandoned her, but left her in the sense that he's just gone away. That creates a certain amount of very serious personal isolation and if this should go on for an extended period of time then of course that would increase the problems. But the first part really is the voice of this woman's brother who is trying to comfort her and then she comes in with a response. It's seen on the one hand as a personal thing, but there are other moments when this woman goes back to her childhood and tries to recall her mother and everything. Then towards the end there is one particular piece that actually goes back to the songs of abuse; it's an attack on this other woman who is feeling very jubilant because she had at one time hoped she would have had the man Akofa eventually got married to, so now that he is no longer there she is jubilant. So the lonely woman turns a very sharp tongue on her, expressing some of her frustration.

The other section, 'Moments', has a lot of poems of the kind that sometimes come to you apparently out of nowhere. Some of them tend to be slightly fragmentary, but each one, hopefully, is also making a definite statement.

Something that happened to me while I was in the US was that there were moments when I tried to write letters to friends back home. 'Kwakuvi, Kwakuvi' – Kwakuvi really is Kwakuvi Azasu who recently had a novel, *The Stool*, published by Longman in their Drumbeat Series – I was writing to him as I had just received a letter from him and he was asking me to write back. We had been working on a literary journal in Legon and that time the editor wanted something about my impressions of the US. I started writing the letter and I realized it was in fact something like a poetic composition, so I took a copy down before I mailed the original letter. I later on made a few changes here and there and that happened to a few other letters that I tried to write, so I put all those together in one section.

'Part Five – Mokpoko'. *Mokpoko* is an Ewe word for hope. 'Long Distance Runner', 'They Hunt the Night', 'Our Fortune's Dance', for instance, specifically dealt with the good realization of June 14 1979. Ten days earlier Rawlings had come into power in Ghana. One sometimes has to use specific situations only as starting points, so I talk of the 'raw energy of a certain rolling stone' and I'm really playing on Rawlings's name there, but in that poem I was more interested in the kind of situation that has made that event almost inevitable, a situation in which the master hunters climbed trees, then fell in love with the moon and so forgot to carry on with the hunt. Then the apprentice hunter is going to have to take over if anything is going to be achieved! But again there is that note of sadness:

Our people how soon again in our hive / Shall we swarm around our honeycomb?

At Rawlings's first coming he didn't stay on, he handed over very quickly; there was already a political programme for elections when he came in and his coming in only delayed it for a couple of months. He went ahead and let this happen. But before it could happen one would have one's doubts about at least some of the people who thought that they had a right to become the rulers of this country:

And so the Hippo seeks / our stool of thorns our crown of thunder? / Let him beware the final dance of / soothsayers who now become our praise gatherers.

You may want the stool or the crown, but if you know that it's a stool of thorns, a crown of thunder, you have to beware of what has happened to others before you, who forgot their mission of looking into the future for the people, and became interested only in collecting praises. A little bit of some of the detail there is poetic transformation, images of how the military regime came in and became softened by the joys of civil life and forgot their original mission of carrying through their programme of action.

Legon, 25 March 1987

What *non* African poetry has most interested you, and why?
I have enjoyed poetry from a wide variety of cultures, mostly for the simple reason that it is good poetry. However, I have become increasingly taken up by poetry from African heritage poets of the Caribbean and the Americas. Clearly there are natural affinities and shared concerns.

Which modern African poets do you feel closest to?
The list is potentially endless, but one could begin with Mazisi Kunene, Kofi Awoonor, Okigbo of *Path of Thunder*, among others of the generation imme- diately preceding ours. Of my contemporaries, there are several whose names may not ring bells in international circles but who are nevertheless ready as the big voices of today and tomorrow, Obiba Opoku-Agyemang and Setheli Ashong-Katai of Ghana, for instance. There are others who have already made the airwaves: Niyi Osundare and Odia Ofeimun of Nigeria, Atukwei Okai and Kobena Eyi Acquah of Ghana. But there are many many others who speak to me in language I'll forever cherish and about things that help me grow.

Reading your poetry, one is aware of a very subtle use of music. What part is played by music (including jazz) in your work?
Let's begin by saying again that the fundamental impulse of my work derives from the oral poetic tradition. Then let's recognize that in that tradition the true *heno* composes *ha* (song), and *ha* is a trinity of word–melody–rhythm. What I write may not deal in obvious melodic patterns, but it is helpless without the vehicle of rhythm. Music is the vehicle that brings my words home. For a literate poet in an essentially oral culture, you cut out the music and you cut out your primary transmission line.

You ask about jazz. Jazz for me holds a unique lesson. Even though it has been co-opted (stolen?) into the so-called mainstream culture of the West, we can't forget how it came into being. Jazz is a celebration of how a people defied death. It re-enacts all the agonies of the tortured journey of Africans across the Middle Passage, through the plantations and into the urban jungles of the New World. Above all, jazz re-enacts how they survived and still survive it all. Elsewhere (in the 1983 *Greenfield Review* article 'They sing the dirge to purge our hearts: introductory comments'), I try to capture the essence of jazz in the following words:

'Some may talk of the Afro-American jazz as a study in dissonance, as a reflec- tion of the spiritual and cultural travail of a people uprooted and flung into the bosom of the storm. There is much historical and psychological truth in this

15

view of a people's art. But the jazzy hoarseness of history's Armstrongs is more than the lyrical agony of the vanquished. Above all else, it is a reaffirmation of hopes once denied, a celebration of that piece of life which survived the storm, an aesthetic definition of an experience which took away their laughter only to find that nature abhors vacuums, and so fills their being with stirring vibrations of the soul.'

By way of conclusion, could you say a few words about *Earthchild?*
Earthchild is my third poetry book, released in Ghana by Woeli Publishing Services. The title piece is a celebration of jazz and that whole historical experience jazz re-enacts. The book is therefore dedicated to:

All of Africa's Children / who live die and still live / in the diaspora / especially for those / who still stand so tall among the cannonades / and smell of mists and of powdered memories.

Earthchild is actually a combined volume of two separate collections. The first part, titled 'Late Harvest', features the 'Earthchild' collection proper, mostly poems written during my six-year stay in America, a few written just before I went over. The second part of the book presents what I call 'First-fruits', gathered under the title 'Brain Surgery', a collection that pre-dates my first published volume *Elegy for the Revolution*.

SELECTED BIBLIOGRAPHY

POETRY
Elegy for the Revolution (New York: Greenfield Press, 1978).
A Harvest of Our Dreams (with *Elegy for the Revolution*) (London: Heinemann, 1984).
Earthchild, with Brain Surgery (Accra: Woeli Publishing Services, 1985).

ESSAYS
'Atukwei Okai and his poetic territory', in *New West African Literature*, ed. K. Ogungbesan (London: Heinemann, 1979), pp. 45–9.
'Henoga Domegbe and his songs of sorrow', *The Greenfield Review*, VIII, 1–2 (1979), pp. 55–64.
'The poet as a devotee of *se* and song' (paper presented at the 24th annual meeting of the African Studies Association (ASA), Bloomington, Indiana, 21–24 October 1981).
'Kofi Awoonor and the Ewe tradition of songs of abuse (*halo*)', in *Towards Defining the African Aesthetic*, ed. Lemuel A. Johnson, Bernardette Cailler, Russel Hamilton and Mildred Hill-Lubin (selected papers from the 1980 African Literature Association (ALA) meeting) (Washington, DC: Three Continents Press, 1982), pp. 17–29.
'They sing the dirge to purge our hearts: introductory comments', *Greenfield Review*, X, 3–4 (1983), pp. 124–31. Precedes sampling of recent Ghanaian poetry.
'Ewe funeral poetry as a rite of passage' (paper presented at the 24th annual meeting of the ASA, Boston, Massachusetts, 7–10 December 1983).
'Historical realism and the visionary ideal: Ayi Kwei Armah's *Two Thousand Seasons*', *Ufahamu*, XI, 2 (1981–2), pp. 108–30.
'African creative fiction and a poetics of social change', *Komparatistische Hefte* (Bayreuth), XIII (1986), pp. 67–81 (paper presented at the 25th annual meeting of the ASA, Washington, DC, 4–7 November 1982).
'Literature and African identity: the example of Ayi Kwei Armah', *Bayreuth African Studies Series*, VI (1986), pp. 23–42.

Kofi Awoonor

The principle of continuity embedded in Ewe religious and cultural tradition is also at the heart of Kofi Awoonor's writing. Born in 1935 at Wheta, he 'grew up on the lap of his grandmother Afedomeshi, a great singer of dirge songs', even if his formal education took place at the Roman Catholic Mission School at Dzodze, the Keta Bremen Mission School and Achimota School, and later at the Universities of Ghana, Legon, of London and SUNY, Stony Brook. He has lectured in English at the School of Administration at the University of Ghana (1960–63), in African literature at the Institute of African Studies and at the State University of New York at Stony Brook, where he became chairman of the Department of Comparative Literature. In 1964, he was managing director of the Ghana Film Corporation. He was a founder member of the Ghana Playhouse and the Osagyefo Players. He has been editor of *Okyeame* and associate-editor of *Transition*. In addition to his poetry collections, novels, plays and criticism, he is co-editor, with G. Adali-Mortty, of *Messages: Poems from Ghana* (London: Heinemann, 1971), he has also collected, translated and edited a selection of Ewe oral poetry *Guardians of the Sacred Word: Ewe Poetry* (New York: Nok Publishers, 1974) and has published a survey of African art and literature, *Breast of the Earth*, as well as numerous articles and essays. After returning to Ghana in 1975, to teach at the University of Cape Coast, he was arrested and imprisoned. He has been Ambassador of Ghana to Brazil and Cuba, and is currently Ghana's Permanent Representative to the United Nations.

2

Kofi Awoonor

The interview was carried out in Rome (2 October 1987), after an international seminar on 'The New African Literatures'.

As you are not only a creator but a historian of literature, I would like you to begin by discussing some of the characteristics of the written literature of your country.
I have a thesis which I tried to work out in my book *The Breast of the Earth*, in which I said a full comprehension of the literature of Ghana – or of any part of Africa for that matter – is not possible unless one goes back to the traditional forms which provide a kind of basis, in terms of the impetus that was later given to the languages these literatures were written in. This impetus was largely missionary, so there was a degree of deviation from the original impulse of the traditional literature. There is a point at which one sees a merger between the traditional literature and what consequently becomes the written literature, even in the received languages of Europe. One can look at the structure of the traditional poem and trace that structure – even today – right into the hymns written by the Christian inspired religious organizations. For example, you see a lot of work being done by the apostolic and spiritualist churches which get *their* inspiration from the form and structure of the traditional prayer and in which you find recurrent elements such as praise, salutation, plea and pleading and even, once in a while, mild rebuke to the deity for not being able to do as much for the people as they expected.

Now, having said that, I want to look at the larger corpus of written literature in Africa in terms primarily of the traditional forms being taken or being shunted aside a little bit for the missionary forms in all our languages, with the exception of the Hausa and Swahili traditions. We're talking now about literature in the vernaculars, the origin of the vernacular literatures of Africa. In Ghana there's been a tremendous amount of work done, for example, in Ewe, in Ewe fiction. I was telling Ndebele from South Africa two days ago that there is a book called *Nomalizo* which I read as a boy in the Ewe. It is the story of a Christian girl whose hand was asked for by a pagan boy. The Christian parents of course objected: 'These people live in darkness!' they said. Ndebele told me the book was written by Enoch Guma and was originally written in Xhosa! So the missionaries – probably the Lovedale group – took it and it travelled all the way to the Gold Coast, where it became an Ewe classic.

Quite a number of other writers – I know at least two in Ewe, anyway, – produced literature that did not conform to the Christian prescription of theme (darkness to salvation; darkness to light, and so on) even though they had been brought up in the Christian tradition. They were all variations on the theme of the pilgrim and of a number of set biblical stories which were very popular in the proselytizing process.

One of these writers was a Roman Catholic teacher called Desewu. He produced a series of books which talked about the Ewe country – our people and our way of life – always with that didactic intention. One of his most famous stories which I knew as a boy was a story about drink, 'Nutsusesema' ('That Strong Man'). The story was about a certain 'strong man' who lives in a house by himself. Now this strong man is very, very quiet. He doesn't talk, he doesn't say anything to anybody; but people love his company and they go and befriend him. And then they see his other side. He's very talkative, he's very boisterous and he's very violent. He destroys homes and families. Or there's the story of a man who travelled, who set himself up as a traveller, beginning in the provinces. Desewu's novel, made up of fact and fiction, opens with the adage that the boy who has never travelled says 'My mother cooks the best soup.' But if you travel you see that there are other people who cook as good a soup if not even better than your mother's. Desewu takes his traveller through the Ewe country and gives details of the various customs he finds: 'When you go to this place this is what you will see that is different and it's very exciting, very interesting . . . It's not like what you are used to in your home, but it's still a very important part of people's lives.' His most famous book was a collection of folktales, *Mise Gli Loo* ('Listen to a Story'), which became a classic. Then he did straightforward novels, short novels, depicting conflict and tension in the traditional society.

What period was this?
He was writing in the '30s. His stories were all set in the traditional communities, but on the edge of it there was always the factor of the missions, the church, what were called the Salems. When the missionaries came they established mission compounds which became home for the rejects of the original society, people who would run to these settlements because of something they had done in their original societies; they called it a place of haven, a Salem. These communities soon began to encroach slowly on the life of the original community and conflict points arose. Chinua Achebe illustrates it beautifully in *Things Fall Apart*. In some situations the conflicts were about simple issues, such as the use of water. A stream passes through the land; everybody uses it. But then the Salem people move a little bit upstream, or, if it's on the other side, they begin to claim the pagans are polluting the water for them. Many of the writers dramatized these conflicts in crisp little novels. A good number were published by a mission publishing house which was based in Togo.

Then came Fiawoo, an M.E. Zion minister of the gospel, who was educated for his higher degrees in the United States and came back to Ghana in 1934. He began by translating the Greek classics into Ewe. Then when he started writing his own works directly, he wrote without any reference whatsoever to the Christian factor. His was mostly a reconstruction of history in dramatic terms. He wrote two very famous plays. The first, called *Toko Atolia*, was published around 1937 in Germany. (A German, Westermann, had done a lot of work on the Ewe language, which had received its orthography from the Bremen missionaries in the middle of the last century, and work was being done on Ewe grammar in German universities.) The meaning of the title is 'The Fifth Landing Stage', and the play is a story of crime and punishment among Ewes long, long before the European advent.

I grew up on this story: it's a kind of morality play, a beautifully drawn out story of a young man whose nature is of great cunning, and deviousness of the most bizarre type. When there was a war he took off for the war but then he went and hid in a forest; when the war was over he came across the corpses of some of the victims, cut off their heads and brought them home as if he was the one who did the killing. He was a great hero until somebody else came and said 'No, no, no, he was nowhere near the battlefield!' He finally seduced the wife of a very respectable elder. This, among the Anlo–Ewe, was a very serious offence. When that final crime was done it was decided he would be taken for trial. The trial was conducted in the deep of the night by the elders. The tradition was that they go into a place where they must hold this trial and when the judgement is given it is announced by a drum-beat. Just after midnight, the town hears the drum-beat saying 'We have gone by night and we have come by night.' And that is the message of the death sentence that is carried out at a place called Agbakute. We've gone by night and come by night means that somebody has been sentenced to death, but nobody knows who. Then of course the executioners will move in on the compound of the victim and lead him away. Fiawoo makes superb use of this fantastic moral and judicial system! What he wanted to say in the book was that this was a highly sophisticated way of crime control and punishment. It wasn't barbarous. It was properly done; it had a moral basis: the survival of the community. And then he also indicated other forms of punishment such as exile or being buried alive up to your head, when they would place roasted cassava on your head for the crows to come and after they had finished eating the cassava they would start going for your eyes.

There was another play called *Tuine Se* or 'Give Your Story to Destiny'. Everyone comes with his own private god, or *se*, and whatever it is you have that bothers you, you must talk to that private god, your individual, private soul as it were. *Toko Atolia* was translated into English – rather badly I think – by the author himself, which was a pity as the Ewe was so beautiful and powerful.

Then of course there were also many other writers, such as Bidi Setsoafia, who did a lot of work in drama – almost modern drama – set in the '40s and '50s. To return to what I was talking about in terms of the written literature itself, we've had a creative literary endeavour which had its duality, as it were, with the original Christian impulse and then forms that were essentially traditional but were now being transposed into the vernacular through writing. The same has been done in Akan, with people like Gaddiel Acquaah in Fanti. His *Ogua Abban* is a long epic poem, or a historical narrative with praise elements in it, using features from the oral tradition, such as when the chief comes out and the drummers are following him with a praise song. He uses this technique even when describing the castles that were built in the Fanti country, telling the history of these castles, what was being done in them, the slave trade: why people were made slaves, where they were supposed to have gone and so on.

In Akan, there was missionary writing which then influenced Akan and Ashanti writers or Akwapim writers like Akrofi, and even the great scholar-poet Kabwena Nketia, who is not only a musicologist but also a very fine poet in Akan, using the Akan poetic form but working from a catechistic impulse as a Christian teacher.

Purely secular writing began as far back as the last century. It drew a lot of its impetus from early journalism on the Gold Coast with people like the Bannermans, who set up a series of newspapers as far back as the 1850s. These newspapers included poems, pieces on native life describing the communities and their events; and then there was always a short story. By the 1860s–1870s, there was the beginning of some kind of agitational poetry and essays, speaking about 'The African', with influences coming mostly from the New World. Most of the writers were mulattos: the Bannermans were mulattos; some of them were educated in England and when they came back they became the elite of the emerging new African society. There was a similar group in Cape Coast; this included Mensah Sarbah, the first African who sat on the Legislative Council in 1880. Or his son, who became a great legal mind: he wrote a fantastic essay called *Fanti Customary Constitution*, describing how the Fanti governed themselves, their political institutions. It was work which required a lot of research, but was also fused with imaginative self-glorification and self-justification, as if to say 'We are not the savages people say we are: this is the way it really is.' And these books are still available. On the creative side, apart from journalistic writing which was also using poetry and so on, there were the Young Turks, led by Kobina Sekyi. This was in the '20s and it was the period of the blossoming of the Aborigines Protection Society, a movement born at the end of the century to fight the British attempt to annex all the land in the Gold Coast to the Crown. Kobina Sekyi and people like Atoh Ahuma in the context of this political movement were talking about rejecting British culture, not accepting to be the cultural imitators that they were becoming. Sekyi's *The Blinkards* is very much a classic play that articulates this position, ridiculing Africans with British manners and British pretensions. Some of them went even further. Atoh Ahuma and others all had European names which they changed (Ahuma was called Solomon originally). They were very much influenced by Blyden with his black nationalist crusade, coming from the New World. Blyden even insisted that the religion the African should embrace was Islam.

Apart from Sekyi, an important writer of that period was J. B. Danquah. Having taken an advanced degree in Anthropology at the University of London, in the late '20s, he came home as a lawyer. But he was interested in philosophy; what is the African's conception of the universe, of God, of creation? Again, it was part of the effort to make the point that these people were not the barbarians they had been made out to be; that they had systems of thought, systems of ideas, epistemologies, if you like, through which their world was directed. He wrote a play called *The Third Woman*. It was beautiful. I read it at about the age of seventeen or so. I don't remember why we were made to read it, but it was just overwhelming. Very bad as *theatre*, because when abstractions become the foci for dramatization, it's difficult for them to assume concrete shape even when you dress them up as human beings. The

22

play used a combination of structures from Greek tragedy and English morality plays, even as its energy came from the pure Akan notion of existence and
African philosophical systems.

The struggle for independence appropriated all these elements as part and
parcel of its self-expression. The anti-colonial struggle gathered momentum
after the First World War with a man like Casely-Hayford who wrote *Ethiopia
Unbound*, which again is the allegory of this general fight for freedom, of
which all these little poems and plays were only tentative expressions, efforts at
giving expression to that African soul which is free, which is unfettered, or
which *must* be freed. So beyond Casely-Hayford we enter the '30s, the '40s,
the war years and of course the coming of Nkrumah.

Before that, one of the most interesting things that happened in the Gold
Coast was again a journalistic event, the founding of the *West African Pilot* by
Azikiwe in Accra. Azikiwe fancied himself a bit of a poet in the Afro-American
tradition. He wasn't allowed back into Nigeria after his American sojourn as a
student and political activist. I think he decided to settle in the Gold Coast
because of what was happening as a result of Casely-Hayford's work with the
West African National Congress. That was until he was deported for some
article he wrote – 'Has the African a God?' – or something to that effect. It
angered the British establishment immensely and they flung him out.

In the wake of all that we are now moving towards World War II, which
aroused an interesting ambivalence of imperialist fervour on the part of some
nationalists, while a number of others were saying 'Well, this war has nothing
to do with us.' In between there had been a lot of other newspapers. It might be
very interesting to look at some of the old newspapers over a period of about
100 years, from the 1850s to the 1950s, in order to see how the modern literature of the Gold Coast emerged. Each paper had a column or a 'Poet's Corner',
and these Poet's Corners were the early beginnings of at least one vital aspect of
that literature of English expression, i.e. poetry.

Which, presumably, is originally imitative of British models?
Very much so. A lot of it was based on Tennyson, a lot on English hymns,
Wesleyan hymns:

I vow to thee my country / All earthly things above

. . . Somebody would take it and turn it around and do all kinds of things with
it, setting it in a proper rhyme and rhythm, the whole works! In Nkrumah's
Evening News, I remember, there was a Poet's Corner, where one poet or
other – either Benibengor Blay, MacNeil Stewart, or, people say, even
Nkrumah himself – would pen a small poem and put it there. These poems
were about Hope, the African Heaven, or the African Woman, the African
Storm . . . abstractions that became part and parcel of that consciousness of
liberation and struggle.

By the '50s therefore, the major names – at least in poetry, because poetry
seems to be always what Ghanaians are most interested in writing – were
Benibengor Blay, R.E.G. Armattoe, who spent all his life in Ireland, and then
the later writers, Michael Dei-Anang and others. All these people became part
of the nationalist movement.

Beyond this period, the younger generation was coming along. These were
the people who were coming out of the universities, or the younger journalists
who were also beginning to write (people like Kwesi Brew, Paa Kayper

Mensah, Adali-Mortty and Efua Sutherland). It's the generation of the early '50s, people who were the teachers of my generation (I'm fifty-two now), people like myself (Ayi Kwei Armah didn't do his growing up in Ghana), like Joe de Graft, who has passed away, like Henry Ofori, a very, very good writer, not a poet but a short-story writer, a humorist.

I don't think I've ever heard of him.
No? He's unbelievably beautiful! I had a manuscript of his for about a year which I've just given back to him. He's done some publishing inside and he has a column in one of the newspapers, under the name Carl Mutt! Fantastic stories of sheer laughter, that's what he does best.

Perhaps it's time to talk about your own writing?
Well, I felt I wanted to write when I was in school: I was always doing poems. I don't know whether any of these things can be found anywhere, I doubt it! This is about '49 or '50.

Were you writing poems like the ones you read at school, or like the poetry you heard at home?
No, at that age I was writing the poems I read in my school texts, which were English:

Half a league, half a league, / Half a league onward, / All in the valley of death

'Daffodils' . . . Until, as I remember, I was home one day, I think I must have been in the sixth form. I had gone to the village as my grandmother or some relative had died. I relived traditional songs and poetry again at the funeral. Of course I had heard all these songs around me all my life and I thought 'These are wonderful songs', so I started writing them down in a little notebook. Now there was one teacher at the university, one of my early lecturers (I had gone to the university in 1957). We were talking one day and he asked 'What are you doing with all these folk songs? I know Nketia has done some very good work on Akan poetry; what are you people doing about Ewe songs in terms of transposing them into English where they could be available to those who cannot read Ewe?' So I did a first exercise. I translated a number of songs straightaway into English. Then somewhere in the translations I would add my own compositions to the original translations. This is really what happened in 'Dzogbese Lisa'. The song is a very short one [sings in Ewe]. That short dirge I translated as:

Dzogbese Lisa has treated me thus / It has led me among the sharps of the forest

. . . And so on. And then I started composing things in that same style, which I did for a short while. I was excited: the first poems were published in the 1961 edition of *Okyeame* and they were done around 1957, 1958. Then I began to develop a more consistent interest in the material, how it works and so on. Meanwhile I took off into my own writing, I was making my own statement. But I never left that original source and impulse, that energy that gave the material its original thrust. Take a poem like 'Hymn to my Dumb Earth' from *Night of My Blood*. A great deal of it is not traditional material, but you'll find the traditional material persisting as its base in:

Oh, someone, / Someone call the dove for me / and it will run to me

24

[*sings in Ewe*], 'Keep quiet and I shall pay the debt' – that's also a snatch – but then:

My friend went to the U.N. / came home talking of the secret service / Thelonius Monk played in the village / There were hymns sung / near the Arc de Triomphe / The fingers were those of Bud Powell / but the voice, the voice is Esau's. / In the upper room the Last Supper is laid / while the redeemed gangster from Detroit / outlined his dream of salvation

And so on. And then later:

I have no sons to fire the guns / no daughters to wail / when I close my mouth / when I pass on / So I shall go beyond and forget

[*sings in Ewe*]. I was sort of weaving into all my experience that traditional-based material that I have received. And that makes for me a continuing process of connection.

The publishers of my latest collection, *Until the Morning After*, or perhaps it was the poetry festival organizers in Rotterdam, wanted me to do a little essay on what my work was and I made a statement there which might be useful: 'I grew up in a typical African Community of relatives, aunts, uncles, some who came as far afield as Togo.' The principle that I believe was at the basis of this community – the community of the thunder shrines and so on in which I grew up – the real world of consciousness, of growth, formed of mysteries, of life, had to do with the invisible living phenomena that pertained to the issues of everyday existence. The principle is the principle of *continuity*. As our people say, *eka xoxoawo nue wogbea yeyeawo do*: 'we weave the new ropes where the old ones left off' [*sings in Ewe*]. To create, you must return to what was there before, advance it. Then I end by saying that:

'in the need for continuity is stressed the principle of survival. [. . .] This is the source of my poetry, the origin of my commitment – the magic of the word in the true poetic sense. Its vitality, its energy, means living and life giving. And that is what the tradition of poetry among my people has always meant. It had as its fundamental thrust the celebration of living itself against a background of suffering. [. . .] Survival in this situation was more than a matter of hope. It was anchored in faith, belief, and the certainty that life is a cyclical process; we fulfill our turn with drums, laughter, and tears, and pass on inevitably to our ancestorhood, to sustain those we leave behind on this wayside farm we call life.'

The rope itself is a cyclical thing. It is not a long, thin thing, it's a winding thing. This is why the snake is always seen as a rope. It's a circular thing rather than a straight thing, you are weaving onto it, but in coils. If you go to the beach, when the fishermen dry their net, the rope part of the net is all done in a coil, bundles of coils, not left out in a long string.

Could you tell me about the experience you had of the oral poetry during your childhood?
I was born in Wheta, which is my mother's town. My father lived eleven miles away, near the town of Dzodze, which was his place of settlement and work: he came from Anyako, which was on the other side of the lagoon, towards Keta. Very regularly I had to go to my mother's town, where I spent most of my vacations as a child. All my uncles were alive then. Once in a while my mother

would come back with me: I remember there were a couple of occasions when my mother and father would quarrel and my mother would go away, taking me away – I was the first child – and we'd go and spend a very, very long time with my grandfather and grandmother and my mother's people. That side of my family was *completely* African in the sense that it was not educated, there was no school, there was no church in that town: it was a traditional village in the purest sense of the word. My grandfather's father had founded a chieftaincy stool, and had also created a thunder house shrine that I was taken to as a baby. It was a world of drums and dirges, the world of the songs my grandmother sang when she was alive (she didn't die until about 1946). So absorbing all these things, this world of mystery to me was *not* a mystery. But then, when I finally moved away to the next town, which was a more developed town, a commercial town with a big school and a church, and I went to the Presbyterian school then up to secondary school, to university, this world receded, it then seemed very far away. But because it is the world of one's mother – my mother is still alive, very much alive – one went back to it. I remember very well when I was in the sixth form and I came home and said to my mother I was having these dreadful headaches. She said 'OK. Then we must go *home*.' So we took the lorry and went back to the village and my uncle, who is a priest-diviner of the Afa cult, was mandated to perform certain rites. He did these, asked these things, asked me a few questions and then went and got some herbs and made a herbal pot which I was told to use in bathing for a number of days. And I was cured; I didn't have the headaches any more!

Did Christianity play much part in your early years?
I was not very serious about Christianity when I was going to school; I never really took to the Christian faith in that strong way which I saw some of my own friends do. Because of the background I came from I was not even baptized early and I was never confirmed into the Church. So by the time I was sixteen, seventeen, eighteen, I had drifted away from Christianity. When I finished university I had begun to think seriously about that original world from which I came. It began as a kind of curiosity. Our people believe that if you are going to embark upon an enterprise, there are things that you must do first. Like when I'm going to go up to college, my mother says 'Ah, we must go *home*!' She provides a small ram, the obligatory bottle of local gin, and I go with her and knock on the door of the ancestral shrine, which is opened to us. I take off my shoes and we go in backwards and kneel down and they make prayers. Then we come back and the ram is killed and there is a feast. Everybody who is a member of that shrine, like my family, comes in and we all eat; and after the meal I go away. I've done this, almost consistently, for the past thirty years and more. Mostly when I come back from the United States or from abroad. Every time I come back I must go there and show myself. My uncle used to say 'When you are prosperous, when things are good for you, it is then that you must always come. We don't want you to come only when you are in trouble.' So it became my second nature. It's a very popular shrine, even with people who marry into my family. And people who travel up country also come there. I'm supposed to be one of the original direct owners or children of the shrine and I see it as a very important factor in my life.

Now there's an interesting thing that happened to me that I haven't written about. When I was in prison, on 2nd March, 1976 – I'd been in prison since December 1975 – I was taken into solitary confinement in Ussher Fort. I was the only person in a big cell in that big, old prison that was a Dutch fort built to house slaves before the transatlantic journey, and for three nights there was no light. I was lying on my cot in that state between sleeping and waking when it's not so much that you're seeing something, but you don't know whether what you're seeing is substantial. Well, as I was lying on my cot, I saw in the corner, right before me, there was my grandfather. He was sitting in an armchair and he was looking at me. He said to me – it was such a quick thing – he said: 'When you are released, you must go immediately and see your mother.' And the thing was over. Was I awake? Was I sleeping or dreaming? To this day I don't know. In due course I *was* released.

Before this happened my uncle had sent me some water in a bottle, with instructions: 'Every day, turn to the East and wash your face with this water. Pour it in your palm and wash your face and say in your mind what you want. You must do it until the water is finished.' And I did it. I started doing it in the communal cell where I was with my friends and I continued to do it when I was sent into solitary confinement. One of the prison warders said he was going to take the water away from me, but I threatened him that if he took it away he would die. So I'd finished using this water before I had this visitation. Then my uncle sent me a message again that I was going to be released very soon – my friends were going to be kept in prison but I was going to be released – because of this water. And, lo and behold, on the day of the trial when they came to take us to the court I was told 'Only eight people will go; you will not go.' So I stayed behind, though later I went and testified as a defence witness for my friends. But a few weeks after that they were all sentenced. Three of them received the death penalty, five of them received twenty-five years, nineteen years and so on. Then one day, a policeman came up to the cell and said 'You are now going to court.' My trial lasted two months and I was sentenced to one year: but when I came down and returned to the prison, they told me I had already served my sentence as I had been in prison for about eleven months or so. And then a pardon had been granted me. I came home that same night and the first thing I did was to go home to my mother, following the instruction I had received. As usual she simply said 'Let's go', and we went to the ancestral shrine. She had bought a ram and a piece of white calico and some local gin. I went through a very elaborate ritual and a cleansing, because the place I had gone to, prison, was supposed to be a place of evil; so I needed purification.

Every time I try to link that dream or vision with the consciousness of what it is that that shrine represents for me in terms of my survival, of being here and doing what I want to do and so on, I become more and more attached to the place. Every time I'm home I go to the shrine and do the proper ceremonies. It's a place of mystery for me, of communion. As I get older I'm getting more and more involved with this world. It's defining for me a very mature perspective on what for me is true religion, the whole business of God, of the relationship with people now, not in terms of the hereafter, but of the ancestral world, that line of continuity that I spoke about.

I've just finished my new novel, *Comes the Voyager At Last*, which explores this question though not in any academic or intellectual way; it leaves a lot of questions unanswered. For me that is the way of expressing sensibility to what is a mystery; one cannot attempt to rationalize it or to understand it.

The publication of this novel has been announced as imminent several times already, hasn't it?
Oh yes! I finished the fourth draft in '74, but I decided I wasn't going to let it out. I've

been working at it and working at it, and now after thirteen years I really believe I've got it. It's very short. When it's published it shouldn't be more than about 150 pages. I think it's better than most parts of *This Earth, My Brother*. It's a more mature kind of work. It's the same kind of mystery I'm dealing with, but this time in a deeper way. It has its frivolous parts. I see frivolity as the other side of the same phenomenon. It's like the religious moments in our tradition, which are also some of the most comic moments.

The theme of the journey is right at the centre of *This Earth, My Brother* as well. Here the journey has a rather ambiguous ending. On the most obvious level the book can be seen as the story of a quest that ends in madness and death and therefore a quest that fails. But if you look more closely at the novel, at its symbols and images, even its structure, the vision that emerges is not so negative. Is this connected with your vision of the artistic process in general?
Your second reading is the correct one, if one can use words like 'correct' for this kind of effort. If you look at the book as a structure, you see I was working out the whole business of separation or fragmentation, dealing with that fragmentation and *moving* consequently towards reunification. So the negative elements become fused in that ultimate unification of the total sensibility of the book. There is a greater degree of fluidity – or what we can call a 'flow' – between the waking world and the sleeping world, the negative and the positive as it were. In other words the protagonist we see in all these vignettes, fragments – all of them are fragments – is the bearer, the man who goes before all of us. To me he is a contemporary Ezeulu; but I wanted him to be a lawyer, the one who went farther than Achebe's Ezeulu in *Arrow of God*. So he's got the legalistic training of the whole colonial structure. His mind goes, as it were – you remember we see him in the asylum, even though we don't meet him – but our final encounter with him was on the beach when the woman of the sea comes. And it is one portion of the book that people never seem to get, that moment when the woman emerges and at the edge of the water they embrace and her smell is the smell of camwood and she's got all the beads and all the beautiful things that were going to be used as adornment for the new people that were going to come. In other words, that self which is the African self in that personality, fragmented in all those experiences, has achieved a reconciliation with that reality by what is almost a kind of self-sacrifice. And I said there was a smile on his face. He was really happy. For once we've seen Amamu really very, very happy. It is the moment for which he had been prepared. And that singular sacrificial act of dying is a continuing act that can be repeated a thousand and a million times. I thought that Christian hymn served the purpose very well as a closure for the book:

Who would true valiant see / Let him come hither / . . . / There's no discouragement / Shall make him once relent / His first avow'd intent / To be a pilgrim.

In that Christian sense the pilgrim is really the man who dares that world of danger for the salvation of the many, unifies all sensibilities and bridges the gulf, for the communal good.

Are you continuing the same kind of theme in your new novel?
I am. What I've done in this new novel really is to move out – the hero is an African-American. This novel opens with a slave caravan which we see in very

poetic terms moving southwards from somewhere up in the northern zones of West Africa. The caravan journey is towards the ocean, crossing some tracks of scrub desert land into savannah, into forest, into savannah again, to a river, then from the river to the sea. And I've peopled this landscape with almost all the elements of life and nature: not only the terrain, the trees, the plants, the shrubs that we have, but also the birds, the animals, the special plants like cactus, lichens, and neophytes. Along the route there are certain events that take place and the story has a back relationship to the story of a young black boy growing up in Virginia. We see him when his father is about to die, his father had worked on the railroad – it's a little history of their family right up to emancipation (they'd moved up from North Carolina to Virginia) with the racial situation of that time (it's set in the '50s) – then he moves to New York, his father has died. He is arrested for some crime he didn't commit, spends some time in jail and is redeemed by the Black Muslims – in fact he meets Malcolm X and becomes one of the bodyguards of Malcolm X and is there when Malcolm X is assassinated. But Malcolm's dream of Africa has fired his imagination and so he decides that he must go to Africa. So the two stories merge, the caravan journey into slavery and the journey from North Carolina, Virginia to New York and to Africa. We meet him in a nightclub in Accra; there's music which I love very much and dancing and lovely girls and so on. One of the people he meets there is the poet. He has just lost his job and has invited his friends to celebrate the loss of his job and they meet this man in this place and then of course things begin to happen. He – the American – is in danger and the poet saves him and takes him somewhere and a lot of other things happen at that somewhere until the ultimate end when there's a waking dream in which he sees a girl of about seventeen or eighteen who has had a nervous breakdown and was being cured at the shrine and she becomes part of him . . . But I won't tell you the whole story!

There seems to be a link between the titles of your works, or at least between the elements of which the titles are composed: 'rediscovery', 'blood', 'earth', 'brotherhood', 'memory', 'sea', 'word' . . . Would you like to discuss this?
I think some of them came quite unconsciously. I mean, I didn't sit down and think 'This will be my title.' But it's true that there's a sense in which they all flow into each other in that artistic consciousness in which I am working. Let me put it this way: if these titles define any concrete tendency towards a return to some place, a return to some elemental community, they don't do this in any traumatized way. They're purely the imaginative effort to respond to immediate things that happen to me. I've had quite rich and interesting experiences, not as dramatic as many other people have, but enough. Then also, at a very early age I had a lot of responsibility, family responsibilities and so on. When my father died, for example, I had to assume the leadership of the family. Everybody looks up to you to do all the things and then when you examine yourself there are times when you think you are a bit too hard and you need to soften that hardness with a little bit of consciousness of that place from which you came. As I said I have become more and more attached to my home place and in that sense I suspect I am more forbearing, I am more gentle with what I sometimes see as general human weakness which God knows all of us do have. I always talk about reconciliation, coming together . . . I don't make friends very easily, but the friends that I have are very good friends. I have five kids and my daughter is my favourite, she is twenty-two now, and then there are the

boys, and I tell them things, about this place where we are and what it is all about. And it is in that sense that there is this 'recovery' and 'homecoming' and 'return' and so on. These titles – 'The Wayfarer Comes Home' is another example – I suspect they flow out of a maybe unconscious vision of home-coming in the truly spiritual sense. I've done some other poems, more recent poems, 'Death's Tears', for instance, this is the kind of thing I keep on doing.

Which other African writers do you feel affinity to? Have any works by other contemporary African authors been of particular significance to you?
I have been particularly excited by everything Achebe has written. There is almost a cord of contact between myself and Achebe in the sense that Achebe – perhaps less complicatedly than I – deals with the same theme of reconcilia-tion, a historical and spiritual return to a place. What Achebe now needs to do is to let it transfuse into a work that will reflect the more contemporary situa-tion and inform it. I hear his new book, *Anthills of the Savannah*, does this, but I haven't read it yet. The work he had done earlier is a very solid work which must inform the contemporary and now consequently the future. There must be that *'eka xoxoawo nue wogbea yeyeawo do'*. He had tried to build the ropes from the old ropes that were there, but we've got to continue to build the ropes into the future. He cannot write another *Things Fall Apart*, there's no need for it, it's already done.

Apart from Chinua Achebe I have been particularly excited by the work of the purely imaginative writer within the very specific frame of a historical condition, that is Alex La Guma. The whole racial nightmare of South Africa is there. But as an artist what he confronts is the drama of human communities, and consequently the drama of individual persons in the throes of very disinte-grative forces, even though he has never worked out a redemptive way. There is no working a redemption out of these dramas. It is as if even articulating it alone indicates there's a possibility of some redemption, because there's the human factor which is most important in all these.

Of the younger poets, of course Kofi Anyidoho's work is beautiful poetry. It's like Kofi Anyidoho is the one who is taking over from me, and I'm excited for him in terms of some of the things that he does and does them better than I, even though there are certain areas where he labours over it a bit. But he has that sensibility to absorb and create it almost naturally.

Unless I'm being very narrow-minded I would also say that a good deal of African writing has been done and very good material has already come out. Whatever will come in the future will have to have links with what has been done already. Take-offs into individual talent, fantastic flowerings of indi-vidual talent do not excite me so much. I'm not interested in great personal statements. I'm interested in individual talent flowering within the total ambience of community. I don't care how small the community is so long as it gives expression to that total African reality. It could be a town, a village, or even a whole country. I have not talked in terms of a whole country, which is why some people have attacked me for just being an 'Ewe writer'. But I say this is ridiculous. I gave an interview once in New York which was published in *West Africa*. I was asked 'What is your first inspiration as a writer?' I said 'The sounds, the music, the sensibility of my Ewe origins' – 'Ah!' some fool said, 'He's an Ewe writer!' But what else could I have been, I say? Where else could I take my inspiration from? Where else could I have been coming from if it is not this? You've got to come from somewhere to be somewhere. For all of us to be

Ghanaians, we must come from some specific place. And only a fool would deny this; unless you pay attention to that specific place that did shape your perspective, or is underneath whatever perspective you have come to have, you will be coming from nowhere or belong to no place. We the writers of Africa must insist that we come from a place, and beyond that, as Anyidoho puts it so beautifully in one of his poems, 'We have people', we are a people.

SELECTED BIBLIOGRAPHY

POETRY
(George Awoonor-Williams), *Rediscovery and Other Poems* (Ibadan: Mbari, 1964).
Night of My Blood (New York: Doubleday, 1971).
Ride Me, Memory (Greenfield Center, NY: Greenfield Review Press, 1973).
The House By The Sea (Greenfield Center, NY: Greenfield Review Press, 1978).
Until the Morning After. Collected Poems 1963–1985 (Greenfield Center, NY: Greenfield Review Press, 1987, and Accra: Woeli Publishing Services, 1987). (Contains all Awoonor's previous collections, together with nine 'New Poems' and an autobiographical note).

NOVELS
This Earth, My Brother (New York: Doubleday, 1971).
Comes the Voyager At Last (Accra: Woeli Publishing Services, forthcoming).

THEATRE
'Ancestral Power' and 'Lament' in *Short African Plays* (London: Heinemann, 1972), pp. 1–11 and 119–28.

CRITICISM, ESSAYS IN HISTORY AND POLITICS
The Breast of the Earth: a survey of the history, culture and literature of Africa south of the Sahara (New York: Doubleday, 1975).
The Ghana Revolution (New York: Oases, 1984)
Ghana: A Political History (Accra: Woeli Publishing Services and Sedco, 1990).

Mohammed ben Abdallah

The ideal rulers, for the griot-protagonist of one of Mohammed ben Abdallah's earliest and most celebrated plays, are 'men who always question', who 'step out of the clamouring mass of living corpses to ask . . . Why?' Involved in Ghanaian theatrical life since an early age, ben Abdallah combines the teaching of Frantz Fanon with the techniques of the West African griots and the interrogative approach of the traditional dilemma tales in his search for an art of 'faction' or 'true fiction'. Drawing on the history and cultural heritage of a variety of West African peoples and on the 'international language' of music, mime and dance, he also seems to be moving increasingly towards the creation of a bilingual theatre where English and Akan can coexist.

After attending secondary school in Accra, ben Abdallah trained as a teacher at Wesley College, Kumasi, where he mounted several productions. After two years teaching at Prempeh College, he enrolled at the School of Music and Drama (now School of Performing Arts) attached to the Institute of African Studies at the University of Ghana, Legon, where he worked closely with Legon 7, a student drama group, developing a touring group, the Legon Road Theatre. He then went to the USA for post-graduate studies, obtaining a Master's degree from the University of Georgia and a Doctorate degree from the University of Texas at Austin. Appointed Secretary for Culture and Tourism in the Government of Jerry Rawlings in 1983, he is currently the Chairman of the National Commission on Culture. He lectures at the School of Performing Arts, University of Ghana, Legon, and directs its resident theatre company, Abibigromma. Mohammed ben Abdallah has also composed plays for children: *Ananse and the Golden Drum* and *Ananse and the Rain God* were produced in the early seventies.

3

Mohammed ben Abdallah

This interview was given in London (November 1984), after the 'New Directions in African Literature' conference at the Commonwealth Institute, at which a video of some of ben Abdallah's work had been shown during a workshop on African theatre chaired by the author.

In a recent talk on Ghanaian theatre you said that the concert party is one of the most interesting forms of theatrical activity in the country and that it originated after the First World War (in 1922) from an encounter between Afro-Americans and Ghanaians, being based essentially on the American minstrel show. Are there no sources for this kind of performance in traditional Ghanaian theatrical activities?

That's not the point really. The form may have been inspired by this, but it grew away from it and is now completely Ghanaian. Its only similarity to the minstrel show – and even that is getting lost now – is the painting of the face, the make-up. Actually it has a lot of the elements of the *commedia dell'arte*: stock characterization, expanded and exaggerated acting, an element of satire, of moralization, teaching of lessons, broad acting and slapstick, and the use of the body extensively in terms of dance, music, mime, movement and improvisation, even at times acrobatics. But the relationship with the *commedia dell'arte* is purely accidental. There is no connection whatsoever, it just developed along similar lines. There is no set of characters who are always there, like Pantalone in the *commedia dell'arte*, but there are types who can be recognized. They do all kinds of stories and tales – even Shakespeare! – just improvising without the text of course. I've seen a *Merchant of Venice* in Akan for instance. Then melodrama is a very important aspect: there are lots of tearjerkers. And they are very good at researching. They come into the community and the first thing they do is they find out who is the village villain, who is the prostitute, who the organizer – all kinds of little things – and they make fun of these people.

So it becomes very topical?
Well, they camouflage it of course. And this has become a very, very popular form, not just in Ghana but in West Africa generally. People have to travel around, devising ways and means of surviving. They perform and if they get enough money they purchase a bus – it's a very important thing to be able to travel. So they travel in vans and they can go to one area and perform within that area maybe for a week and while they are performing the driver will be using the van as a means of carting people to and fro from one village to another and collecting money, so he's also making money for the group!

So they're very flexible.
That's right! Then they've also developed a kind of music which has become a peculiarity of the concert party: it's the guitar-band music. It evolved out of the concert party and out of that you get groups like the 'African Brothers International' which is now just a musical group. So besides doing that kind of drama, they also do music and some of them have made very popular albums. So their influence in the theatre and music of Africa has spread and is of very great interest even if it's still underestimated.

How long do the performances last, and where do they actually take place?
The typical one starts at 8 pm and may end at around 4 am! Most of the time, in the big cities, the performances are held in a cinema house or even a nightclub. In the villages they'll be held in the village square or the town hall or the community centre. In the villages what they do is they come in the daytime and everybody knows they have arrived because they go on top of their car or bus and play their music as they drive around the town. Then they set up their stage and people come from smaller villages around (they have been known to carry their chairs and lanterns with them). When the performance starts it starts with music while the audience is getting seated and then there is a series of opening numbers which are usually accompanied by vigorous dancing by the comedians of the group. Then they play a few numbers and do short sketches that make fun of people, like the story about a young girl who quit going to school simply because she wanted to make some money. So she started selling bread and one day some young man calls her into his room and says he wants to buy some bread. Before she knows it she is seduced and then becomes pregnant and has a baby. She can't do anything, she can't go anywhere, because she has the baby at such an early age. Then the actor says 'Well now, that girl, tomorrow morning, if you look out you will see her carrying her tray with bread in it: she's still selling bread!' That's the kind of thing they do, based on their local research. These little sketches take up quite a long time. The actual concert proper, the story they call the concert, begins maybe about midnight and goes on very long. They take their time and it's very simple. They don't have a stage. They use a big piece of cloth they tie up to dress behind and they set up their instruments and play in front of it. In the cinema houses there's not much room on the stage. There's a big wall and maybe about six feet or so in front, but it's enough for them.

You are supposed to feel free to interrupt the performance: people talk to the actors, the characters, insulting them. The wicked stepmother for instance gets insulted by the audience and when the stepdaughter is ill-treated in her tattered clothes, people have been known to get up and give her some money while she's singing her sad song!

It's a form that has really established itself. Its problem right now is time. People don't have time any more to sit down all evening way into the early morning, so they are forced to change and adapt and the plays are getting shorter. They're also learning the techniques of modern theatre. Some of them are even using stage lighting.

What sort of audiences go to the concert parties?
A cross-section. It's not just your ordinary illiterate public. Ghanaians love Highlife music, and there is such a variety of things they do that they attract different kinds of people. They perform mostly in Akan, I've never heard any of them performing in any of the other Ghanaian languages. But it's not surprising as they started on the coast, with duos and trios, the Azim trio . . .

How many companies do you think there are? Or is it impossible to say?
There are quite a few of them. Some of the big ones – the Kakaiku Concert Party – are still around even if Kakaiku himself is dead. Okukuseku – they like these names – the Royal Brothers . . . Some of them have been in the system for quite a long time. They've established a reputation, though some of their leaders are dead. Bob Cole, for instance, is a legend in Ghana. He used to lead a trio, the Azim trio or the 'Two Bobs'. Even their names are interesting. The first one said he was called Bob Johnson. He goes back to the Minstrel show and Al Jolson, that's why they called themselves the 'Two Bobs'. Bob Cole is still alive and does a lot of work. One of these concert parties was turned into a national concert party by the late President Nkrumah, a sort of national troupe: 'The Arts Council Concert Party', based at the Arts Centre.

Do they still maintain their spontaneity despite this official standing?
They don't do scripted plays. They just keep creating on their own. So this is the one and probably the only traditional professional theatre company that exists in Ghana.

In Nigeria research has shown that there existed a traditional professional travelling theatre even before colonial times. Was there anything similar in Ghana?
The only thing I can think of along those lines is what they used to call the 'storytelling theatre'. But there are very few places where it existed as a *professional* form. I find that term very difficult to deal with by the way. By professional in the Western sense you mean something people get their livelihood from, in the sense that it's all they do for their living. In that sense it's very, very hard to see people in Ghana who are professional performers. There are performers who have professional standards, but so far as saying that is all they do for their living, well, they have other things that they do: they farm, they hunt, but they are very well known for being excellent performers. There are one or two areas – there's a place called Atwia, a village in the central region of Ghana – where they have professional storytellers who don't just tell the story, they perform it. Efua Sutherland has done some research on them. It's a very old tradition which must have started at least as early as the early eighteenth

century, and it still carries on. They pick up the *Anansesem* tradition – the Ananse story form that is all over Ghana – but here they've developed it into what they call *Anansegoro* (Ananse play), so they don't just tell the story. It's a call and response thing. All over Ghana the person who starts the story sees that the audience responds and then as he says the story somebody will start a song and everybody will join in and get up and dance and so on. But in this community they *perform* the story and have developed professional performers who just go about performing these stories.

Presumably it's a very different tradition from that of ritual theatre?
Yes. Ritual theatre is a very, very religious thing. Storytelling theatre is mostly educational. It's a means of educating the community and the children at large on the traditions and customs and morals and values of their society.

Would you say contemporary Ghanaian drama derives more from the storytelling tradition?
I think from both. My theatre, for instance, is heavily influenced by ritual – sometimes too heavily, I'm aware of that. I can't think of a single play I have written that doesn't have that heavy ritual aspect. Maybe because for me the ritual – the mask and the dance which are all part of the ritual anyway – provides a very important medium for the regeneration of society. I don't believe in theatre purely for entertainment.

What effect did the impact of Western culture have on Ghanaian theatre?
I think a lot. The developments have to be connected with Christianity, the coming of Christianity to West Africa and to Ghana specifically. With it came the attempt by the Church to use drama as a means of educating and converting people. When schools were started, part of the process of cultural imperialism was to educate people: they had to learn Shakespeare and so on, and this was actually introduced into the system. The early drama performances were mostly performances by expatriates to entertain themselves. They used to meet at the European Club to have a drink and chat and eventually they formed drama groups and did plays by Shakespeare, Shaw, and so on. Then there were the schools, the old schools like Achimota school which was later to develop into the University of Ghana. Achimota still has a tradition of Gilbert and Sullivan. Every year they do one Gilbert and Sullivan – *The Mikado, The Pirates of Penzance* – and recently they have added Molière to it. In Cape Coast there were quite a number of these schools and eventually the inter-schools drama competitions developed.

Were these competitions entirely for productions of plays by foreign dramatists, or was any original work by the students themselves being produced?
No, they were all productions of plays by Shakespeare, Shaw, Sheridan and they were doing quite a good job with them.

What period did all this happen in?
It started when the first schools, the first secondary schools, were founded, way back in the 1920s in Achimota, I don't remember the dates. It was considered part of education, the education of the Ghanaian. But then there was also a play called *The Blinkards*, by Kobina Sekyi . . .

'Africa's George Bernard Shaw', I think he's been described as!

That's right! One of my dreams is, when we have rehabilitated our studios, to really do a film of *The Blinkards*. I think it evokes the atmosphere and environment of Cape Coast at a time which would be fantastic to capture on the screen, realistically, I mean. It would take a lot of research, of course. It was only discovered fairly recently. One of his grandchildren discovered the script, but it was not published. It's not like some of these old colonial scholars whose works were published and who were appreciated by people. Sekyi's works were lost. It's a biting satire.

It's also interesting from the linguistic aspect, isn't it? I mean, it was not just in English.

That's right, parts were in Akan. This is one of our very earliest Ghanaian writers, but he was virtually unknown until recently and all this time people were still doing drama that was Western, mostly British. The only non-British playwright who seemed to have broken in was Luigi Pirandello. As a sixteen-year-old I saw his *Six Characters in Search of an Author*. I don't remember now which group did it. Towards independence there were visits by European performers and groups.

Was there a change in theatrical activity with the approach of independence?

Independence was reflected in the selection of the kind of plays which were put on. But Ghanaian and African playwrights were not feeling confident enough to come out and do their own things and write their own scripts. Even someone like Wole Soyinka was not on the scene. He didn't come out until just before independence when he did *The Lion and the Jewel* and even then it was when he was in London at the Royal Court Theatre. Then of course he wrote *A Dance of the Forests* for the Nigerian independence celebrations.

So modern Ghanaian theatre is really a post-independence phenomenon.

That's what I'm leading up to. Modern African theatre is a post-independence phenomenon and in Ghana particularly. First of all there is the development of the African writer from the colonized writer, giving evidence of his mastery of the literature of the colonizing power. And you could really see that. People like Joe de Graft who was one of the leaders, or even Efua Sutherland: what they did was to show a mastery of Western theatre. Efua's first and probably one of her best works is called *Edufa*. It's based on a Greek tragedy. And Joe de Graft for a long time was known more as an actor than as a playwright. He was a fantastic actor and did all kinds of Shakespearean roles. The first 'African' thing that he did was when he took *Hamlet* and made a film of it called *Hamile* – the name of a town in Northern Ghana, which is where he set the play and costumed it, Africanizing it only by changing the names of people and places. He maintained most of Shakespeare's language. And he kept on doing that kind of thing. He did another play called *Mambo* just before he died. It was rather a radical adaptation of *Macbeth* where he changed the language a bit, maintaining some of the poetry. Lady Macbeth became three women: three women in one, a schizophrenic kind of character. But before he died he had begun to break away from Shakespeare. He did several of his own things, *Sons and Daughters*, for instance, and *Through a Film Darkly*. He was one of the very earliest Ghanaian playwrights. With Efua Sutherland he started the School of Music and Drama at the University of Ghana, but the interesting thing is that quite a few people came from Nigeria to study the model and then went back, and suddenly Nigeria took over. There was Wole Soyinka, J.P. Clark, Ola Rotimi, Duro Ladipo. It became a habit for Ghanaians just to pick on these and do justice to them in Ghana.

So Ghana developed theatrically more in the sense of its theatre than in the sense of theatre literature. There were quite a lot of good theatre groups. There was a group called the Freelance Players. Then Mrs Sutherland managed to get some foundation money and started the Ghana Drama Studio, which is now a building – a very interesting structure – in which a lot of experimental work is done. Since then theatrical development has followed the ups and downs of the country's political situation. Another interesting development is coming from little dance groups. They're experimenting, doing what they call dance dramas, using the traditional dances to create new things. I think eventually there will be some kind of meeting point between that and the developments in drama. There, too, people are saying we cannot go the way Europe has developed. It's alright to have *The Bloodknot* and *Sizwe Banzi is Dead*. But that kind of drama people think will not *grow* in Africa. I have my doubts about it. I think eventually the two will exist side by side. But I think the most powerful kind of theatre in Africa would be the type that combines the celebrative aspects of the festival and the original essences of the ritual with the self-criticism of modern theatre as you find it in Britain and the USA and so on. Our rituals are as essential in life as eating, drinking, breathing, living. Europe and America have reached somewhere through their rejection of certain aspects. They have moved up to a certain point. We have their example, but we happen also to have a lot of the things they have left behind. For me there is an implicit advice in the images of people like Brecht, Artaud, Genet, Peter Brook [laughs] who are looking all over the place, even in our backyards in Africa, for what we have to bring life into their theatre. I think Peter Brook says specifically that he's looking for a theatre that's as important as breathing, eating, sex . . . I think again that is dreaming too far, but I don't think we can ever *really* capture that if we insist on theatre in the Western sense of the word. Once you have banished the gods, which we are doing rapidly in Africa, it's very hard to maintain that essential aspect.

What relationship do you see today between the work of the major Ghanaian dramatists and traditional theatrical activity in Ghana?
I think there is a unanimous acceptance of the need not to go the Western way in terms of not compartmentalizing, removing music and dance from drama. Some writers are even very religious about this. It's probably one of the easiest ways to identify a piece as African as opposed to something that is purely Western. That's one thing. Then I think it will also take some time before African playwrights move away from politics. They, more than poets and novelists, tend to see their work as linked up with the politics of Africa. Ngũgĩ, for instance, has never been apolitical in his novels, but he comes out as *most* political when you look at his playwriting. Maybe it has to do with the form they use rather than their intentions.

Presumably there is quite a lot of theatrical activity still in the schools and universities?
That's where most of it gets done in terms of the theatre we've been talking about, the theatre of people like Wole Soyinka, Joe de Graft, Ama Ata Aidoo,

Efua Sutherland and so on: in the universities, the teacher training colleges, the secondary schools. Outside of that the only other places where you see them performed may be community centres, like in Accra the Arts Centre, or in Kumasi the Ghanaian Cultural Centre. All these places have their own resident amateur drama groups. Kumasi Cultural Centre has two drama groups, one of them called Anokye Players, named after the priest who unified the Ashantis.

The Ashanti kingdom was not a nation. It was a group of different tribes and groups who spoke different dialects. The legend says that there was a Queen Mother who could not have a child, so she went to this High Priest to seek help. Eventually she had a baby and she named the child after the god of that shrine, Tutu: Osei Tutu. It was also the custom in those days to send the prince to another palace of a different king – I guess there's the feeling that you can't teach your own son – so this boy was sent to another court, which was where he met this young priest and they became friends. He also met a girl and they had an affair. The girl was a princess and she became pregnant, so he ran away and went back to Ashanti and that developed into a war between Ashanti and Dentyira, a war that lasted for a long time. Osei Tutu eventually became the King of Ashanti and he invited the priest to come and stay with him in Ashanti. Later the priest became his adviser, his major adviser. And it was this priest who one day called all the Kings of Ashanti and told them he had had a vision: they were going to become a great nation. So at that gathering he asked every king to pull a lock of his hair and to cut their nails from their fingers and toes. He collected all of it and put it all together and mixed it with something. Then he chanted some incantations and the skies split open and a golden stool – solid gold – fell down from the sky and he said the souls of all the Ashanti people were in that stool. They were to stay united and that would be the source of their power and their strength. So the golden stool was very important for the Ashanti. There are all kinds of stories about how when the British went finally into the city of Kumasi they wanted the stool as the symbol of the surrender of the Ashanti people. Nobody knows what the real truth in this story is. It was said that the Ashanti gave the British that stool and it was brought to London and returned to Kumasi only after independence. But the Ashanti also say that when the British requested it as a symbol of surrender, the goldsmiths – all of them – went underground and produced a copy which was given to the British and that the golden stool never left Kumasi!

Anyway, this company was named after Anokye, and then there is another company too at the Arts Cultural Centre. And there are so many little groups like that, most of them amateur groups, teachers, nurses, students and workers who come together in the evenings and do performances.

Do the children study Ghanaian drama as part of their school programme?
This is becoming more and more frequent – African drama, not just Ghanaian. It used to be Shakespeare, the usual set books for literature, but now they include African authors. That also provides some of the incentives for people to do these plays. When I was a student there was the Legon Road Theatre: about seven of us who came together and formed this group. We would rehearse short things during the week and during the weekends we would take off. Sometimes we would do scenes from some of the plays they were studying in the schools and would visit these schools and do performances for them. At one point we even did a series on television: we'd do a scene and somebody else would talk about that scene, it helped develop an

interest in theatre. Besides that, there were the interschools drama competitions, which still go on.

Starting, I suppose, in colonial times?
That's right. They have maintained the tradition, but now most of the plays they do are Ghanaian or African even if every now and then some of them still do Shakespeare or adaptations from Shakespeare.

Do the students do any of the playwriting themselves?
Sometimes, yes. A lot of playwriting has come out of this. There was a student of Achimota school called Joris Wortenberg, a very interesting name for a Ghanaian! He came out of Achimota and was part of the tradition of *The Mikado*, *The Pirates of Penzance* and so on, and he was very strongly influenced by Molière. He wrote a comedy called *The Corpse's Comedy*. He picked up Molière's comic techniques very quickly, and eventually did an adaptation of *Le Tartuffe*, which he called *Osofu Moko*, which is the nickname of a quack priest who used to preach on Sundays against drinking, while he was known to be indulging in drinking. He moved from there and used a concert party technique to develop a series for television called *Osofu Dadze*. It became a very popular series and ran for a long time, every Sunday evening. It was like *Dallas*: everybody was glued to the screen and if you had a television set in your house and other people didn't you'd find them standing at your window and looking in! It was a very popular thing, but it was forcibly taken off the screen during the 1st December revolution. After that people kept asking for it, and the group that used to do it has turned into a concert party group and tours the country, so they see it just the same. The characters are stock characters, so they keep evolving new stories for themselves. This is a very interesting development: somebody who starts out from the Western tradition and slowly goes backwards into the concert party tradition. He didn't go the Wole Soyinka and Efua Sutherland way. In fact he stopped writing completely and it's the concert party people themselves who are carrying on.

Is there now much writing for television?
Yes, both spontaneously and induced. Radio Ghana keeps requesting scripts and encouraging writing competitions.

So there is not much imported stuff?
Very little. Except where there are exchange programmes, with Radio Netherlands, or Germany, where they send you a film in exchange for something else, both West and East Germany, I think. Television has suffered greatly from our economic problems. It was one thing that was set up properly along the correct lines. It was structured into the curricula of the schools. You can tune in and there will be music lessons, or other kinds of lessons: it was tuned in to education. It worked very well and was improving rapidly, but with the onset of the economic problems in Ghana everything collapsed. Television was black and white, all the cameras and technical things were outmoded and because of the developments in the electronics industry it was more expensive to maintain those old things, because if you ordered parts they had to be made specially. So everything really collapsed. About a month ago we signed an agreement with a Japanese company to change the whole thing, the studios are going to be completely overhauled and the whole system turned into colour. The hard-

ships in Ghana have developed in Ghanaians a sense of 'We will do it our-selves', which I think is very good.

How about cinema?
Again, there's the same kind of problem. Nkrumah did something which was very good for his time, but which has caused us a lot of trouble. Ghana has the best film industry technology in the whole of Africa. Nkrumah put the film industry under the Ministry for Information, because he saw information dis-semination as a very, very important thing. He was using film to make sure Ghanaians would know what was going on. If you went to see a movie the movie-house would lose its licence in the days of Nkrumah if it didn't start by showing the Ghana News Reel, which starts with the national anthem, the eagle, a few patriotic songs and then shows the highlights of the day's news. It was very good, there was a sense of pride in Ghanaians. He was using the film industry for that, so there are thousands of metres of footage on all kinds of things – speeches at the United Nations, the building of the Volta Dam – but I think that emphasis on documentaries and so on really killed film-making in Ghana. You really have to have some courage to get up and say you'll do things yourself. That's why you find people like Sembene Ousmane in Senegal doing things, while in Ghana we don't have anything, even though we have the equipment. What makes it sad is that Ghanaians are great filmgoers, they love the movies. There are theatre-houses all over the country and people flock into them to see films. When I grew up I saw things I'm sure people my age in the US haven't seen: I used to go to the movies three times a day. They'd start at 12.15 with the matinée: that's when they'd show the cowboy films. At 5 pm they showed what we called 'Dancy dancy', which is all dance, these were the musicals, that's when we got to see Ginger Rogers and Fred Astaire, Gene Kelly, *Singing in the Rain*, then that one in Paris . . . Then at 8.30 there were the 'heavies'. That's when you saw *The Thief of Baghdad* with Sabu, or *Gunga Dhin*, or *The Charge of the Light Brigade*, or Victor Mature in *Samson and Delilah*. Then later on there was the influx of Indian films, which are popular in Ghana, even though people don't speak a word of Hindustani.

They're not dubbed?
No, I'm quite serious! People will go in and sit there and follow the story. Some of them can sing all those songs. And some of those Indian films are long: three hours, three and a half hours. So it's a pity. It's not that we didn't have the expertise, but we were very late in coming into it. There's an Institute, the National Institute of Film and Television, the only one of its kind in Africa, built with the aid of the Frederick Evert Foundation in Accra. It was started by the Germans. For about four years they ran it and then they handed it over to the Ghanaians. We get students from all over Africa and some of the people who are coming out of it are really very good. So there is hope for the future.

What languages are used in the theatre productions?
The only theatre that really does everything in the Ghanaian languages is the concert party. In the other areas there is always a combination. Efua Sutherland, for instance, has a group called Kusum Agromma. It was a concert party group which she cut down. They maintain the concert party format: they use the guitar – the concert party relies very heavily on the guitar – and she put in more and more dialogue. What she does with them is that the group

makes the play, she doesn't write, she works with them on the play. *The Marriage of Anansewa* for instance was done like that. I was one of the original performers in it. It was done in Akan by the group, with her, and then when they finished she wrote the script in Akan and then translated it into English. More and more people are doing that now. You can go into a place where most of the people don't speak English so you do the play in Akan. In the urban areas you'll do it in English. The churches are also doing something interesting. In every church there is a drama group and a lot of them are doing things in the Akan language or in the language of the area.

Mostly religious dramas, I suppose?
Not necessarily. There was a play called *Kakabunka malabuna*, for instance, which was written by a Roman Catholic priest, he played a leading role in it. The advert for it on TV was great: 'Kakabun malabun, kakabunka malabunka!'

What does it mean?
Nothing! Anyway, a lot of these things are going on. The theatrical scene in Ghana is really very alive and I hope with the recent improvement in the economic situation we are going to see more. The problem is that the publishing houses have a limited interest in African writing and then plays don't sell nearly as well as novels, so they're not interested in publishing plays. One of the things we're doing now at the Ministry of Culture is to barge into publishing. We've already started setting up the machinery for the rehabilitation of the Ghana Publishing Corporation and Printing House and a few other printing houses that are government owned.

Actually publishing really started fairly early in Ghana, didn't it?
That's right! And it's been going on for a long time. What happened is that the printing presses got very old and for a long time there was no money to change them. Then the money came and everything changed. But then the economic problem set in and there was no paper, no ink. So we are left with this fantastic machinery and we can't do anything with it. Things have now started improving. But until somewhere in the middle of next year no novel or poem is going to come out of the Publishing Corporation. It's a priority we have to set – there are kids in our schools who don't have books, not just reading books, but even exercise – so there's feverish work going on to produce things for the schools.

Could you tell me something about your own experience in theatre?
The first play I wrote was when I was a student. I started this travelling company and we decided that we were going to go touring the country coming back in time to go to school on Monday. Then I realized there were no scripts. You could do Joe de Graft's plays a number of times. Wole Soyinka's plays had come out, but we felt we wanted to deal with the situation of Ghana and there were no scripts! So that forced me to write my first play called *The Alien King*. It was going to be an epic, a three-hour epic, very long. I showed it to my playwriting teacher, but he took off everything except the last three pages. Then he gave them to me and said 'Your play begins here, all the rest is nonsense!' I went home with it and my wife was cooking in a little coal pot thing and I crushed it up and threw it in the fire! Two days later I came out with a shorter version,

very tight and compact, and that was *The Alien King*. From that time onwards I decided I was only going to write one-act plays and I think that's a very good training exercise for any playwright.

After that I wrote *The Slaves*, followed by *Verdict of the Cobra*, which won first prize at an annual playwriting contest in the US, run by the National Association for Speech and Dramatic Arts. Then I went to the US. Before I left I wrote a children's play, called *Ananse and the Golden Drum*, which was to be part of a series. I used to work at the Cultural Centre in Kumasi: I was the Drama Organizer for the Ministry of Education in the Central Region – it was in 1973 or '74 – so we sent a letter to all the schools saying they could send their children to come and see the play. It was to start at two o'clock, but at one o'clock I went to the Cultural Centre and it was as if somebody had opened the flood-gates: children coming from every part of the city! There was no way you could contain them and the place was packed. The first children's play was an experiment, but it opened my eyes to a need. So, from then onwards I wrote something like one children's play every six months: *Ananse and the Golden Drum*, *Ananse and the Rain God*, *The Witch of Mopti*, before I left for the US to do my Master's degree, and that was where I wrote *The Trial of Mallam Ilya*.

Then I went to the University of Texas and for my PhD I wrote three full length plays. That's when I took *The Slaves* and expanded it. Then I did another play called *The Blind Hippopotamus* and the third one was called *The Fall of Kumbi* which is a historical drama. Kumbi was the capital of the old kingdom of Ghana in the Sudanic Empire. And the story is about how Kumbi was captured and destroyed by the Moorish army. The city is destroyed and the women are captured and taken away to be sold into slavery. There's an exodus. Before the city fell, some of the men decided it was useless to fight and it was better to come down south. That was the beginning of the movement southwards. I included a lot of fiction, plus history, fact, some of the things I looked up in history books about the origins of the Ashanti people and other people of the southern part in the movement from the Sahel region. The women slaves were taken to an island off the coast of Senegal, which is a kind of foreshadowing of the castle that was to develop on the island of Gorée. A serious thing happened there, a kind of community suicide rather than be sold into slavery, by one of the women, who led the rest of the women, offering herself as a sacrifice but at the same time encouraging them to go on and live. She made a prophecy about how from out of their loins will spring forth a generation of men and women out of slavery, who will one day be the beginning of the end of the civilization which has bathed mankind in blood, and so on. It's a rather wild and crazy play. We were going to do it in Ghana last year with the Abibigromma group, but we decided our audience was not ready for it, so we shelved it, but we enjoyed rehearsing it. It was one of the plays we used as a training piece and one of these days we'll come back and do it for the public.

Is this your latest work?
No, there's another one, a very short one called *Saman Ba*. I wrote it in Akan and then translated it into English. It means 'Child of the Dead'. It's about a girl. I wrote it in Georgia – I was in Georgia from 1974 to 1976 – a quick draft of it. I did it in one night and then put it aside: it scared the hell out of me! Then about three months ago I picked it up and finished it. One evening we were going through all kinds of problems. The play begins in a grove, a forest, which is also a graveyard. There is a big tree out of which has been carved a kind of seat.

On the seat is one of these things with a hole in the bottom and there's a woman sitting on it. Underneath the seat is a big black pot. The woman is pregnant, but she's dead . . . It comes out of an Akan tradition that they never bury a pregnant dead woman with a baby in her stomach; the baby has to come out. It's believed that a pregnant woman doesn't die. A woman dies in delivering a baby, but for a woman to die with a baby in her stomach there is something wrong and they have a way of finding it out. They put her in that position for three days and three nights and the High Priest is supposed to go away and confer with the gods. All kinds of things happen and if there is no foul play in her death the baby will drop out into the pot and will be buried in the pot. But if the baby doesn't fall out then there is really something wrong. The belief is that if whoever did the wrong comes out and confesses, the baby will drop out into the pot.

I use that as a confrontation theme to deal with the past. So the play opens with the sound of the High Priest's bell and his gong and the dead body is sitting there, a man is sitting over here and his wife over there. From their conversation we learn that he is the husband and she is the professional mourner. It comes out that the dead body is actually the body of the wife's younger sister who has been living with them. She was in school, but she became pregnant and they wanted to find out who was responsible for the pregnancy. So the story unravels, but in between there are all kinds of things. The High Priest comes back and performs some rituals, there is some dancing – I use it also to reveal some of the ritual behind death and specially that particular kind of death. It's very uncommon that you see anything about the death of a pregnant woman. It's a soul-searching thing, with a flashback to a couple of scenes between the man and his wife and her sister, the relationships in the family. Eventually it comes out that the girl was made to confess that she was pregnant with another boy who is a student also. It would have meant that he would get into trouble and afterwards she feels really guilty that she has put the blame on him when really . . . And then the scene reveals that there was a relationship between her and her sister's husband. The priest's role is also very interesting. He is not in on the conversation, it is between the husband and wife, and at the climax of the play, when he is coming back, the bell rings closer and closer and closer . . . and by the time he comes in the revelation has been made and there is a popping sound – pop! – the baby drops into the pot and that's the end of the play! It's a one night thing, the kind of thing you write in winter, when it's very cold outside, but you are drenched in sweat! So I just put it away and forgot about it. I've revised it, finished it, but I haven't given it out to anybody yet.

Are you going to have any of your work published?
I don't know. What has happened is that I find myself accepting the stage presentation as a kind of publishing. I'm working on another play, a full-length play. It's actually based on Brecht's *The Good Woman of Setzwan*. When I came back from the States there was a joke about Nigerians, how they referred to Ghanaians. In Ghana you are paid something like 20 cedis a day, and the average worker pays the equivalent of that for transportation from his house to his place of work and that doesn't take into account what he eats for breakfast, for lunch and dinner, what his wife and children eat, his children's school fees, his rent and everything. But everybody still survives. So the Nigerians nickname Ghana 'the land of 12 million magicians'. As soon as they told me that I

thought of *The Good Woman of Setzuan* and came out with the draft of a script called *The City of a Million Magicians*. It's in a market city, where everybody is finding a way to survive. A long time ago I used to live in a place called Nima, a ghetto. An American friend of mine came to visit me and said it reminded him of Harlem: it was difficult for anybody to grow up in a place like that and not become a 'hustler'. And when I read *The Good Woman of Setzwan* it reminded me of quite a few people there who had to survive and it was 'impossible for them to be good and survive at the same time'. It was totally against their nature. There are quite a few people in Ghana like that today.

SELECTED BIBLIOGRAPHY

THEATRE
The Trial of Mallam Ilya and Other Plays (Accra: Woeli Publishing Services, 1987). Contains: *The Alien King*, first produced in January 1971 at the University of Ghana Commonwealth Hall and already published in part in James Morel Gibbs, 'Mohammed ben Abdallah and the Legon Road Theatre', *African Arts / Arts d'Afrique*, V, 4 (1972), pp. 34–5, 63–8; *Verdict of the Cobra* and *The Trial of Mallam Ilya*.
The Fall of Kumbi and Other Plays (Accra: Woeli Publishing Services, 1989). Contains: *The Witch of Mopti*, *The Slaves* (the first non-American play to win the Randolph Edmunds Award of the National Association for Speech and Dramatic Arts in 1972) and *The Fall of Kumbi*.

Chinua Achebe

The return of Nigeria's most celebrated novelist to the genre he had abandoned in 1965, after the defeat of Biafra, has encouraged a renewal of interest in the work of Chinua Achebe, whose decision to react and respond to the colonial writers' distorted images of Africa had produced, in 1958, what was to become the most widely read and loved 'classic' of African literature in English, *Things Fall Apart*.

Born in Ogidi in 1930, Chinua Achebe was educated at the Government Secondary School in Umuahia. He then went on to study medicine, which he soon dropped, and later literature at the University College of Ibadan. After a brief period of teaching, he worked with the Nigerian Broadcasting Company in Lagos, becoming Director of External Broadcasting. After the Civil War, in which he was actively involved on the side of Biafra, Achebe devoted himself to poetry, short stories and essays, but also to encouraging the development of cultural activity in his country through his lecturing – at the University of Enugu, where he was Director of African Studies, and at the University of Nsukka – and editing. The founder of *Okike*, one of Nigeria's major literary journals, he has also co-edited several works, including, with Dubem Okafor, an anthology of poems in honour of Christopher Okigbo, *Don't Let Him Die* (Enugu: Fourth Dimension, 1978). An important sideline is represented by his books for children. Chinua Achebe has received a number of awards, including the Nigerian National Merit Award and, for his book of poems, the first Commonwealth Poetry Prize, of which he was joint-winner in 1972.

NIGERIA

4

Chinua Achebe

This interview was carried out shortly after the launching of Achebe's latest novel, London, 17 September 1987. It has previously been published in Africa America Asia Australia, *Rome, IV (1988), pp. 69–82. An abbreviated version has also appeared in Italian in* L'Indice, *VI, 2 (February 1989), pp. 21–2.*

You said recently that the label 'The Novelist as Teacher' has haunted you ever since you used it as the title of an essay in 1965. At the launching of *Anthills of the Savannah*, you seemed to be encouraging listeners to look upon the novelist rather as an explorer, or perhaps as a teacher who can be seen as an explorer. Could you enlarge on this?

You are right. I don't think I was completely aware how narrow people can be in their view of the teacher! I was never really thinking of the teacher in a narrow sense at all. I was thinking of the teacher in the sense of the great teachers, like Jesus Christ or Mohammed, Buddha or Plato. These were the people I had in mind, not some little fellow who is really oppressed by life and can't find any other job except to stand in front of people and punish them. This seems to me to be the problem. As there is this tendency to think in categories, perhaps I should have used some different kind of person rather than a teacher. Anyhow, I was not thinking of the kind of teacher who prescribes. A good teacher never prescribes; he *draws out*. Education is a drawing out of what is there, leading out, helping the pupil to discover . . . to explore.

The kind of relationship you want with your reader is presumably a very active one.

Yes, we are interacting: the teacher is learning from his pupils at the same time, so that he can sharpen his tools. I like your use of the explorer image, that's really what it is.

You seem in all five novels to be exploring the roles, responsibilities and limits of intellectuals in Africa. In *Things Fall Apart* there is a distinction between the man of action and the intellectual – Okonkwo and his father – but the distinction tends to blur in your later novels, where the problem is rather how the two figures – the man of action and the artist/intellectual/creator – can combine.

That is a continuing problem. Even when I am not dealing with it specifically, it is always there. It is the man of action who is always at centre-stage: the political leader, or the priest who is also a political leader, the Minister, the Minister of Culture, these are all men of action. The way society is organized, they are the ones who make things *happen*. All we are saying really is that they should *listen*, they should listen to the voice of the artist even when the artist is not visible, for what he stands for. The artists are the other side of the truth, the side of gentleness where there is too much violence, humaneness where there is too much concentration on efficiency or strength, the voice of the mother who cares for life continuing. This side must not be suppressed. This is what I was really saying. But it was not clearly brought out again until *Anthills,* where I have an actual character who is an artist, maybe because I felt that what I was doing, leaving the voice of the artist hanging in the air, was not enough and that there should be somebody labelled 'artist' to take part in the action of the novel. I didn't think of it like this, but now that you raise the point I'm trying to understand what may have been going on in my mind.

These two roles, these two views of the world are very much at the centre of my thinking: action and reflection. It is these two working together that can save the situation. In Ezeulu I tried to combine the two in one person. It had its interest, but it did not solve the problem. It's something I have to keep coming back to again and again, because it will never be really resolved. These are the two polarities of our reality and we must expect them sometimes even to be at loggerheads. There is certainly a lot of this conflict in the contemporary African situation, the artist and the regime, and this is a manifestation of the same thing. If we can create this consciousness that the two need to work out a way of surviving side by side, as I think our traditional societies tried to do, we would really be much better off.

This leads to the problem of commitment and 'Non-Commitment', the title of one of your poems. Here you suggest that 'wisdom' and 'sensibleness' may be a bar to sight, a 'diaphragm' against what you call 'seminal rage'. How do you view commitment as a writer?

It is at the root of the writer's being: his commitment to his vision of the world, to truth as he understands it, including the truth of fiction, which is a slightly different kind of truth from the truth you encounter when you are buying and selling; the commitment to the integrity of language, commitment to excellence in the use of your talent so that you don't tolerate from yourself, in your work, something that you know can be done better by a little more attention, by waiting, by some more patience. So it is commitment over a wide scope of things really. The writer, any artist, who defaults in this is betraying the nature of art. This is why it is so difficult for me to accept legislation from some kinds of people who cannot see the world in its complexity: the fanatics of all kinds, of right or left, the fundamentalists of all kinds. These people do not understand, they cannot possibly understand, the kind of commitment I'm talking about. They use the word 'commitment' more frequently than artists do and they use it so frequently that the word has become debased and is now in the service of fanaticism. That is not what I had in mind. It is not what I mean by commitment: not commitment to a narrow definition of the world, to a narrow perception of reality, to a narrow view of politics or economics or anything, religion, race. One can become committed to any of these things, but that's not what I'm talking about. I'm talking about something quite different. When you are committed to your art, you are very different from the man who is committed, say, to his religion. I cannot see an artist being a fanatical person in terms of religion, it seems to me to be quite contradictory. You may have artists who are good churchmen, but if they are really good artists you will soon discover that they cannot be fanatical in their religion. The same goes for politics. What they are committed to is bigger, something of infinitely greater value than what church you go to, what race you belong to, what language you speak.

There is a strong focus on the problem of communication in your books and on the possibilities and limits of language. You yourself use a very wide register of language, probably also because you are reflecting a multilingual situation. Could you discuss this?

The integrity I was talking about is also reflected in one's ability to listen, very carefully, to all these registers. If I'm going to explore a certain kind of character, I must *listen* to this character. Before I can understand how his or her mind operates I must also know how he or she uses words. This is the first and most obvious level of judging whether I am truly looking at this character or not: I must know what they sound like, I must know *how* they speak language. It's not simply a matter of making the novel sound like real life, it is really part of a wider integrity. This character deserves to be listened to seriously, so that when I introduce what he's saying, I'm doing this with integrity and you can recognize him through the way he uses language. Of course if you have the kind of linguistic richness that we have in a place like Nigeria, it's an advantage to the writer. But you've got to learn to listen. Not everybody has learnt to listen; we all live in the same linguistic environment, but some writers bring their dialogue from I don't know where. This dialogue must come from the source, from the people. This is part of commitment to the people: I think it was Danquah who said we must pay one another's gods the compliment of calling them by their proper names. It is very, very important that you give people the respect that is due to them by presenting them properly, not through some kind of travesty, jazzing it up to make it sound nice or because this is what is expected. Somebody was just telling me about a book written by an Englishman living in Lagos, where the Pidgin is a sort of *Uncle Tom's Cabin* dialect, rather than the real Nigerian Pidgin, which is a language in itself, not something you can just cook up. There are some people who are not bothering to listen, who are just using what you might call the 'packaged' Pidgin: the 'I love Massah too much' kind of thing, but that's not what people actually say. So the beginning of this kind of integrity and commitment is that we must listen carefully and learn how people speak and convey it carefully.

The style and structure of your two poems to Christopher Okigbo – one in Igbo and another, 'Mango Seedling', in English – differ considerably. When you write poetry in Igbo do you tend to reproduce the traditional structures?

Sometimes. The Igbo poem on Christopher Okigbo is actually structured on a traditional dirge format, the song that people sing when one of their age-grade dies. The age-group goes around chanting. They don't accept that he is dead yet, so they are looking for him, wondering whether he has gone to the stream, or to the forest. It is a very old song, no doubt, and it's that form that I use in the Igbo poem, expanding it and asking more questions than the traditional song would ask.

In a 1970 interview at the University of Texas at Austin you explained that you were unwilling to write another novel because you were 'not at ease'. You felt that the novel was not appropriate for 'creating in the context of our struggle'. Judging by your essays in *The Trouble With Nigeria*, the past few years have been just as uneasy. Now, twenty years after your last novel, you have published a new one. Is this made possible by a change in your view of the genre?

I've tried to answer this question a number of times already, but without complete satisfaction. I don't really know, as a matter of fact, why it is only now that I have succeeded in bringing the novel to fruition. I started writing it about fifteen years ago and put it away completely. When I picked it up again about five years ago I had to read it carefully to see who and what were there and it still didn't advance at all, so I had to put it away again, thinking perhaps it was for good. I had the characters, these four people, who were there, but I hadn't got anything I considered adequate for them to do. But three years ago – I don't fully know why three years ago it was different – I picked the thing up again and reread it in order to get acquainted once more with the characters, and the story seemed to be there this time. So it is possible that I don't fully understand; perhaps the fact that I had rested and thought about our condition and written a rather angry essay about this, *The Trouble With Nigeria*: perhaps all that helped to ease the passage of the new story.

Do you see *Anthills* as being more related to your previous novels or to your other post-war writing?

I think they are all related. What I am trying to do is look at the story of Africa in the modern world, looking at it from different angles, according to what's happening at the time, according to what I've just been through, according to what I have just learned, or even just to be different from the way I looked at it previously. It's like the masquerade I talked about in *Arrow of God*, which is dancing. If you see the story of Africa in the modern age as that masquerade you just have to keep circling the arena in order to catch the various glimpses which you need in order to approach anything like a complete image of its formidable presence. If you stand in one place you see one view, and it's not enough. That's what I try to do: even the essays, even the poetry. I think they all come from the same concern, to tell as complete a story as possible. And of course our situation itself is not standing still, it's adding to itself all the time – and subtracting from it! The Civil War, for example, was not there, it had not happened, when I wrote the first four novels. Now it's a melancholy part of this dance, so what comes after it is going to be informed in one way or another by this tragedy. I'm not quite sure that I can say 'This thing in this book has been caused by this specific experience', but I have had to assimilate the Civil War experience, and so it must be there, in this new book, which is the first since that horrendous event. So in a way perhaps it's going to be the first of a new generation of books.

Anthills **seems to differ from your previous novels, which alternate between past and present, or in which past and present interrelate, in that it projects more explicitly into the future. Do you agree with this?**

Yes, I think it does, in the sense that it ends specifically with the birth of a new generation and with the possibility of some of the survivors picking up something from the wreck of their recent past that may help them as they make their way into the future. One of such gains being their awareness of the totality of the community as opposed to an elite sitting up there and not even knowing the names of the people they were dealing with or where they lived. Again, the same plea to respect the integrity of your fellows; to accord to everybody the respect that is due to them as people. They may be only labourers or taxi-drivers, but they are full people: they have total humanity which is no less than that of anybody else and has to be accorded full respect. The Igbo people say that when you appear in a crowd the greeting that you give is 'Everybody and his own', because you can't go round shaking hands with 400 people or call each of them by his title, that would be impossible, so you say: 'Everybody and his own', or 'To every man his due'. I think this is a new lesson that is insinuating itself into the consciousness of the survivors of *Anthills*. Beatrice particularly is aware of this and she is also aware that it is something new, something that even Chris did not know, or was just beginning to know at the moment of his death. So this is something that points to the possibility of better performance, to put it crudely, if they should have another chance. Now that kind of thought was actually present in my mind in *A Man of the People*, but I didn't dwell on it specifically. I just left it to my readers' imagination to understand, for instance, that if Odili were to have another chance to go through the same experience he would do rather better, would be a better person than he was before. But clearly I seem to have once again overestimated the imagination some readers can bring to fiction!

Perhaps your irony in presenting the character was over-successful. The reader tends to view Odili as an unreliable narrator.
One thing that he wasn't unreliable about was his own feelings, and that saves him as a human being, as somebody who puts his own feelings under the microscope and analyses them honestly, seeing where he's behaving badly and so on. I think such a person is worthy of respect. Anyway, that was certainly in my mind there. But you are right, there's a more specific overtone in *Anthills* of what would happen in the future if the right lessons are learned. There's always a big 'if', of course.

What about the youngest member of the new generation, the newly born baby, the girl who is given a boy's name?
Well, it's really a name that could belong to anybody. The fact that it was appropriated by men in the past was an indication of one of the flaws in the society. Amaechina is a real name and the implication of the 'path', 'May-the-path-never-close', is really that it is only a boy who can keep the family homestead alive and the path they are talking about is the path that leads to the family's compound. Girls don't count because they go out, they marry elsewhere. It is only the boy who stays in the compound. If there is no boy, then the compound closes. This is why if you find a family that is having difficulty having a male issue, but finally succeeds, they are likely to call him Amaechina: their hope of immortality hangs on this one person. This is a masculine view of the world, so that to suggest that a girl can have this kind of name is of course saying that this arrangement in which only boys count in terms of maintaining the name of the family is really out-dated, because the

family can survive also through the women. So it's more than just a name, it becomes something more complex than 'My name is *A* so that if I have a son he will answer *A* and *A* will always be answered by someone.' It's something more important than that mechanical succession and survival through a specific name. It's something bigger. Even if Shakespeare didn't have children he still survives as a name. That kind of awareness is important for people who are trapped in this notion that you are finished if you don't have a son, that your line will come to an end and you will come to nothing. It was very much the thinking in the past, not only in Africa but in Europe as well, certainly among the kings: if they didn't have a son they would put away or even kill off their wife, or something! This is all a narrow view of survival, which the naming ceremony in *Anthills* is challenging and calling into question. The fact that the old man accepts it without too much difficulty is a very encouraging sign.

You've mentioned 'surviving' several times. This is connected with the title of your novel as well, isn't it?
Well, it's simply that there is a proverb, or rather a saying (the word 'proverb' does not quite cover all the oral sayings that we have in Igbo). The saying which I'm using for my title is really an observation of what happens after the dry season in the grasslands. Generally the grasslands tend to be burnt down during the dry season, before the next rains. Everything is burnt down and the only things that cannot be burnt are these structures of earth made by termites. If you go to the savannah country, after a fire you will see that this is really all that's left standing, these very interesting structures. So the people say these are the remnants, these are the survivors. When the rains come, the new grasses will grow – there's no problem there – but will they have a memory? There's no way they can know about the fire of last year because they were not there and they're likely to think that the world began with them, that the world is always green. So they need these experienced structures of indestructible earth that are standing in their midst and are very soon to be dwarfed, in fact, by the grass, which soon grows taller than they, but which are there as a memory: they know, they remember, and they will be there again when there is another fire and all the present grass is burnt. It's a very concise statement when it is said in Igbo, an effective image drawn from exact observation. You see, our people are very observant about nature and all these proverbs, quite apart from how you can apply them as a metaphor and so on, are also very exact, actual observations of what goes on in nature and in society. This is what gives them their power, because they operate at different levels.

The setting of *Anthills* is an imaginary African country called Kangan, with its capital, Bassa, and a rebellious drought-stricken northern region, Abazon. But there are also many references to Nigeria, which the non-Nigerian reader may not be able to appreciate. Would you like to explain this double level?
Well, it is inevitable, it always happens. If the writer is using his own knowledge and experience he is then located somewhere in space and time and the other people who occupy contiguous positions will see more than others further afield. But an important thing about stories is that they are also not *locked* in any particular place and time; a good writer tries to ensure this. This is one reason why I decided not to call the country Nigeria. I wanted it to have this possibility of application elsewhere, apart from wanting to avoid the possibility that someone will say 'Oh, this is me here, this is my brother' or something

like that, to give the story this air which a good story has of being anywhere. You actually lift it out of wherever it is and put it where it can stand for many things. This in itself becomes a metaphor on a big scale, not just for one country but for a whole continent. Having done that I decided it wasn't perhaps necessary even to insist that everything here must be fictional. There are certain things which we now know which are common knowledge, certain names of real people, which I have deliberately left in: people like Nkrumah, Mazrui, names of Nigerian singers. It seemed to me that there is a value in doing that, making it both out there in space but also attached to events and people that the reader might recognize. If the reader doesn't know that there is somebody called Mazrui it doesn't really matter very much, but if he does it adds to his understanding, I hope.

Is there any relationship between Beatrice and other female characters in previous novels, such as Eunice in *A Man of the People*? Could you explain why you give Beatrice a double identity and why the relationship to the goddess Idemili?
Well the Eunice connection you raise is interesting. I didn't think of it. What it means is that I have really been worried about the woman's role for some time, although I didn't have that scope for it in *A Man of the People*.

There is an ambivalence to women in traditional society. There is a respect, a very deep respect, which is implied in such names as 'Mother-is-supreme', which is quite a common name, and in certain customs like the burial of a woman: she has to be taken back and buried with her people, because in her husband's place she may just be treated like an outsider but when she dies she must be taken back, because she belongs to her father's people, she is just like the men. So there are these attitudes that suggest that there are two streams in the minds of our people: one in which women are really oppressed and given very low status and one in which they are given very high honour, sometimes even greater honour than men, at least if not in fact, in language and metaphor. I think this suggests that in this situation the role of the woman has not yet been fully worked out, that we are still ambivalent about it. And then we find the situation where in actual life the men fail politically and the women are called upon to take over the running of things. We see that in the Senegalese film-maker, Sembene Ousmane: there is a film in which this happens, in which the men give up the struggle against France and leave their spears where they staged their last dance and go away in disgrace and ignominy and the women then arrive on the scene, take up the spears, have their own dance and take over the running of affairs. This is a very, very powerful metaphor. Now in real life, in my own society, there was a case where the women took over. It was when the British first came and began to tax the population. The men surrendered and allowed themselves to be taxed like slaves, but the women said no and came and took over and really caused the downfall of the system of colonial administration: the British had to think again. So I think we have this in our metaphors, in the names we call people and also in actual life, where situations can arise in which women are not the underdogs but can take over the affairs of society. I think we must re-examine this situation and find a way in which the modern woman in Africa will have a role which is not just something we refer to once in a while, but brings her talents and her special gifts to the running of affairs. This is one of the things that I was tentatively exploring in *Anthills*. I think that one of the ways we can do this is to allow the women to speak on this issue. It's not enough for men to work out what women should do now. I think women should organize themselves to speak, from a real understanding of our situation and not just from a copying of European fashions, women's lib and things like that, but out of our own traditions to work out a new role for themselves. This is the challenge I throw both to the men and to the women, but particularly to the women.

You say that Beatrice does not actually know the legends but that she has an inheritance. Is Idemili a very well-known figure in Nigeria?
In my own part of Igboland, yes. She is the daughter of God and there is a river of that name – Idemili – from which my local government area is named. It goes back to the idea that the Almighty has a daughter.

Is the legend also behind some of the imagery connected with Beatrice, the water imagery, for example?
Yes, 'Idemili' actually means the 'pillar of water', literally. The source of Idemili River is a lake. It runs through a territory throughout which the python is held sacred, and flows into the River Niger.

At the end of the novel you refer to Mazisi Kunene's epic poem *Emperor Shaka the Great* and to Shaka's 'smiling' and 'beautiful' death. Were you also thinking of how Kunene's 'Palm Race' sing of how Shaka's children shall 'rise, scatter the dust of our enemies and make our earth free for the Palm Race'?
Well, I was trying to invoke that particular incident and other incidents like it in our literature and also to suggest that in our literature and in our lives as Africans today we should make a habit of invoking these powerful images from our history, legend and art. Because this is really what history and literature are about: that we can use them as a shorthand to say things which then start off resonances in the minds of everybody who has this kind of experience and history and is aware of it. You don't have to repeat everything that Kunene said, but just mention the keyword, the password, and the whole image is called up in the imagination of those who know, who are aware, who are literate in our traditions. I think this is very important. It's like a sort of short cut, saving a lot of time and energy, and in its result way beyond the size of the effort you make. But also I think that as writers we have tended to imitate the politicians who do not invoke the men before them. Even great politicians like Nkrumah: if you lived in Nkrumah's Ghana, for instance, you did not hear a lot about the people who laboured twenty or thirty years before: names like Aggrey, perhaps because they were too moderate for the taste of later times and we therefore forget that no matter how moderate they may have been they were actually in the field before us and made a significant contribution. And I think the same thing can be said in the literary area, for the negritude/tigritude argument, for instance. By renouncing that whole movement we were really cutting ourselves off from a source that could have helped us. I am saying that we should not behave like politicians who think that the good things, the revolution, the change only began when *they* arrived on the scene. We must recognize that there has been a ferment in Africa for a long time and that different people through the ages played a role according to their light and their ability and perhaps according to the constraints of the time. We must make use of all this to give us momentum. If you don't have a long history you won't have any momentum, you'll be starting again every day, you'll be a new man in the world every day and this is terrible . . .

I also wondered if in the emphasis on beauty there was not a veiled allusion to Ayi Kwei Armah's *The Beautyful Ones Are Not Yet Born*.

I don't know, but it's quite possible. I believe that Ayi Kwei Armah's title is a very powerful image. It's a book that I taught for years when I was in the United States. Perhaps it was from teaching it that I was able to see some fundamental flaws that I then pointed out, causing a kind of rupture in our relationship, so I don't want to get involved in his work again! But I think it is possible. The image of the beautiful ones waiting to be born is a very good one and a very powerful one.

A consciously intended allusion is surely made to Christopher Okigbo when you speak of the 'complex and paradoxical cavern of Mother Idoto'. To what extent is Okigbo present in *Anthills*?

I don't recall having him clearly in front of me as a model, but I would like to say that his presence as a friend, when he was alive, and his presence as a poet have been so powerful in my experience and in the experience of my generation that it is inconceivable that I would be creating a poet without somehow having reference to my experience of Okigbo as *the* poet. Now you mention it, thinking back on some of the actions of Ikem, the poet in *Anthills*, I think some of the things he gets into could easily have been got into by Okigbo. So you are probably right, to that extent. He was probably there, at the back of my mind.

As to the reference to the paradoxical cavern of Mother Idoto – which comes straight out of Okigbo's poetry – it is the end of the journey of the prodigal, who is the poet, who is Okigbo, who is ourselves, discovering the roots again, searching and finally, after a long search, being accepted by the goddess Idoto into her paradise, a paradise, in my view, that is the paradise of artists and poets. It is paradoxical, it is complex, it cannot be described in one word. There is a very detailed description of the passageway, for instance: all this phosphorescence and these geometrical forms and figures appearing. It is something beyond words, and Okigbo simply *hints* at it. For me, this is where we are all headed, all artists, all those who work with words, all those who create stories. To be accepted here is to have one's work endorsed by the Owner of stories, this goddess . . . It is a *complex* place and I repeat that: it is not a place for fanatics. Okigbo was the very opposite of fanatical. He wanted to experience everything. He wanted to get to London through Barcelona one day and through Rome the next, as he said. He was striving to discover the secret of his ancestors, but he had also read the Latin and Greek classics and he wasn't going to renounce those. That was the kind of person he was. The kind of paradise where he was going to be would be a paradise where this kind of openness was possible, not a paradise where narrow visions, *one* vision of the way and the truth and the light would dominate, but where everything is possible. This is one of the things I was trying to say in this passage. Of course if you hadn't read Okigbo you might say 'Oh, this is very nice' and that would be that, but if you had, then all kinds of bonuses in echoes and resonances would be yours.

Could you tell me something about your teaching experience, how you present African literature and what African literature you present?

Teaching African literature in America and teaching it in Nigeria are very different things. Students in Nigeria are having more and more trouble simply being literate, being able to read extensively. To many students coming to the

University, reading a novel is a huge chore. To plough through a novel is intimidating to many of them. Some will even run away and do linguistics because they imagine there is very little reading required there. So you have to coax them into literature. Many of them had never read before, except for what they had to read for their School Certificate. What I did was to introduce short stories, African short stories, that anybody could manage: the scope is small, the time required is small and there are some stories that can really trigger off discussion and interest. People could really come alive in discussing what happens in this story in a way that they would never have imagined before: they had thought of these stories as something dead, that you had to struggle to master. Once this was done with the shorter things then they were readier to tackle a longer novel.

In America the problem is different. Here you are dealing with students who are coming out of a tradition where Africa is not really like anywhere else they know: Africa in literature, Africa in the newspapers, Africa in the sermons preached in the churches is really the Other Place. It is the Africa of *Heart of Darkness*: there are no real people in the Dark Continent, only *forces* operating; and people don't speak any language you can understand, they just grunt, too busy jumping up and down in frenzy. This is what is in the minds of these students as they come to African literature. So I find that the first thing is to familiarize them with Africa, make them think that this is a place of *people*, it's not the Other Place, the opposite of Europe or America. This is quite a task. But once you've done it – going into the history of Africa, showing how this is something that could have happened to anybody – the reaction is often quite interesting. I remember a white American boy who came to me very tense, after reading *Things Fall Apart*, and saying 'This Okonkwo is my father!' Now I'd never in my wildest dreams thought of Okonkwo as a White Anglo-Saxon Protestant! But this is what literature is about and why it's worth doing. Otherwise why go to America to teach African literature?

Do you connect the written literature with the oral tradition?
The oral tradition is dealt with extensively in the introduction. I begin with issues, all kinds of issues, in African literature: the history, philosophy, negritude, African personality, issues like racism, like African language, before we begin to deal with the texts. And the oral tradition plays a very important part here, and also in actual handling of the texts, like for instance in Amos Tutuola, *The Palmwine Drinkard*, which I always teach. This is quite a useful peg on which to hang a discussion of the oral tradition.

As for the people I teach, Amos Tutuola; Cheikh Hamidou Kane, *Ambiguous Adventure*; Camara Laye, *The Dark Child* and sometimes *The Radiance of the King* as well; Ferdinand Oyono, *Houseboy*; Mongo Beti, *Mission to Kala*; Alex La Guma's stories and his short novel *A Walk in the Night*, which is very effective: he says more about the South African situation than anyone else, I always teach him. This time I'm including two women, writing out of the Islamic tradition: an Egyptian, Alifa Rifaat, whose collection of short stories, *A View from the Minaret*, is absolutely stunning, and Mariama Bâ, *So Long a Letter*.

You have also been working on the collection of oral literature in Nigeria . . .
This is really a matter of life and death. You see, there are some elements of tradition that will keep struggling on for some time, but there are some that will

not. Where the environment no longer exists for a particular art form then that art form will disappear. Epic poems and poets flourished in a village society in which there was a planting season, then a harvest season and then a time of rest after the harvest, and the way they used this time was for the village to come and listen for a whole night, sometimes for five nights in a row, to the poets reciting the stories of the heroes. Sometimes there would be a contest between two poets and the village would be the audience. Now the form I have been studying, which has been going on through the millennia, no longer has a viable audience, because these communities are dispersing and the people are no longer handing down the art to anybody because the children have gone to school and gone on to the towns. The men are all very old, in their seventies, in fact one of them started off his recital for us but couldn't continue from physical exhaustion, and said we must come back another time. So it's a life and death thing. We were able to put as much as we could on video-tape so that we will be publishing extracts with translations. We have in fact started a new journal, *Uwa ndi Igbo* ('The World of the Igbo') in which the first extracts from these recordings were published side by side in Igbo and in English.

SELECTED BIBLIOGRAPHY

NOVELS
Things Fall Apart (London: Heinemann, 1958).
No Longer At Ease (London: Heinemann, 1960).
Arrow of God (London: Heinemann, 1964).
A Man of the People (London: Heinemann, 1966).
Anthills of the Savannah (London: Heinemann, 1987).

SHORT STORIES
Girls at War and Other Stories (London: Heinemann, 1972).

CHILDREN'S BOOKS
Chike and the River (London and New York: Cambridge University Press, 1966).
(With John Iroaganachi), *How the Leopard Got his Claws* (Enugu: Nwamife Publishers, 1972).
The Drum (Enugu: Fourth Dimension Publishing Company, 1977).
The Flute (Enugu: Fourth Dimension Publishing Company, 1977).

POETRY
Beware Soul Brother and Other Poems (London: Heinemann, 1972).

ESSAYS
Morning Yet on Creation Day (London: Heinemann, 1975).
The Trouble With Nigeria (London: Heinemann, and Enugu: Fourth Dimension Publishing Company, 1983).
The World of Ogbanje (Enugu: Fourth Dimension Publishing Company, 1986).
Hopes and Impediments. Selected Essays 1965-1987 (London: Heinemann International, 1988).

Odia Ofeimun

Although for many years Odia Ofeimun's first collection of poems, *The Poet Lied*, was difficult to obtain, it quickly became one of the best-known books to have been published by a Nigerian poet, even if the motives for its fame were not entirely literary. The author's work had however already been discovered and admired by poetry-lovers thanks to Wole Soyinka's anthology, *Poems of Black Africa* (London: Secker and Warburg, 1975), and to literary journals such as *Okike*, *Nigeria Magazine*, *Idoto* and *Opon Ifa*.

Born in Iruekpen in 1950, Ofeimun had a haphazard, constantly interrupted and largely self-organized education. After undertaking a variety of jobs, he studied Political Science at the University of Ibadan. From 1978 to 1982 he was private secretary to one of Nigeria's major political figures, Chief Awolowo. Two years later he joined the editorial board of *The Guardian* (Lagos) and became General Secretary of the Association of Nigerian Authors. In 1989 he moved to Oxford, where he has been researching into the life and times of Awolowo and collecting his own many and varied articles and essays (both literary and political) for publication. During his stay in Britain he has also worked with Adzido, Britain's leading African dance company, whose 1990 production of 'Under African Skies' makes use of several of the author's recent, unpublished poems.

5

Odia Ofeimun

This interview was carried out in Oxford in September 1989.

You've had a very varied life, could you think back over your early life and tell me about some of your different activities?
I wouldn't know where to start, it's like asking me to tell you the story of my life! Well . . . I think I had a very normal childhood. I mean, looking at the life of other people of my own age who grew up with me. Nothing particularly extraordinary took place. My parents were living at Akure, some 300 or so kilometres from the village in which I grew up. My mother had eloped to marry my father. There's a streak of independence in the family which almost every other daughter in the house appeared to have followed, in the sense that they picked their own husbands and got their parents to approve.

When I was born I was brought to live with my grandparents. They are perhaps the best grandparents anybody could wish for. My grandmother was already fairly old when I was a child, but she was also a very considerate person. She did not like controversy; in a polygamous home in which women are normally quarrelsome, she controlled others by the force of non-intervention. She had a very quiet way of expressing whatever she considered was right, and she did it in such a manner that you had no choice but to listen to her. She was not the kind of person to control children by force or threats, so I had a lot of freedom as a child.

My grandfather – my maternal grandfather – was also that kind of person. He was a very hardworking man. He enjoyed the kind of wealth he had acquired: he was one of the first few to build a storey-building in the village, one of the first people to buy a lorry. He was a very well-travelled trader before he became a big cocoa farmer. He saw himself as someone who was partici-pating in the modern economy, who needed to be very well heeled in the pro-cess. All his children he insisted had to go to school, so that in fact my mother and the rest of them who broke out of that plan were like rebels against his wishes. But whoever entered that family had to get an education. That was how I too had to go to school. All his grandchildren – I was his eldest grandchild – had to go to school. It was mandatory. This was before Awolowo's free education came in, which made it compulsory for every child.

I had this luck of having an uncle who worked at the SIM bookshop. He enjoyed reading and acquired a fairly large library. So as a child I had books to play with: all sorts of books! And he had a very good collection. Looking back now, the books weren't that many, but they were very well selected. When I was in secondary school I always had to be sent out of school for one reason or the other, either because I didn't pay my school fees, or because I was ill. So while my mates were at school I would find myself at home and that was how I gravitated towards these books. At first I was interested in just looking at the photographs and drawings, but by the time I got to secondary school I had started reading them. In my first year at secondary school, largely because of reading poets like Wordsworth, Shelley and a few others, the idea of becoming a writer crystallized: I was quite positive about that. Even if I did nothing else in the world I would be a writer.

When did you first encounter poetry?
My first real contact with poetry! Although I had read *The Ancient Mariner* in my last year in the primary school and had thumbed Wordsworth and the rest of them it didn't hit me as such until I read Martin Carter, the West Indian poet. There was this small collection titled *Poems of Resistance*, which he smuggled out of prison in 1952.

How old were you?
Eleven or twelve. It seemed he made it easier for me to understand Wordsworth and all the other poets. Reading Martin Carter it was no longer a matter of relating to poetry as a book, you related to it as life: something that actually happens to people. That prepared me for most of the other authors. Incidentally, I found myself reading Jean-Jacques Rousseau's *Confessions* before I was fifteen! I had the luck of finding the series of letters written by Nehru to his daughter from various imprisonments. One found the world literally opening out. So I did not have to go to school like most people did in order to learn. Staying at home was like going to school. I must confess one of the things I resented then was being sent on errands, being asked to go to the farm with the labourers, going to the cocoa plantation: it was as if every such thing was taking me away from what I was beginning to see as my life's work. My life's work had to do with books and anything that took me away from this did not appear normal. The abnormal thing was to get involved in household chores and things like that! Books opened up a world for me which I'm still trying to live in.

Did you do all your schooling then in Akure?
No. I did not live with my parents in Akure. I lived with my grandparents in the village, at Iruekpen-Ekpoma in Bendel State (what was then Benin Province). As a child I didn't travel much. The first time I travelled out of my village (beyond attending festivals in neighbouring villages or going to farms) was when I had to go for the entrance examination to the secondary school I later attended, which was about six kilometres away, in Ujoelen-Ekpoma. It was an

Anglican Grammar School. I spent only three years there. By my fourth year my parents couldn't pay my school fees so I had to drop out. In fact apart from my very first year in that school almost every other year I spent there was truncated with suspensions due to lack of fees. Annually I spent only about three months out of the nine you are normally supposed to spend in a school year. I won't say I enjoyed my secondary school days: I did not. The only thing is that each time there was an exam I managed to smuggle myself back into the school, do the exams, and run away! During the exams the Principal never bothered to find out whether you'd paid your school fees or not: I benefited from that lapse. That way I was able to finish the third year. But in my fourth year there was no way I could continue. My grandfather had a large constituency and my father's motor mechanic business had hit the bad times.

I spent almost a year plus at home doing next to nothing. It wasn't fun. I allowed myself to be cajoled into tapping rubber for pocket money but I hated the diversion. Even the idea of just going on reading did not make sense any more because I needed to learn to feed myself. It was very desultory reading. I read mainly romantic novels, Marie Corelli, Rider Haggard, Bertha M. Clay to fill the more disorienting periods, but towards what purpose? I wanted to sit for the School Certificate at home. Somehow it didn't work out. That was how I left my village for Benin, about 78 kilometres away. Benin was the headquarters of the newly created Midwest State. I didn't really know why I went there. I didn't particularly want a job but if you were in a place and people fed you, you had to justify the way you were living. So I decided to learn something. But for a whole year all I did was to ransack the libraries in Benin. I woke up in the morning and at eight o'clock, when they opened the libraries – there were three very good libraries in Benin then – I'd be one of the first people to go in.

In 1967 just before the war broke out I almost joined the army. I actually went for one of the recruitment exercises, but I suddenly saw people showing certificates and I had none. So I rushed back to pick up the certificates I had acquired to show that I'd finished three years of secondary school education. By the time I returned they had lowered the stadium gates. That was how I did not join the army. To think of it, I really did not want to join the army. It was just something to do. I did not like the army or the war that came after. At that time I had started writing poetry in earnest and very many of the poems I wrote about the war reflected the way I felt. I believed that the people on the Federal side really had no moral authority to castigate the secessionists, because they committed all the crimes they accused Ojukwu of. Ojukwu was silly, alright, declaring secession. If he had stayed, if he had refused to declare the state of Biafra, that crisis might have been resolved in a way that would have been more helpful for Nigeria's future. The tall and short of it is that I did not join the army. The story of my life went back again to the village because once the Biafran crisis really picked up, especially after the Biafran invasion of Bendel State, one just had to go back.

It was only after the Biafran forces were cleared out of Bendel that I went back to Benin. This time I stayed with another uncle. My intention was to study for the GCE, but that was regarded as a very long route and this uncle of mine – a very nice uncle by the way – thought I had to do something fast so that I could earn a living. They wanted me to be apprenticed to one of these roadside 'rewire' electricians. I didn't want to listen to them, so they sent some other uncle from home to come speak to me and he went on and on about how I had better listen to reason or it would result in far-reaching consequences. But the way I saw it nothing was going to make me deviate from this business of becoming a writer. So I explained to this uncle, 'Look, my father could not pay my school fees, that was why I had to come to this uncle and I'm now being advised to be apprenticed to this roadside electrician. Maybe someday I'll have my own children after becoming a "rewire". And because I won't be able to send my children to school I'll have to farm them out to other relations who will do exactly what is happening to me now. They will advise my own children to get apprenticed to some motor mechanic.' Incidentally, my father was a motor mechanic and I didn't want to repeat the circle so cheaply. If it was a matter of making a choice, nobody was going to make this choice for me. But he was a nice man as I said, so they made an arrangement for me to learn typewriting and shorthand, something which I detested because I didn't want to be a copy typist. I learnt typewriting for a month and I just got fed up. But now I must say, looking back, it was one of the best things that happened to me, otherwise I wouldn't know how to type!

How was your writing proceeding in the meantime?
Somehow while I was doing all this I managed to write some poems for a newspaper, *The Midwest Echo*, a local newspaper in Benin. The sub-editor happened to come from my own village. He showed them to the editor who liked them very much. They were terribly bad poems! I hope nobody will ever get to see them! On the basis of the things I wrote for them they decided I was good enough to be a reporter. That was how in 1968 I was employed as a reporter. So I was able to convince all my uncles that I might somehow become a writer some day! It gave me a chance also to relate to the other side of my nature: I'd always liked politics. Being a reporter brought me close to the problems of my immediate environment in an eye-opening sense. I did court stories mainly and then I was lucky, I had to report the Rebel Atrocities Tribunal during the Civil War. It was like opening up the power bracket in the State for me to look into. And, man, the seediness and corruption of the system was bare! The way public figures present well-honed faces to the public when in fact they had done atrocious and heinous things behind the scenes. It was all so clear to me. Many of the poems I wrote during this period were really based on the way I saw public figures: how those who try to present the symbols through which we interpret our lives are themselves horrible characters. *The Poet Lied*, frankly, started with this court reporting, seeing how public figures – military governors, soldiers, court judges and all the people who were regarded as the big men of society – lied profusely and confused themselves and the whole of society in the process.

This brings me to the explanations I give about *The Poet Lied*. *The Poet Lied* is not really just about a poet. It is based on an assessment of the symbol manipulators, the leaders who manipulate symbols by which the whole society interprets the life that people live in the country.

I did not work in that newspaper for more than a year. It was a very small newspaper. They couldn't pay the workers, so that you sometimes found that in March you'd be receiving half the pay for January. It was painful to see married people with wives and children who at the end of the month wouldn't get their salary. We wanted to go on strike and it suddenly occurred to everybody that we didn't even know how to! I was considered the most knowledgeable among the workers because most of them were compositors. When we met the labour officer at the Ministry of Labour and I wanted to present our case, the man demanded to know our jobs. The others said they were compositors and I said I was a reporter. He said 'In that case, you can't speak for them!' Anyway, we went ahead and we went on strike. In the end they played a very fast one on us. The people who ran the newspaper called me aside and doubled my pay. They knew that if they did that I would soft-pedal and not get the other workers to go on with the strike. But I suddenly felt I was being insulted. What made them believe that giving me this money would change the situation? I worked with these people! So I simply came back to the office and told them what had happened and told them that the strike had to continue. The next day I was called and threatened viciously. I could see that the boss was bluffing. It was a game of wits just to make sure we went back to work. Well, they thought I was reasonable. They didn't know I was just like the rest of them! In the end, they had to close down the newspaper and all of us had to go home.

I was back to square one, but this time around, I didn't want to go back to my village. Now I felt I ought to stand by whatever I got. I stayed with a friend for some time and realized I couldn't stay on in Bendel. I planned to go somewhere where I would not be known by anybody, where I could do any odd jobs to survive while I wrote poetry. I tried my hand at several things then, trying to write a play, trying to write short stories, but poetry was easier to reach.

I left Bendel and went to Lagos. I stayed with an uncle of mine – the same uncle who bought those books of my childhood days. But we were always quarrelling: we never agreed on anything! He thought I was silly wanting to be a writer and we used to argue all night. I remember one night arguing with him till about three in the morning. He got so fed up and angry with me he started abusing me and calling me names. 'Look, why not sit down and think properly like every honest young man? Why do you think you can become a writer?' He asked me to give him the names of any writers I knew who became writers after having my kind of education. But unfortunately for his argument I had known so many I reeled the names off my fingers! I would start with Amos Tutuola, Bernard Shaw, Dickens . . . Once I won that argument I knew I would have no problems, but in the end we just could not stay together.

Because I knew I was going to have to leave I started work as a petrol attendant, selling petrol. I did it for a few weeks, but I couldn't continue. Luckily I got a job as a factory labourer with the help of another uncle who was a big civil servant at the Public Service Commission. It was a very interesting job because there were all sorts of things you had to learn. It wasn't always a matter of carrying cement for people who wanted to build concrete floors and things. I also found I had to help the technicians, many of them brought in from abroad to fit new machines, new textile machines and things of that nature.

It was while working in that factory that I started reading for my GCE examinations. I'd always wanted to do this: to prove to myself that I could pass it. So I registered for the examinations and it was probably the most purposive period I ever had in my life: I knew precisely what I wanted and I allowed no distractions. I was living very far away from Apapa, where I worked. I was living at Oshodi, some 15 kilometres from Apapa. I had to take the train at six o'clock every morning and get the train back about six thirty in the evening. Usually I read all the way, to and fro. I just did not allow my books to rest. I passed the exams – I knew I would. I did two A-level papers and three O-level papers. Incidentally the only subject I failed was literature at O-level! *Annoying*! So the next year I decided to take it at Advanced level. And of course I enjoyed the feeling that I got a B! Of all subjects, why should I fail literature?

I wanted these certificates just to find a job that would allow me to do the things I wanted to do. Then I visited this uncle of mine and he just said 'Why not go to the university?' I told him I hadn't any money and he said he would pay. I gained admission to the University of Ibadan. I'd told him I could pay for my first term by myself but before the end of that term we quarrelled. He wanted to control what I bought with my money. He saw me reading all sorts of magazines, some of these current affairs magazines. I didn't want to depend on the libraries, I wanted a collection of them. I came to visit him on a weekend from Ibadan holding a copy of *Afriscope* and he said 'These are the things you do with your money? Buying useless magazines?' I didn't like that part of it. He had not yet started paying my fees and he wanted to tell me what I should read? So we quarrelled. And thereafter I simply refused to take his money. I won't lie to you, because of that I had a rotten period during my university days. It was horrible.

You were studying political science, weren't you?
Yes, I went in for Political Science, although the faculty tried to make me change to English for which I had my highest grade. I insisted on taking a course in English poetry, while remaining in the Social Sciences. Poetry, as a course, was terrible. I almost failed it!

Anyway, the most serious matter was to find a way of surviving. After the first term I was thrown out of the hall of residence because I couldn't pay my fees. So I put my books with some friends, I put my clothes with some others and I slept between as many friends as possible. One of them, Segun Oyegbami, was particularly helpful. We met in the English class. So I managed to survive that first year. In fact by the end of that first year I was almost about to give up university because I couldn't really think how to continue. I applied for loans which the Federal Loans Board farmed out to students for their education. Although I got a loan I never received the money until the end of my second year at the university. That meant that I had to find some way to survive anyway. And – many people can't understand it – I tried to live a life as full as possible! Nobody knew I was a very indigent student because I took part in university debates, discussed politics and literature and I ran for the presidency of the Students' Union. If I had won that presidency I probably would not have been allowed in, because I had not then registered for the second year because I couldn't pay my fees. To be frank, I was also trying to win that election because I wanted to make a case out of the fact that indigent students had a right to survive in the university. At that time they'd just started the Youth Service Corps for university graduates. And my argument was that if the Government could afford to pay students £200 at the end of their university education, why not slash the money by some percentage and make university education free? If I was going to work for the State at the end of my education I felt the State owed me a crisis-free university education. But that was not an argument we could win.

In the end, I managed to finish my university education with the help of friends. One of the people I was later to meet who was perhaps the most helpful was Bola Ige, who became a Governor of Oyo State in 1979. He was one of the few radical lawyers in town. There was a friend in Benin, Mr Obahiagbon. He was the man I worked for at the *Midwest Echo*. When I was having difficulties I decided to go to him.

Despite everything?
Yes! He was so nice, he was surprised I'd managed to break through and get a university admission. He said he would like to help me, but that he was not in a position to. So he decided to contact somebody who was from my part of the state, Mr Enaboifo. He helped me survive one very bleak period, so that the idea of dropping out of the university, I had to shelve it. And then, later on, I met Bola Ige. He was the one who literally made it possible for me to finish my university education. In fact, he was a blind supporter: blind in the sense that he did not mind what I did with the money he gave me. Once he was convinced that I was actually a student at that university, he had known me by reputation as a student activist and that kind of thing, he gave me all the support he could get.

It was while I was in my second year at university that I wrote 'The Poet Lied'. It was largely like trying to tell myself 'Now, if you must be a writer, what kind of a writer do you want to be?' And that poem was really like trying to write a manifesto, as I explain in the interview you will find at the end of the latest edition. 'What kind of a writer do you want to be, and what kind of a writer *don't* you want to be?' So within Nigerian society as it was in 1974, it was like trying to build up symbols with which I could identify. As I enjoy saying, if I had said 'The Politician Lied', it wouldn't make any difference to most people: people expect politicians to lie anyway. As a title, 'The *Poet* Lied' made more sense to me, because there just happened to be a poet at that time who fitted the pattern. Most of what I say about the poet does not directly refer to him, but he provided me with a very fine foil. It was like venting all my frustration on him!

So it was during your second year at the university?
Yes, in 1974. The poem eventually won the university prize. I had done a series, the 'New Broom' series, and then 'The Poet Lied', and I entered the two separately. Like so many things that have happened in my life I was very sure I would win that prize. But somehow I did not expect 'The Poet Lied' to win; I expected the 'New Brooms' to win. And it was only after it had won that I started taking a second look at the poem to see why. And somehow, largely because of the controversies, it's beginning to look like a poem I can't forget and I'm getting worried it's beginning to look like the only poem I've ever written!

Otherwise my university education was fun in its own way. I was used to the financial crisis: that had always been my lot. But if I was to look at my university education to see what I got from it I would say it was some kind of diffidence. I was no longer as confident after as I was when I entered the university. As somebody who wanted to be a writer, my university education dented my confidence, largely because I became more ambitious, probably over-ambitious. I no longer just wanted to be a creative writer. The idea of being a social scientist, a social philosopher of a kind, invaded my way of looking at the world and I haven't been able to get out of it. These days I'm only just beginning to think that I can marry the two positions. I've always had this conflict within me. In politics there are so many things you can't say. You have to be deferential to positions and opinions that you don't like very much; you don't want to offend or run too far ahead of what you regard as your constituency. And there's always this tendency to try to be more subtle than you need, which I consider a process of telling lies. Very many public figures have to do it. Thankfully, I had to work with a public figure who did not like the role at all: to lie in public. It helped to shore up something I cherish.

Who was this?
Awolowo. He suffered for it. Trying to speak his mind meant hurting those who could help his political ambitions. Even when he realized he was hurting himself, he just went ahead and said what he felt. Because of this, even those who liked his ideas and would have liked to support him did not know how to do it. Of course in a situation like Nigeria's where you have structured groupings, all of them with petty interests they want to defend, it's easy to hurt people when you are straightforward and when you try to tell the truth.

I must say this argument between the artist and the politician, between the man who should just go ahead and say what he considers right and the man who needs to realize that coalition building is the soul of politics, this almost created immobilism in my attitude towards creative writing. I have only just realized that it is possible to do the two at the same time. It is possible to tell the truth and on the basis of the positions you take try to change public policies. Trying to marry political positioning to my view of creative writing is something I find I cannot get out of: I cannot do one without the other. I think a writer will be deceiving himself if he believes he can draw a line between himself as an artist and himself as a citizen of society who has positions that he considers right and deserving of expression. Maybe I'll never succeed in resolving it completely, but I realize that unless I resolve it I won't make much headway.

You had problems with the publication of _The Poet Lied_, didn't you?
In 1976 I sent the collection to the publishers through their general editor then, Professor Echeruo. It was not published until 1980, and then somebody – a journalist, Chuks Iloegbunani – reviewed it in _Punch_, a Nigerian newspaper published in Lagos. He was a very clever reviewer. What he did was to take quotations from Chinua Achebe, quotations from Soyinka, quotations from J.P. Clark before he started his review, so that at the end of the review, on the basis of the quotations, you could tell who was the poet that lied. When J.P. Clark read that he wrote a letter to Longman, threatening he would sue them if they continued to distribute the book.

In my view the Longman people were intimidated for two reasons. One was that J.P. Clark was one of their biggest writers. He was in the school system, and when a writer has entered the school system it means that in terms of profit he's an asset. And then, J.P. Clark was very well connected. One of his brothers had been a commissioner, a minister in Government, another was fairly powerful in the Foreign Affairs establishment. I think he was then in London. So it was easy of course. If it was a matter of putting pressure on the publishers he had the weight to throw. And then there was this other problem. If he decided to sue, Nigerian courts could not be relied upon to give the kind of judgement that would make sense. The good judge may be on holiday when the matter comes up.

I think the publisher took a hard look at the situation and realized it was a market they were trying to catch, not save a small writer who may not get far. So they removed the book from the market. They tried later to explain all sorts of things. In fact, some people thought that what J. P. Clark was worried about was that I'd plagiarized his works! If he had accused me of plagiarizing, it would have been fun. I'd have enjoyed going to court! But that was not the argument. They didn't let me see his letter. What they did was to make quotations from the letter to show aspects of 'The Poet Lied' which J.P. Clark objected to. He said lines like:

fishermen in their canoes, hounded by tides, / swimmers drowning, hounded by tides

. . . steeped in riverine figures and images, easily would suggest to the reader that I was making references to him. On the basis of some of these things, they wanted me to remove 'The Poet Lied' from the collection so that they could go ahead with the rest. But I refused to withdraw the poem and insisted that if that was what they wanted they might as well withdraw the book from the market, and that was what they did.

In Nigeria, presumably, not everywhere?
Everywhere! Some booksellers kept copies aside. At least, when I started looking for copies to buy, people bought copies for me in the West Indies, Kole Omotoso bought copies for me in Nairobi, and I got copies to buy in London, in bookshops that did not send their copies back to the publishers. When that happened, I was beginning to enjoy it, because it wasn't as if I wrote *The Poet Lied* to make money anyway. What he did by threatening to sue was to make the poem more popular than it would probably ever have been. People who did not know about the poem started asking what was it about. In Nigeria there was this hue and cry about literary critics not giving enough space to the younger writers. So most teachers of literature who wanted to be with the new wave started looking for younger writers to teach and many of them latched upon *The Poet Lied*. So the poems were being taught from school to school in xeroxed copies. Samizdat Nigerian style. Some lecturers would just take them to the photocopying machines and roll them out for the students. In Britain they got a very fine review by Lalage Bown in *Index on Censorship*. It was as if J. P. Clark really helped me to popularize the poem.

At the end of the day it is important for people to know that it wasn't so much about J. P. Clark: he merely became the foil. I grew up reading and believing in writers who saw the role of creation as that of truth-telling. I must confess I am quite married to this Shelleyan position that writers are actually unacknowledged legislators in a lot of ways. But not just poets. All people who manipulate symbols are legislators. A politician, writer or public figure who makes a statement in public is providing images with which to live a life. I don't think it is right for anybody who is in a position to do this to disclaim responsibility for the effect it's having on people. You may not necessarily have the effect you intend, but what you have produced, the symbol you have thrown out, has a way of conditioning consciousness. So when J. P. Clark in his collection *Casualties* started quoting Yeats and Auden to the effect that we have no art by which to make a statesman wise, that poetry makes nothing happen, I just felt that that was a lie. What *The Poet Lied* is really saying is that a writer who takes that position is telling a lie. And I believe Yeats was lying when he took such a position and I believe Auden didn't know what he was talking about. In fact I see these as positions they took in their years of deterioration. I mean, what a writer says may not have an effect on a one-to-one basis. But it has an effect. It's not as if when a writer says 'May the man die' the man dies, or that a reader will necessarily go ahead and do what the writer suggests. But we cannot therefore say that the writer has no effect on the people who read him. In *The Poet Lied*, what I was really doing was trying to say that J. P. Clark in taking the position of these other poets was lying.

But there was another aspect to this. In *The Man Died* Soyinka wrote about an incident involving J. P. Clark, in which he told all sorts of stories about him in various literary conferences outside Nigeria while Soyinka was in detention. Now as somebody who wanted to be a writer I always identified with writers. You sometimes imagine that writers are not human beings: they are close to the gods, they cannot do bad things, they cannot afford the ways of evil which they see all around them. So it was my first real taste of the literary process: writers are just human beings, like tailors, carpenters and what not. And they can lie just as frequently! But knowing that they have such pervasive influence they ought to try to be above board. When they put their pen to paper or sit in front of their typewriters, they are supposed to be so aware of the difference between words as tools and the implements of other artisans to try to present a position of value, a moral position. It's not as if they're holier than other human beings; they may be able to plumb and present a moral position because many of them in fact are either amoral or very immoral in the ways they live their lives. The important thing is for a writer to be faithful to his own and other people's experiences.

Therefore, when I was reading *The Man Died* it just struck me that there was something particularly wrong with this noble profession if its purveyors allow political propaganda to distort experience. Since a writer necessarily has an impact on his readers, he ought to see his role as a very responsible one. He ought to try very hard not to confuse people, not to lie to them. It is in his own interest and it is in the interest of everybody that writers at least give a picture of the world that will help people understand the world, so that they can try to lead better lives. It doesn't matter if the writer isn't able to live up to much of what he preaches, but he ought to try to live up to it. And in fact it is in trying to live up to it that he probably may write better.

The Poet Lied was really my own manifesto. This is the kind of writer, the kind of public figure, the kind of manipulator of symbols that I don't want to be. I believe if everybody who has a profession applies this kind of principle to whatever he or she does the world will be better for it.

This collection is divided into five parts, with five different titles. How do you explain the division?
There is a sense in which there was a thematic underlining. In the new edition some of the poems have been shifted in order to fit them into new sections. My attitude towards the poems generally is really like my attitude towards 'The Poet Lied': it's as if all the poems can be brought under that title: 'The Poet Lied'. They are nearly all a reaction to those manipulators of symbols as I call them. They are writers and leaders, they are people in a position to provide the means by which other people live or interpret their lives. You find, for instance, 'How Can I Sing' relates to a matter of personal self-expression. Social expression is touched upon in the poem which deals with 'Our Model Democracy'. Now they have to do with the relationship between those who wish to express themselves and the social environment within which they have to express themselves. The social environment is not particularly helpful to certain forms of

expression. All that section is simply an attempt to give you a taste of what it is like. Then 'The New Brooms' is really a reaction to military rulers. Two poems were removed from it which I have still not added. One of them is called 'The Cockerel in the Story': a reaction to Gowon's nine years in power. I deliberately removed it for reasons which are not literary. What I wanted to do was to provide a picture of military rule without necessarily indicating a difference between military rulers and other kinds of rulers. As far as I am concerned, soldiers are just like all the other kinds of rulers. Most of them – even those who regard themselves as democratically elected leaders – did not come to power by democratic means. They rigged elections; they falsified voters' registers and became leaders. So in fact whether they came by guns or through the ballot they tended to have this hood of illegitimacy around them. The other poem I removed started by talking about soldiers who wear this hood of illegitimacy. The section 'Where Bullets Have Spoken' deals with the Civil War. Very many of these poems were written during the Civil War. Some of my earliest poems written between '67 and '69 belong to that section.

The section on 'Resolve' is really about a possible world. The poem 'Resolve' itself was written after the Civil War. It ends by saying that rather than mourn, what we should do is make sure that the locust will never again visit our farmsteads. It ought to have been a much longer poem, but I slashed the other part of it because it was like an attempt to explain. I did not want to explain. If I did it would become dated. What I was really trying to do was say 'Look, the Civil War took place. We all know what happened, but for God's sake, all the things which led to the Civil War are still with us! What we ought to be doing is try to make sure that those things never again play into a situation of crisis.' Well, we're still there, and I don't think we've left it behind us yet! The Civil War is still very much with us.

How about 'The Neophytes' – that was the last section?
'The Neophytes' is largely about people who are about to break into some form of social commitment, like the students, people who are about to take decisions. I call them neophytes largely because they are new, they have not yet become part of the establishment, they are just about to take decisions. Some of these decisions have been taken wrongly. So they are really neophytes both in the sense that they are new and because of the kind of mistakes that they are making. One of the poems is saying that they are merely making the mistakes of their fathers. It is partly self-critical too, because I was part of what I was criticizing. We are new in this business and we are just making the mistakes that our fathers made.

So this order has changed in the new edition?
Many of the poems are still in that order, slightly rearranged. Many new poems have been added to 'Where Bullets Have Spoken': they were originally published in Soyinka's *Poems of Black Africa*. In fact it was during my second year in the university that I got this letter from Secker and Warburg saying that I should give them permission to publish some of my poems. I then recalled that when I was a factory labourer and Soyinka had just been released from prison, I went to Ibadan from Lagos to see him on a weekend. I was writing poetry and I just wanted somebody who was really a poet to see them. You meet a lot of people who say what you're writing is fine, but you know their opinions are not quite expert opinions. It's as if they were saying nice things just in order to make

me feel good and I didn't like that. So I went to see Soyinka in '70–'71.

He was just coming out of his house – he used to drive this small jeep – and I stopped his car and told him I wanted to show him some of my poems. He started reading some of them in my presence, one after the other, and said 'Are you sure you wrote these?' That's what he said and it made me feel good! Then I didn't hear from him for a very long time. By the time he decided to publish them in *Poems of Black Africa* I was in the university. He didn't know I was in the University of Ibadan, so there is no autobiographical sketch for me because he didn't know where I was. So all the poems that had been published in *Poems of Black Africa* have been included in the new collection. There were some poems, too, published by Chinua Achebe in number 3 of *Okike*. I've inserted them, too, in the new edition. One poem which appeared in '69, '70, in *Nigeria Magazine* has also been added.

Have you changed them at all?
No, I didn't have to. Except for the one that was published in 1969. I think I removed a line from it. The new collection is really like an attempt to bring all the poems together. If *The Poet Lied* cannot get a wide circulation what I am going to insist on doing, for every other poem I write, is simply to add it to *The Poet Lied* so that all the poems I will ever write will come under the same title! If people are feeling so bad about the title *The Poet Lied* they will just have to go on encountering it! Almost every poem Walt Whitman wrote became *The Leaves of Grass* and I don't mind if all my poems just have to go on as *The Poet Lied*.

How about your second collection of poems *A Handle for the Flutist*? When did that actually come out?
As General Secretary of the Nigerian Authors I had to organize a conference for Lagos in 1986, and because a lot of people were wondering if I was still writing poetry, I wanted to give a taste of the kind of things I was writing, so I decided to publish that slim collection, *A Handle for the Flutist*. It includes some old poems, but I decided to bring all of them together, because there's a sense in which the language is slightly different from the language of *The Poet Lied*. I wanted people to see something different. Usually people reacting to my poetry tend to give the impression that I write only political poetry.

There is quite a bit of love poetry in the new collection, isn't there?
Yes, I wanted that collection to give a different reading. It was my way of trying to confuse the critics who enjoy holding onto the one end of the stick and bashing away. So the new collection was really an attempt to give a different reading of my poetry.

Can we catch up with your job activities before we come back to your poetry?
I left the university in '75 and did my youth service in Katsina in the North. Then, when I returned I worked briefly as an administrative officer in the Federal Public Service Commission in Lagos. I really wouldn't have made a good civil servant, in fact in the few months I spent there I was already having problems.

Having read your poem 'A Civil Servant', I can't say I'm surprised!
I couldn't take the very staid atmosphere, no! I went back to the university for a post-graduate course, which I have not finished. Incidentally, I didn't go back to the university because I wanted to get a second degree, it had more to do with

myself. I knew what I wanted to do, but I knew I couldn't do it immediately, so I went back to the university. My original intention was to do a thesis on corruption in Nigeria, but along the way even that didn't look particularly appealing. While in post-graduate school I was doing part-time teaching in Ijomu-Oro Grammar School in Kwara State about 50 kilometres from the State capital, Ilorin. Early in the week I'd go to Kwara State about 280 kilometres away from Ibadan. I'd teach from Monday to about Thursday and then come back to Ibadan till Sunday and then go back again to Kwara. It was at Oro, on a Saturday, I trekked into town and bought an old copy of the *New Nigerian* whose columnist, Candid, was famous for Awolowo-bashing and the defence of the north in Nigeria's political arithmetic. The column on this occasion was reacting to Awolowo's advertisement – which I had not seen – asking for involved and committed researchers. I was already late but I wrote a letter in which I said 'You've asked for involved and committed researchers. If by involved and committed you do not imply that I cannot disagree with my employers when I feel very strongly about anything, then I will be prepared to work for you as your secretary.'

When I was invited for the job I was asked a tricky question. It was Alhaji L. K. Jakande who asked me the question. He said 'You indicate in your letter that there are certain things you could disagree with in Chief Awolowo's ideas. What are those things?' He thought he was being smart, but I had worked it all out. I told him 'I have read Chief Awolowo's books, and he seems to give the impression that class analysis is not very helpful, that in fact political activism on the basis of class is not something quite helpful in our kind of situation. But I don't see how he can press that argument even in Nigeria. For one thing, if you want to come out with a new land law, you ought to be able to tell which classes will support you, which class of people will oppose you, and therefore which groups you will mobilize in order to sustain your political position. If you rule out class analysis and class position you will find it very difficult to come out with a good strategy in political organization.'

In the end that is really where my political position and that of Awolowo diverge. Awolowo takes cognizance of the class position, but he doesn't believe in the political practice based on it. He will apply it intellectually sometimes, but he doesn't want to make it central. It was a very crafty way of operating. The reason was that he realized that he could not play politics based on working-class organizations. The working class – properly speaking – is a very small minority in Nigerian politics and any wise politician can see where not to make it central to strategy. So I could see where Awolowo's theory and his practice fused. Whereas he would accept the Marxist position on a lot of issues, when it came to practical politics he would not accept the class-based politics of the Marxian type.

He was very religious, at least in public life. He started as an agnostic, but I think when he went into politics he realized that an agnostic would have a rough time in a very religious society like Nigeria. He became so religious it was really sometimes embarrassing for somebody like me who cannot be said to belong to any of the established religions as a church-goer or whatever.

Awolowo was a very interesting person to work with. He was a very well-organized person: he knew what he wanted and he went at it doggedly. There are certain confusing moments – all right – but he worked very hard at eliminating all the things he considered his weaknesses. He was not very successful in the end in dealing with them, but he worked harder than any Nigerian public figure I know. He had this very straightforward view of politics which I consider vital to any public role. He saw the position of the leader as one which involved a contract with a constituency. A leader ought first to conquer himself, eliminating from his life all those things that could excite wrong decision-making. The leader must avoid alcoholics, must not allow sexual relationships to influence his positions, must try as hard as possible to live by a certain logical code. And then of course you would not find Awolowo dancing in public, ever. In fact he built a strong mythology around himself for being a very puritan person. He worked very hard at it, and he believed that it is only on the basis of that kind of self-conquering and the provision of a social philosophy which benefits a putative constituency that anybody could claim to want to lead others. If you cannot conquer yourself you cannot lead others. And to that extent he became a kind of exemplar against which other people, other leaders are measured. And all through his political career it became a matter of his political opponents trying to show that he was not living in accordance with his code. In a lot of ways that improved the climate of public decision-making.

Has Awolowo figured in any of your poems?
'Papa' in the 'Memos to Papa' series is Awolowo. 'On Your Birthday' is actually for Bola Ige after he became Governor. 'The Condemned' is a poem for Chief Awolowo. He told us his story: how when he was in jail the people on the other side of the wall were condemned criminals. Every day they would start singing this song 'I know Calabar'. When I got hold of that I just wanted to reproduce this:

'I know Calabar', the prisoners sang / from the other side of the wall. / You could hear their voices breaking bread / beyond the storybook lesson / of the kings and freedom fighters exiled there.

Incidentally, Calabar was where Ovonramwen of Benin was exiled when Benin was sacked by British adventurers in 1898.

Wasn't he the protagonist of one of Ola Rotimi's plays?
That's right. That was where he died; he died in that same prison where Awolowo was jailed, or thereabout. That was why I talked about the kings and freedom fighters exiled there. [*Reads the rest of the poem*] That was how Awolowo saw himself. Any time he sat down in the evening he enjoyed telling stories. Many Nigerians were never given a chance to see Awolowo in that light-hearted mood. Once Awolowo came out of the house he was the quintessential politician, always telling people this is what we must do, this is where we must go. He was that kind of politician. He really believed in building projects and designing means for carrying them out. He had his own problems, which are some of the things that I bring out in the biography of him that I am doing, but, for me, as a man in public life he was the perfect exemplar of how to do it. You hear many Nigerians saying that Awolowo was a very cunning, very deceitful fellow, very tribalistic . . . They may be right in a lot of ways. But he was a man who saw the need to change society for the better. Awolowo worked very hard. He may even have been more tribalistic than people said he was, but he also provided Nigerians with the strongest cross-ethnic pillars in our national life. During the Civil War he was Nigeria's Finance Minister and no Nigerian has been able to say that Awolowo did not manage the economy

well. People referring to the war period look at it as if it was Awolowo who fought the war. The Biafrans or the Igbos have not forgiven him for that: they believe that, but for Awolowo, Biafra would still be a country; they believe it was Awolowo who smashed it because of the way he managed the economy. Some of the things he did give a fair idea of what he probably would have done had he become Nigeria's Head of Government.

When did he die?
In '87.

And were you working with him up to that time?
I stopped being his private secretary on 8 April 1982 – I was sacked! I have always refused to tell the story of how I was sacked because there is no way I can tell it in a short way. I want the whole story told properly. That's one of the reasons I'm writing his biography: I want to be able to explain how I was sacked, because how I was sacked tells the story of Awolowo's life, of how a leader is really a victim of his followers. He takes decisions on the basis of the information that he has and if that information is wrong he takes silly decisions. I was sacked because it was said that I leaked a letter that had been written to him. I must say that until the day I was sacked I did not see a copy of the letter. True, I was his private secretary and nobody would absolve me if I said I was his private secretary, but I didn't see the letter. It was only after I was sacked I sat down and had to do all sorts of unimaginable espionage to find out how it happened. The day I tell the full story I just hope that most of the people involved will still be alive!

After I was sacked people expected I would go to the press and go to town – I refused. I wanted to find out first of all what had happened. Eventually I got what to me was a very satisfactory answer. I spoke to the man I was supposed to have leaked the documents to. In fact, in the story I am doing I start with the day I went to see him, M. K. O. Abiolo. At that time he was the ITT boss for the whole of Africa and the Middle East region. By the time I went to see him I had reached the conclusion as to who did what I was supposed to have done. I was ready to go to town. I wrote to Awolowo to say he owed me an apology. When *This Week* magazine interviewed me early in 1987 I told them Awolowo owed me an apology and he must give it to me! I wanted it in the open. In Nigeria it is like asking God to apologize to you, but I knew nobody could come out and challenge what I was going to say if it became a matter for public debate. I was strong enough by that time, I had enough information. Nobody responded. His own nephew, who became a very good friend of mine, came out in the open. He wrote a letter to the magazine and said it was true that Awolowo owed me an apology – he knew what had happened. Chief Awolowo did not react. I understand he gave the magazine an interview for a Monday. They wanted to find out what he felt about what I'd said. He died the Saturday before.

I liked the man a lot: maybe that was why it pained me, the way I was sacked. I thought he had ways of finding out the truth before he sacked me, but I was wrong. Looking back now, as a student of political organizations, the story of how I was sacked is like trying to tell the story of the whole of the organization, how the information flowed, how he himself created the very cage that led to many of his problems. As a political leader who was worshipped by his constituency, Awolowo could never go out. If he was found anywhere in Nigeria, the shout of 'Awo!' would ruin whatever was taking place. If he attended a wedding, the wedding would be turned into a political rally. He couldn't ever go out without the event he attended becoming something political, so Awolowo hardly went out. People had to bring him information. And those who could catch Awolowo's ears ruled his decision making. True, he was a very agnostic person: he doubted. But there were people Awolowo was not disposed to question. They were very close to him and, if they lied to him, too bad for whoever they lied against. It was a struggle for succession. They wanted to succeed Awolowo. It was like running into a fight between elephants, and I was in between!

SELECTED BIBLIOGRAPHY

POETRY
The Poet Lied (London: Longman, 1980).
A Handle for the Flutist and Other Poems (Lagos: Update Communications, 1986).
The Poet Lied (and Other Poems) (Lagos: Update Communications, 1989). Contains the poems of both of the author's previous collections, together with other, separately published poems and an interview with Onwuchekwa Jemie that originally appeared in *The Guardian* (17, 23 and 31 August 1983).

ESSAYS
'Criticism as homicide: a reply to Femi Osofisan's "Literacy as Suicide" ', *Afriscope*, VII, 6 (1977), pp. 31–2.
'Breaking the deaf wall in Nigerian literature', *The Guardian* (14 November 1984), p. 11; (21 November 1984), p. 13; (28 November 1984), p. 13.
'The Nobel paradox', *The Guardian* (20 November 1986), p. 7.
'My romance with *Anthills*', *The Guardian* (20 November 1987).
'Character is still destiny', *The Guardian* (4 January 1989), p. 13. An appreciation of Salman Rushdie's *Satanic Verses*.

Ben Okri

The strange, fantastic and often intensely disturbing world that is opened up by the stories of Ben Okri, a cosmopolitan writer with wide-ranging cultural interests who has been resident in London for over a decade, has been described by other writers from his country as distinctively, even realistically Nigerian. For it is impossible to write about Nigeria, the author has said, 'with a logical mind. You have to suspend judgement and education and see it afresh.' Born in Nigeria in 1959, Ben Okri left for Britain at the age of nineteen and studied at the University of Essex. His short stories have been published in various journals, including *The New Statesman, Firebird, Paris Review* and *PEN New Fiction*. He has been poetry editor of *West Africa* and has also worked for the BBC Africa service. In 1984 he was awarded an Arts Council bursary and in 1987 he was the winner of the Commonwealth Writers' Prize for Africa and the *Paris Review* Aga Khan Prize for Fiction. His latest novel *The Famished Road* was awarded the 1991 Booker Prize. In addition to novels and short story collections, Ben Okri has also published several poems (in journals such as *PEN International, The Guardian* and *West Africa*, and in *Colours of the New Day*, an anthology of poems for South Africa), as well as numerous articles of literary criticism. He is currently completing a collection of his poetry for Jonathan Cape.

6

Ben Okri

The interview was held in London, July 1986, and completed on 12 December 1990.

Tell me about your beginnings, your childhood, where you grew up . . .
I'd rather reserve that for the complex manipulations of memory that only fiction can provide. The writer's childhood is an important part of anything he writes. That's the only way you can explain why some writers seem to be secretive about aspects of their lives. It's an area that they want to keep inviolate for their writings. It's the only reservoir they've got and they want to keep that for themselves, for the benefit of those who are interested in reading them. I prefer to talk in terms of writing, of when I first started consciously writing.

When was that?
1976.

And how did it come about?
My father returned from his law studies in London with a library of Western classics from Dickens to Mark Twain, the Greeks, the Romans, Austen, English essays, books he didn't actually have the time to read. Those books were my beginnings. While I read Aristotle he said 'Look, Africa has got everything: it's got Aristotle, it's got Plato, it's got all these things and more.' And it was from his library of undiscovered books, books that were just there, mouldering away in this amazing landscape, eaten away by cockroaches and dust and heat, that I started to read and discover the extraordinary quality of the imagination, of fiction.

And that inspired you to write, in your turn?
Not inspired, but gave me my beginnings. I began writing from my own failure, my failure to get a place at a university in Nigeria. I wrote while

waiting, I wrote as a way of waiting: I wrote stories and poems. I wrote a play and a novel. I got a job in a paint company, and in 1976 I had my first article published which was about the failure of rent tribunals in the ghetto, how landlords could charge you what they wanted, without anyone being able to control them. So from the beginning there was a dim awareness of social inequalities, of injustice. This is the thing: you cannot separate the environment from your conscience. Those were my beginnings, but I've not even begun to describe them.

What literature did you do at school?
I didn't do literature at all. I was studying to be a scientist, a doctor or an engineer. In fact I had very little interest in studying literature, as far as I remember. The books of literature that I read were my own secret pleasures. My earliest readings were of folktales and myths, Greek myths, German myths, Roman myths, African myths, African legends. And my mother always told me stories. All of them were intermingled. I didn't separate one thing from the other. Aladdin was as African to me as Ananse. Odysseus was just another variation of the tortoise myth. Literature depends first and foremost on the fact that one person can write something that another wants to read. How is it possible, if it weren't for the fact that essentially there's something that's shared? All this ghetto criticism ignores that essential point. You can't read a book, you can't absorb it, you can't appreciate an oral fable unless it speaks to you in some way. We are talking about the outer and inner dimensions of literature. As a kid you don't make these distinctions, you just read what enchants you and listen to what fascinates you. It's as simple as that.

You were talking before about your writing while waiting. Did you actually consciously desire to become a writer, or was this a gradual development?
I had been writing for years actually, without knowing it. I'd been writing since I was twelve. All the essays and stories I wrote at secondary school were preparing me for it. The books that I'd read and that I enjoyed and the music that I loved were shaping my aesthetic frames. Reading prepares you for writing. It's an inseparable process. I'd always felt with the books I'd liked that they were written for me, that they were speaking to me. The readers select themselves in the process of reading. It is a secret aspect of writing. Writing begins in the secret recesses of the self, places that you don't know about, for reasons that you cannot find. I'd always enjoyed writing essays, but I'd never felt that I was actually writing till out of indignation and frustration I wrote about a social injustice. I had been affected by the high rents in the ghettos. Nobody could control the landlord. The rent edict was useless. So I wrote about it, collecting as much data as I could, and my essay was accepted. From that moment I understood something of the relation between what you *see* and what you have to *say*. The minute you see it, you have to say it. That's where responsibility begins.

When that article was published, I knew I was going to be a writer. I was seventeen.

And how did you go on from there?
I just wrote, I just continued. I wrote many other articles, none of which were published. And when the articles were not published I wrote short stories based on them. The stories were published. People read and liked them, not for the

reasons that I wrote them, but for the fact that they could be read and enjoyed as fictions.

Where were they published?
In women's journals in Nigeria and in the evening papers. I was surprised when they actually paid me: the joy of being able to write and of actually seeing my work published seemed enough at the time. I wrote about charlatans: our society lends greatly to writing about charlatans. And then I found that one of these stories in particular just kept on growing. It just grew and grew and all my friends thought I was mad because I spent so much time on it. That story became *Flowers and Shadows*.

Writers share the same thing that readers experience when they're reading something that interests them: curiosity. They're writing something and they think, my God, how did this person get here? What are they going to do next? How do I follow this sentence? That's what they mean when they say writing's connected with ability, it's connected with that irreducible, indefinable thing that they call talent. It's being able to just do it. The intuitive extraordinary ability to tell a story is a sign of talent. People who have talent think not of writing but of stories, moods, possibilities. They think in terms of narrative situations. You look at their work and somewhere in the first ten pages you see a set of predicaments, you hear someone speaking truly, you catch the music of a unique identity, you see the vague outlines of an individual, of human beings, caught in their peculiar fates, in their peculiar societies. It's very different from mathematics, but it shares the same thing in terms of logic, because good writing is impossible without logic. But good writing has got something else that's higher than logic.

How long did it take you to write *Flowers and Shadows*? Did you take a long time going over it, revising it afterwards, when you'd got your main story out?
I didn't discover my main story till after I'd written it twice. I wrote it once and it was quite awful and then I started writing it again. You see I discovered what I was trying to say, the story I was trying to tell, while I was writing it. As I got deeper into it I realized that what I was writing wasn't really what I should be writing. So I rewrote it and the story came out of the predicament that was most fictionable and most true. The set of opposites, youth and experience, that lent itself most to narrative. Because narrative essentially is tension, opposites, anything that pushes forward. Mathematics works itself backwards and forwards, but fiction, like music, presses in all directions.

Was *Flowers and Shadows* autobiographical?
This is the astonishing thing. I'd written the thing so much that it had become autobiographical. And when it was published every reviewer, anyone who liked it, said it was an autobiographical novel. In fact nothing could be further from the truth! It was *not* autobiographical at all. My parents did *not* live in Ikoyi, my father was *not* a successful businessman who had reached his peak and was now being torn down by jealous relatives. If it's autobiographical, then it's autobiographical in terms of all the people who were young in Lagos at the time I was writing. By that I mean it shares the place, the mood of that time. But in terms of details of life it's an imagined piece of writing. You see it's when I realized this that I could begin to really accept the book, after it had been published. After I'd written *Landscapes*, I'd begun to want to distance myself

from it. When I came to this book of stories, *Incidents*, I looked back and realized that *Flowers* is not about my life, it's not about the details of my life, which is the best place to start from for a writer. I'd actually invented a different set of propositions, a different basis. If there's any point in the book that's autobiographical it's where it ends, in the ghetto. I'm only saying this because people had always thought that some of Henry Miller's books were autobiographical and had dismissed them for that reason, till they realized that in fact Henry Miller's life was the direct opposite. Then they appreciated the imaginative quality of it. Not only was it imagined, but to the reader it felt as if it must be autobiographical. That's an achievement you can't dismiss easily.

What about *The Landscapes Within*, with the lonely artist figure?
That is more autobiographical in the landscape. I knew every detail of the terrain.

When you talk about the terrain are you talking about the landscape without or the landscape within?
The landscapes without. The landscape within is imagined, the external one is autobiographical. The details of his *condition* are not mine, the details of his *predicament* – to some extent – were.

There are continual references to art in one form or another in the book. Are you reflecting consciously on the condition of the Nigerian artist?
The thing about *Landscapes* that has been misunderstood, and misunderstood for good reasons, is that it's often thought of as being about the possibilities of art in that particular environment, when in fact if you look at its centre, my entire thesis was how to convey the *chaos* of life in Lagos, in Nigeria. And I thought that the best way to do it was to show it through the artist who was trying to organize it. So you got two kinds of realities. That was the tension, the internal tension, to show the life, the place, the environment, what it was doing to people, and then to show the artist, this young artist, who was not totally aware of the artist in him yet, organizing all of that. I mean it showed first of all the perniciousness of the environment and then the difficulty of art in that environment. It's a double mirror. It could reflect back and forth, for infinity.

And I suppose all his 'scumscapes' are expressing the same sort of thing; particularly the one he calls 'Drifts', but perhaps even his painting of a Lagos traffic jam.
Exactly, exactly.

But there were also references to art that seem to go beyond this, reflecting the young artist's relations to art in Africa. His visit to the Ebony gallery, for instance:

'Photographed terracotta. Sculpted heads. African children. Negritude in ebony. They all glared reproachfully at him from the black walls. He looked at the crowding presences and the flimsy thought skimmed his mind: you are all dead.'

Omovo, the main character, is at a very awkward point there, when the new is simply crowding out the old. The lucidity of that worldview expressed on the gallery walls spoke of a simpler universe, an older universe of nostalgias, untouched by everything I'd been describing. That kind of nostalgia will die because the environment will either render it impotent and useless, worthy only for tourists and devoid of power. That is why when he confronted his own painting, its rawness shocked *him*.

Were you thinking of a possible way of writing?
I wasn't, no. But I've come to realize you can't write about Nigeria truthfully without a sense of violence. To be serene is to lie. Relations in Nigeria are violent relations. It's the way it is, for historical and all sorts of other reasons. In a way, for me, Omovo is an ideal artist. It's astonishing how people keep talking about him as the 'young artist'. When I think of Omovo it's not just as the young artist: he's what the artist in his progression through time, through age, through experience would end up as. So that's what you are when you're young, but that's what you *should* be, on a higher level, as you get older: seeing experience *pure*, seeing without preconceptions. The elucidation of what you see depends on how clearly you see it. People emphasized Omovo's youth, but they've completely ignored the fact that his innocence does not distort what he sees or what he paints. He's an ideal filter, a prism: in that sense he's an ideal artist. He's a complete contrast from the artists who have ideas, distort the world in terms of their ideas, and then reflect an idea-distorted universe. So it's not the world they're really writing about but something produced from a refusal to see.

You see, the sub-text of all that is the American writer who said that art coming into this world does not disturb anything. But in an atmosphere of chaos art *has* to disturb something. For art to be distinctive it either has to be very cool, very clear – which, in relation to chaos, is a negative kind of disturbance – or it has to be more chaotic, more violent than the chaos around. Put that on one side. Now think of the fact that for anything new, for something good to come about, for it to reach a level of art, you have to liberate it from old kinds of perception, which is a kind of destruction. An old way of seeing things has to be destroyed for the new to be born.

You say Omovo should be seen as the artist, not just as the young artist. But he is also a young man finding himself, isn't he? At the end of the novel he is learning about surviving, about becoming a 'life artist' and 'going through the familiar darkness, alone', which sounds like someone who is reaching maturity.
He's going through a passage. At the end of that passage it's impossible to say whether there's maturity or disintegration.

I suppose I shall have to ask you the question that is always put to African writers in English: Who are you writing for?
Everything you write, the way you write, answers that question. In *Landscapes* I was obviously writing for those who are essentially interested in looking at the relationship between the environment and what it does to you inside. In *Landscapes* I was writing about something that hurts a lot of people.

In *Landscapes* you write 'Everything is alien and nauseating. The English language leaves him empty and deeply tainted: he cannot think freely. [. . .] The common language, in its profound betrayal, stings, coils, means nothing. Meaning and language clamour in the voids of several layers of alienation.' What is your position on the language question?

To write in a language you have to be inhabited by it. That's basic. The thing about language is frames. You have feelings, mood – a way of life. A language inhabits you; if you know the language well enough and you know your feelings strongly enough and you're deeply rooted in your world and if you care enough about your art and about life you can get any language to say what you want to say. Even Shakespeare seemed to me to write from an invisible handicap. Where there isn't a handicap you have to invent one.

How do you relate to the older generation, the 'pioneers'?
I accept them.

Do you disagree with the view that the new Nigerian poetry must do away with the external influences and quotations?
All I can say is that poetry should be luminous and should affect you by its mastery and its superior consciousness.

From the novel to the short story. How did that come about?
Time, poverty, homelessness, desperation, hunger, fear. I had to go back to the basics. By the time I got around to putting this collection together I'd been so distanced from my two novels that I felt as if I was just learning to write, as if I was writing for the first time. My attitude to writing changed. My sense of an audience changed. My sense of words changed.

Would you like to be more specific in your 'sense of an audience' and your 'sense of words', the way they've changed?
The short story form is one of the most neglected forms in fiction generally and African literature in particular. It's the most neglected and requires the most discipline. It is the closest to the essence of fiction: legends, myths, fables. The fact that I found myself writing short stories after the novels required a radical alteration of perception. It consisted of an atomization of the way I looked at craft. I had to look at words with new eyes. A novel is a river, but a short story is a glass of water. A novel is a forest, but the short story is a seed. It is more atomic. The atom may contain the secret structures of the universe.

Why did you choose the title of 'Incidents at the Shrine' as the title of your whole collection?
That's an interesting question. First of all I think because the story itself is the most central. It refers to a new orientation, a return to origins, a different set of perceptions. The world is the shrine and the shrine is the world, as the image-maker says: the way we worship is the way we live, the way we live is the way we worship. These short stories were pressured by the desire to catch as many layers of reality as I could. I wrote the stories the way poems are written.

You move back and forward between Nigeria and England in these stories, which is something new for you, isn't it?
Yes, I suppose so. But I see that book of stories as being unified by the shrine.

There are a lot of dreams in your work.
Dreams are part of reality. The best fiction has the effect on you that dreams do. The best fiction can become dreams which can influence reality. Dreams and fiction blur the boundaries. They become part of your experience, your

life. That interests me. Dreams interest me. Writing is sometimes a continuation of dreaming. I enjoy inventing lives.

(London, 12 December 1990)

The title of your new book, *The Famished Road*, raises memories in the reader's mind of Soyinka's *The Road*.
No, there's no connection. My road is quite different. My road is a way. It's a road that is meant to take you from one place to another, on a journey, towards a destination.

It seems to me that there are two processes involved in your road. One is as you say a journey that may take you from one place to another. The other is a road that seems to be circling round itself as part of a kind of labyrinth.
Well, this really refers to the cycle of coming and going, the *abiku* cycle, the road of birth and death and life. I know people will see connections with Soyinka's road now, but perhaps in fifty years they won't.

How about the structure of the book? It's very carefully structured, with its divisions into three sections, with each section divided into books, each book into chapters. But it also seems to connect up with the idea of divisions not really being divisions in the sense of separations, but suggesting a continuity. Could you talk to me about the divisions in your book?
The book is really intended to be a flow of life. So the divisions would be akin to moments in tidal waves, sea patterns, the way rollers race towards the shore, the way the water beats and then there are lappings and then it retreats. So that within each beginning is an ending, and within each ending is a beginning. It's like the process of birth and rebirth, and it's hard to say where it starts and where it stops. In some cases it's actually starting and stopping simultaneously, or it's being lived out simultaneously. So many things that will seem puzzling in the book are actually in the possibility of a life being lived simultaneously at different levels of consciousness and in different territories.

You said 'puzzling'. 'Puzzle', 'enigma', 'mystery', 'riddle' are key words or leitmotifs running through the book. There are a series of variations on the theme of the riddle, for instance, that seem particularly significant. First you have 'The world is full of riddles that only the dead can answer', then a reference to the 'drama of the living that only the dead can understand', then about 150 pages on another to there being 'many riddles of the dead that only the living can answer', till finally there is the assertion that 'There are many riddles amongst us that neither the living nor the dead can answer', as if you are refusing any attempt to solve the mystery or enigma.
The novel moves towards infinity, basically. You're dealing with a consciousness, like the consciousness that emerges in the book – it's written in the first person, but the consciousness is not my consciousness – which is already aware of other lives behind and in front and also of people actually living their futures in the present. I suppose what I'm really trying to say is that the novel as a form, if it is not going to be artificial, can only move towards infinity.

It must be a kind of open-ended process . . .
It must open towards infinity. Otherwise it would have to end with a death,

and this book cannot admit a death, because it began before death, outside the realm of birth and death.

This openness seems to flow over into the characters themselves, not only Azaro, the *abiku* protagonist, who obviously contains within himself all his past and possibly future lives, but also some of the other characters, who also have something of the *abiku* multiplicity. I was thinking of Madame Koto who seems to echo the figure of the goddess of the island who appeared at the beginning of the book.

This raises a question, from the main character's point of view. Isn't it just possible that we are all *abikus*? I don't say that of course, but why should there be some and not others? Why should the universe be distributed in that way? Essentially we're talking about reincarnation, though I don't want to use that word because it has metaphysical connotations. But it's impossible for a character like that, who sees that there are no divisions really in life, just a constant flow, forming and reforming, and who is looking at other characters, not to see that they themselves knowingly or unknowingly are flowing and reflowing, forming and reforming. That's why you have the three deaths of the father and the three births of the father. There are many, many ways in which the *abiku* set of variations takes place. It can take place on smaller, more visible levels and it can take place on larger levels, but it's all there.

There seems to be a kind of opposition to this in the attempts that are made to appropriate the identity of the protagonist by characters who are trying to seize him and use him, reducing his identity potentials as it were. The island goddess, the police officer and his wife who try to make him assume the identity of the son they have lost, Madame Koto, the thugs, the spirits, the blind old man: they all seem to be trying to pin him down in one way or another.

I wouldn't say they were trying to pin him down. There is something unique about his destiny. One of the central oppositions in the book is the choice between living and dying. Remember there's a pact at the beginning with his spirit companions. This can be interpreted in many ways; I don't want to go into that now. What I'm trying to say is that because of the unique nature of his consciousness he is accompanied by certain forces. Madame Koto perceives him as a lucky child, as a magnet . . . What seems like a constant attempt to pin down his identity is just that all of these different phenomena are different attempts to pull him one way or another: towards life or towards death. And it is part of his choice that he always has to move towards life.

Life being a possibility of constant metamorphosis, change, growth . . .
Consciousness, and allowing infinity – and therefore possibilities – to grow in him. Because that's what infinity means when it's incarnated in the human consciousness. That's the opposition: infinity and human life.

Can we go back a moment to the characters and their metamorphic capacities? You say for instance of the king of the spirit world that he has a hundred different names and faces and all sorts of incarnations: one can see him throughout the invisible book of world history. Mum, too, you see in all the different market women and all the things in the market. Both she and Dad, although they're very distinctive individuals, are also all people: all the people who are suffering, all the martyr figures . . .

Well, that's the 'famished' in the title, isn't it? For me one of the central themes in the book is suffering, probably the only paradoxically democratic thing about our condition: suffering on the one hand and joy on the other, but especially suffering. Suffering is one of the great characters of the book, the different ways people suffer. It defines the boundaries of self but also breaks down the boundaries of individual identifications. So when Azaro sees Mum in all the market women, they *are* Mum. Any one of their children telling their stories would be telling a story just like this one, but with its own particularity. There are hundreds of variations, but there is just one god there, and that god is suffering, pain. But he's not the supreme deity. The higher deity is joy. Again, that's just part of the paradox. Paradoxes keep running through the book, about what it is that redeems the suffering of that continent and what all the people go through. What is it that redeems it? How do people go on living?

One aspect of that is myth. Myth is important in the book too. I never state it particularly. We forget the value of myth, and we forget it more when we give the myth its name. When it's a living, sustaining thing, it's not myth. You give it that word – 'myth' – when it has left that vital territory of living. But, when it is in that territory of life, myth is what makes it possible for those who suffer and struggle, whatever the suffering, to live and sleep and carry on. That's when it's most important. So the 'famishment' has its shadow side in the book, which is joy, which is myth, which is the spirit. There are many mirrors in the book – if I start talking about one thing it leads me to talk about another.

Of course, everything is connected. But going back to the subject of myth, the book itself has a mythic opening: 'In the beginning. . .'. And then we see myths as they form, events or people that are actually becoming myths: Madame Koto, the photographer, Black Tyger . . .
And Mum, underneath it all and surrounding it all.

There is an oppositional relationship between Madame Koto and Dad at the end of the book, when she appears as a sucking, devouring incarnation of power and he is the desire for justice. But there is also a relationship between Madame Koto and Mum, between a devouring mother and a protecting, giving one, surely?
Yes, there is, of course. And it's Madame Koto who has the *abiku* trinity in her. But Madame Koto is actually an ambiguous figure. I feel a great compassion for her. But at the same time I think she's quite terrifying.

A kind of fertility goddess, with an infinite capacity in her for both good and evil – and also suffering.
Yes, very much. That becomes visible when the boy goes into her room. But she's also connected to the *abiku* cycle in her own way. That's why the spirits are attracted to her. There is a great magnetic force in her. But it's difficult for me at this stage to say anything very coherent about this book, probably because it's not meant to be coherent. It's against the perception of the world as being coherent and therefore readable as a text. The world isn't really a text, contrary to what people like Borges say. It's more than a text. It's more akin to music.

Or an infinity of texts, texts within texts within texts.
Texts without words. That's why I probably lean more towards dreams. The blurring of dreams and reality is also crucial. And that will have to take place if you're going to talk about the road in any meaningful sense. That's why there's so

much about blurring of boundaries. The book does begin with 'In the beginning', but it ends by saying that it's quite possible that there aren't any beginnings or any endings. So it does pull away from even the basis of its beginning. The way I read the world through it, it's just quite possible we're all living different phases and at different levels.

This brings me to the time scheme of your novel. There are one or two references that give us some sort of clue as to how to place it but even then one isn't quite sure. Past and future blend into each other and coexist. But there are two references to 'our white rulers'. This suggests a possible pre-colonial setting, but on the other hand not necessarily . . .
It could be. That again depends on how you want to read the book. You could simply ask yourself: Yes, while it is true that everybody in a place like that could be affected by the colonial presence, isn't it just quite possible that within it there may be people who are living their lives almost completely unaware that it was happening? They were affected by it but they were almost completely unaware of it. Questions like that need to be asked, because there's been too much attribution of power to the effect of colonialism on our consciousness. Too much has been given to it. We've looked too much in that direction and have forgotten about our own aesthetic frames. Even though that was there and took place and invaded the social structure, it's quite possible that it didn't invade our spiritual and aesthetic and mythic internal structures, the way in which we perceive the world. Because if one were going to be investigative, one would probably say that a true invasion takes place not when a society has been taken over by another society in terms of its infrastructure, but in terms of its mind and its dreams and its myths, and its perception of reality. If the perception of reality has not been fundamentally, internally altered, then the experience itself is just transitional. There are certain areas of the African consciousness which will remain inviolate. Because the world-view it is that makes a people survive.

Towards the end of the book there are more and more references to history. Earlier history is presented as a 'weird delirium', but it is a delirium you are in no way seeking to escape from. The novel itself could be seen as an attempt to come to terms with history and to understand history, seen here as the 'undiscovered continent deep in our souls'. When Azaro's perception fuses with that of the duiker, in the last part of the book, he sees the whole of African history, its various phases; but it is also, as we see for example in the transcultural nature of the previous lives of the other explicit *abiku* character of the book, Ade, a universal history.
I am very interested in history and this book is also about history. It's one of the reasons why some of the spirit-children choose to – or not to – be born. If you know something about the life you are going to come to, the suffering or whatever, you may or may not choose to be born into all of this. History is actually in the book right from the beginning. But I prefer to say suffering rather than history. There's a great celebration of history, the great accomplishments of various kinds: space travel, moon travel, things like that. They are invisible histories and we have to change our perception of how we speak of people's accomplishments. Pyramids is one way, but there are pyramids of the spirit. And they can have their fruition in many, many different ways. One form of that could simply be the elasticity of a people's aesthetics, their sur-

vival. And Africa has an incredible capacity to not die and not be destroyed. Unlike China that was always unified and had this great wall to prevent invasion, Africa had no great wall, yet it manages to remain unique. It's things like that, the resilience of the spirit, the great dreaming capacities, the imaginative frames that are visible in the art, an art that has not remotely been understood. All these things are within the terrain of the book. But they're not different things. It's just one subject I'm addressing: the famished road.

Then of course there is the story of the road – the unfinished road – that is told within the novel itself: the road that has been being built for 2,000 years and that must not be finished in order that there may always be something to strive after. So that whenever the road is about to be completed catastrophes take place and a new generation comes along and begins again from the wreckage.

I think in our age you have to posit a different conception of history, because the facts of history alone are not enough to give an account of our consciousness and what we need to do with our age. We are in a very, very interesting age: we could go either way. We could go towards destruction still and we could go towards the greatest stage of creativity yet, world creativity. But unless we change the way we perceive history, we're not going to be able to do this. This book is my modest effort to do that, just to alter the way in which we perceive what is valid and what is valuable, different measures and different values. Also, you can talk about small things in big ways and you can talk about big things in small ways. It's not the size of the subject that's important, it's what it leads to. As I said at the beginning of this interview, for me it has to lead to infinity, to endless possibilities within our limitations. I'm offering this to Africa and to the world. We can look at our condition in Africa in despair. On the other hand we can look at it and say 'Well, we are some of the luckiest people at this time because we've got so much to invent and fight for.' Time is actually a short thing and the future is all there to be created.

To return more specifically to aesthetics and to different ways of seeing the African aesthetic, I would like you to talk about Dad and his developing interest in books – books of all kinds and origins – the books that he gets Azaro to read to him.

Well, first of all, the father can't read, so he goes to a bookshop and just picks up any old book: they're not books that he chose, they're just picked at random. That's why they involve everything from Chinese medicine to Homer's *Odyssey* and the tales of Sundjata and so on and so forth. But, if we're going to talk about affinities, the fact of having accidentally or by chance chosen those books could suggest that the African aesthetic could be found almost everywhere. I personally find the African aesthetic in Homer and in a lot of the Greeks, and that's not surprising because the Greeks got a lot of their aesthetics from Egypt, they got some of their gods from Egypt. So that's not surprising at all, that journey of world-views through world history and world literature. Even the *Arabian Nights*, I find a lot of African aesthetics and African world-views there.

Moving away from the book now, I'd like to propose that we stop making so narrow what constitutes the African aesthetic. It is not something that is bound only to place, it's bound to a way of looking at the world. It's bound to a way of looking at the world in more than three dimensions. It's the aesthetic of possibilities, of labyrinths, of riddles – we love riddles – of paradoxes. I think we miss this element when we try to fix it too much within national or tribal boundaries. I think it's more fluid and more interesting than that. When I read *Beowulf* I see Africa in that. A lot of the texts that Okigbo bounces off in *Labyrinths* are texts that he found an Igbo affinity with, otherwise they wouldn't fit into textual manipulations. They are affinities along those lines. They're not just literary affinities, they're aesthetic affinities. I'm not saying that they're universal. I'm saying that they've been travelling through history and they still remain quite pure. They're very strong and they can be picked up 2,000 miles away from where they originated. But who knows where they originated anyway?

My personal experience of reading your book was in fact to recall Fagunwa, Tutuola and Soyinka, but also the vast transnational literature of dream vision and vision generally; forests of the night together with forests of symbols, but also countless forests and labyrinths of literary modern cities.
I think when reading the novel one should just think of my primary sources as being the invisible books of the spirit. My primary sources are those invisible books. And I mean that very seriously.

And your visible books?
Many of them I haven't read yet. And when I read them I'll feel I've always known them. But the great source finally has to be something that keeps flowing, not something that's fixed, and a book is fixed. This is why I tried to write an unfixed book, a river.

Towards the beginning of your book you say something to the effect that life should be a movement towards vision, from blindness to vision, though very few people ever achieve it. And vision is constantly to the fore (as is blindness), even on the physical level of the references to eyes and to seeing and watching and of course photographing. The photographer, surely, is another mediator between what is seen . . .
And what isn't, what is made visible that is not seen, like the ghosts. One of the things I wanted to do was just to make visible one of the stories of the river, that's all. Just one. Not even a life, or many years. Just one of the phases of consciousness. I'll go back to what I said earlier. It is consciousness, it is the way we perceive the world, it is our mythic frame that shapes the way we affect the world and the way the world affects us. It's these invisible things that shape the visible things. I'd like us to go back more often to our aesthetic and mythic frames, even while we're moving into the twenty-first century. For all our technology, we shouldn't abandon those invisible things in our world thinking, they're what shape us. In my last volume I wrote about visible things, visible history, objects, an assault of chaos. In this book I want to go to something more serene and therefore more hopeful. The unbreakable things in us. One shouldn't offer hope cheaply. One should be very, very serious when one is going to talk about hope. One has to know about the very hard facts of the world and one has to look at them and know how deadly and powerful they are before one can begin to think or dream oneself into positions out of which hope and then possibilities can come. It's one of the steps I try to take in this book.

SELECTED BIBLIOGRAPHY

NOVELS
Flowers and Shadows (London: Longman, 1980).
The Landscapes Within (Harlow: Longman, 1981).
The Famished Road (London: Jonathan Cape, 1991).

SHORT STORIES
Incidents at the Shrine (London: Heinemann, 1986).
Stars of the New Curfew (London: Secker and Warburg, 1988).

ESSAYS
'Fear of flying', *West Africa* (3 November 1980), pp. 2177–8. (Autobiographical sketch.)
'How reality overwhelms good fiction', *The Guardian* (Manchester) (26 September 1985), p. 25.
'Soyinka: a personal view', *West Africa* (27 October 1986), pp. 2249–50.
'Meditations on Othello', *West Africa* (23 March and 30 March 1987), pp. 562–4 and 618–19.
'Fresh interpretations' (review of Italo Calvino, *The Literature Machine*), *West Africa* (25 January 1988), pp. 132–3.
'Redreaming the world', *The Guardian* (9 August 1990).

First African Nobel prize-winner (1986), Wole Soyinka is one of the most versatile and eclectic writers of our times. The years – and places – of his childhood (he was born in Abeokuta in 1934) are recounted in *Aké* and returned to, more indirectly, through an imaginary reconstruction of a period of his father's life, in *Isara*, his most recent work. Welding myths and legends from the cultures of Nigeria and both East and West with his reactions to contemporary events, he has described his writing as a '*danse macabre* in this political jungle of ours' – a jungle that belongs both to Nigeria, Africa and the world.

Wole Soyinka

Educated at St Peter's Primary School, Abeokuta Grammar School and at Government College, Ibadan, Soyinka went on to University College, Ibadan, where he studied English, Greek and History, and then to the University of Leeds, where he was awarded an Honours degree in English in 1957. Although his writing had begun during his school days, it was at Leeds that Soyinka composed what were to be his first published plays, *The Swamp Dwellers* and *The Lion and the Jewel*.

After working for a time at the Royal Court Theatre in London, Soyinka returned to Nigeria at the beginning of 1960 with a Rockefeller scholarship to study drama in West Africa, and began writing and producing plays for both theatre and radio. The author's harrowing 27 months' detention during the Nigerian Civil War is described in his prison notes, *The Man Died*. In 1965 Soyinka had been appointed senior lecturer at the University of Lagos, and on his release from prison he became director of the school of drama at Ibadan. After going into voluntary exile in 1970, Soyinka became editor of *Transition* (re-named *Ch'Indaba*) and was elected Secretary General of the Union of Writers of African Peoples. On his return to Nigeria he took up a professorship at the University of Ife, and it was in Ife that he formed the Guerrilla Theatre Unit that presented his 'shot-gun sketches'.

Beside composing plays, poetry, novels, short stories (published in *The Gryphon*, Leeds, and *New Nigerian Forum*, London), biographical and autobiographical writing and a vast number of essays and articles, Soyinka has directed theatrical productions and given university lectures and courses in various parts of the world and produced both films – *Culture in Transition* (1962) and *Blues for a Prodigal* (1984) – and a record, *Unlimited Liability Company* (1983). He has also edited an African poetry collection, *Poems of Black Africa* (London: Secker and Warburg, 1975) and translated the major classic of Yoruba literature, D.O. Fagunwa's *The Forest of a Thousand Daemons: a hunter's saga* (London: Nelson, 1968). Soyinka has now 'retired' to Abeokuta.

7

Wole Soyinka

The first of the three interviews included in this volume took place in L'Aquila (Italy), 7 June 1985, during a conference on African theatre; the second in London, 16 July 1986; and the third in Rome, 24 May 1990, after two 'Meetings with Wole Soyinka' at the Italo-African Institute, where the author talked on 'The World of Wole Soyinka' and 'Beyond the Berlin Wall'. Extracts from the first and second interviews were published in Italian in L'Unità, LXIII, 259 (2 November 1986), p. 13, and Rinascita, XLIII, 41 (25 October 1986), p. 24, and from the third in Rinascita (nuova serie), I, 19 (17 May 1990), pp. 72–4.

(L'Aquila, 7 June 1985)

What would you say are the major problems facing the Nigerian writer today?
I don't know that there are any major problems facing the established writers – I don't think so; I don't imagine that writers like Chinua Achebe, Wole Soyinka, the younger writers like Femi Osofisan, Iyayi, Osundare have any major problems. The only problem which we all face is one which besets not only writers but citizens in Nigeria: the problems of our unbelievable and unacceptable socio-political situation, which gets more and more reactionary and inhuman with every succeeding regime. So that's a general problem. For the younger writers I think the main problem is what I call an ideological confusion. During the last decade, I think there has been far more criticism than creative work and this I have attributed to the stridency of what I call the ideologues *vis-à-vis* the kind of literature Nigerians should be producing. I take the attitude that it is better to have lots and lots of literature and creative material for people to work on according to the various ideological and critical schools than to have none at all. I have in fact accused these critics of inhibiting younger writers by confusing them about certain priorities that are not even very clearly defined. There's a very crude, vulgar school of Marxist criticism,

or so-called Marxist criticism. Placed side by side with criticism, Marxist criticism, even from the Eastern European countries like Hungary for instance, Poland, even contemporary criticism from the Soviet Union, this kind of so-called Marxist criticism – not just Nigerian – also of socialist thinking countries, its level of crudity is a form of authoritarianism, back-to-Zhdanov-Stalinist school. The damage it is doing to very talented writers is incalculable: they're inhibited, they're threatened, they're bullied – some of these critics are their teachers who have a captive audience among these students, some of whom are very talented. And the problem is that some of these new writers cannot give free range to their creative bent without constantly having hovering over their head accusations of being reactionary, subjective – all the usual terminology which in the end means absolutely nothing. This for me represents the greatest problem that the Nigerian writer has, though naturally people like me are totally impervious to this crudeness and in fact we respond only because we are also teachers and we feel that certain wrong things are being taught. Otherwise I don't see any particular problems.

You don't think the crisis in publishing in Nigeria is creating difficulties for the young writers?
Yes and no. I don't really consider that a major problem. It is true that Western publishers have shown less interest in African literature since that first flush of curiosity for what was coming out of the newly independent countries. Now they've become far more circumspect, more critical, more choosy. Frankly, a lot of literature got published that should never have seen the light of day and most of those writers have fallen by the wayside, because there was never really much talent there. As we say in Nigeria, 'water has been finding its own level'. The other point I wanted to make is that there has been a growth in indigenous publishing: Ethiope Publishers, which is constantly looking for scripts; Fourth Dimension, which has a *number* of writers, especially from the Eastern Region post-war school: literature, criticism, poetry, essays; Onibonoje Publishers; Fagbamigbe Publishers; so there has been a lot of very healthy growth which is very good for Nigerian literature. In fact I began reserving all Nigerian rights for my works from about ten years ago: Ethiope is publishing a couple of my plays, for instance. So there has been compensation for that loss of foreign outlet. In fact the situation seems very promising.

How do you see the present political situation in Nigeria?
Very sad. Very distracting. In a statement I made last year I referred to my generation as the wasted generation and I was thinking in terms of all fields, not just the literary: the technological talents that we have which are not being used; but I also had in mind our writers of course, the fact that a lot of our energy has really been devoted to coping with the oppressive political situation in which we find ourselves. A lot of our energies go into fighting unacceptable situations as they arise while at the same time trying to pursue a long-term approach to politics such as, for instance, joining progressive-looking political parties, but of course each step is always one step forwards and about ten backwards. I find the political situation very, very frustrating, personally frustrating. I mean, forget even the amount of let us say personal work one could have done, writing and so on, and just think in terms of the amount of time one could have spent on training, in theatre for instance, would-be actors, or devoting more time to would-be writers, many of whom are constantly

inundating one with cries for help; the qualitatively different kind of creative community atmosphere, structures that one would really love to give more time to – look at what we started in the early '60s, the Mbari club with its movement, its discovery of new writers, workshops. I know, very definitely, that I feel a great sense of deprivation in terms of what I could have contributed to the general productive atmosphere of the country in literary terms and I'm sure a lot of other writers feel the same. That is one of the penalties of the political situation we've been undergoing since independence and which has got *progressively* worse, progressively more lethal. The penalties for the wrong kind of political action in this situation have become far more depressing.

You were talking yesterday evening about problems of censorship. Would you like to go back to that question?
Censorship is a very real thing. First of all, the decrees that have been passed amount to a total penal control over all activities. There is first of all Decree No. 4 which was aimed primarily at journalists, at the media. Two of the journalists, Tunde Thompson and Nduka Irabor, were jailed in very disgusting circumstances: the imprisonment, the judgement, everything about it was criminal. They were jailed in effect for publishing the truth. The decree says it is not a question of whether what you print is factual or not, if it can be proven that it's brought the Government into ridicule or created disaffection – not just the Government but any official, any servant, any employee of the Government – that decree gets you. Now this has affected a number of things one can say to people, because the media have to practise self-censorship. But, as if that were not enough, the Chief of Staff, a few weeks ago, bothered perhaps by the fact that universities and university writers and intellectuals carry on business as usual at least within their own walls, made new threats. Universities are saturated, literally *saturated*, with the NSO, the National Security Organization, so maybe they had reports on seminars, lectures and symposia on the state of the nation, on current affairs. Not so long ago there was a production, a convocation production, which was an adaptation by Biodun Jeyifo of Brecht's *Puntila and His Man Matti,* and the opportunity was seized to call attention to a number of those who had been detained without any trial, for a year without any trial whatsoever. You should have seen the kerfuffle! There were letters from the Chief of Police, the University Vice Chancellor had to call a meeting and I went to represent the department and told them in no uncertain terms that this is part and parcel of Brechtian theatre and Brecht is not just talking about Puntila, he is talking about actual social contradictions, social injustice; that we're a teaching department and that it's our responsibility to adapt and to relate whatever we're teaching to the actualities of the moment, especially if it's a playwright like Brecht, and therefore we're not going to apologize to anybody and we can tell the Chief of Police what to do with his protest. So they had to contend with all of that plus the symposia, student movements and so on, the statements – because the papers carry a lot of the statements we make, as much as possible, in fact they seize the chance. We also ran a workshop for which I used Femi Osofisan's text *Who's Afraid of Solarin,* which in itself is an adaptation of Gogol's *The Government Inspector.* I chose that deliberately because Tai Solarin, an educationist, a forcible spokesman, a real fighter against the oppression of the masses, deprivation and exploitation and so on, has been detained for a year and a half. So I imagine there were

regular reports of all these activities and that's what led Idiagbon to give a press conference in which he said that people should remember that Decree No. 4 does not affect merely what is published in the newspapers but all subversive lectures and symposia in the universities, which have become the hotbed of sedition and subversion, and that they're going to deal with the universities under this decree. Sure enough, they have moved to stop public symposia in Ibadan. In other instances the university authorities have forced student bodies to cancel lectures and symposia . . . So it's a really fascist situation: all the gloves are off and these people are letting us know just what they are, as if we needed to be instructed, but the struggle continues.

Tell me about your teaching of theatre at Ife. What sort of plays do you put on and teach?
Well, the emphasis is very often on African theatre. Naturally we teach comparative drama, theatre of the world. Three years ago I taught *commedia dell'arte*, which in fact became very cogent for the final year students, as the theme of their long essay. Two years ago it was Russian contemporary drama; three years before that it was Irish theatre; this year it's Nigerian theatre. So we teach all forms of drama: Japanese Noh drama at one time. We make sure that it's a very catholic range. I don't believe in teaching just African theatre exclusively, that's daft, it just limits the horizons of our students.

Do you believe in national or racial categorizing of literature? Do you think African books should be published in a series on their own or alongside writings from other countries in miscellaneous collections?
I look at series like Heinemann's as a kind of time-specific event. The European world, the Western world, suddenly had a hunger for literature coming from this part of the world. The series, of course, was very uneven; quite a large portion of it was total dross, but a fair amount, quite a good amount, was excellent literature. So it fulfilled its purpose. It all depends on the content. If for instance the Heinemann African Series had been more discriminatory I don't think I'd even have thought twice about the whole question of publishing literature from a continent, a race, in a series on its own. The reason why I have considered it at all is because it occurred to me that the series was adopting a policy of anything goes because it's African and therefore it must be published. If that series had been run by African intellectuals I would suggest that at least one-third of what was published would never have been published and then this question would not have bothered me in the slightest. So it depends entirely; I think it's a very relative question and it doesn't even occur to one if one can dig up any book in a series and find that at the very least it's average, at the very least it matches what is published in any other society and you've not got the feeling that this only got there because there's a large series which can accommodate everything. That's about the clearest explanation I can give of my attitude. But obviously good literature, for me, is very, very important, no matter where it comes from.

You have urged very strongly for the adoption of Kiswahili as a Pan-African language. Would you explain this?
Well, for me – I think this is true of most African writers, most Anglophone writers, not so much the Francophone ones, they went through this assimilation programme, which we never did – for writers like me, there has always

been a resentment, an underlying resentment, that I have to express myself and create in another language, especially a language that belongs to the conquerors. I think that is true of anybody: I know the English for a long time resented Latin and French, so it is a very normal phenomenon. Now it is as a result of my recognition of this resentment, that's one. Two, the problem all Nigerians in particular and I think most nationalities in Africa have had to confront: the question, the political question, what should be our national attitude to language, what is going to be the official language? Now, I know that in Nigeria if an attempt is made to impose any of the major languages there will be another Civil War; that is clear. I don't want another Civil War. It's my duty as a writer whose tool is language to think in terms of strategies for creating a national feeling, a national sense of belonging, while making sure that it's not yet another form of cultural colonization.

Then, I had always looked with envy at the kind of homogeneity of Arab culture – *comparative* homogenity, because Arab cultures are also very diverse – and I know that this has been due to two factors: religion, which also has affected the language – and vice versa – for Arabic is considered *the* language of the Koran, and of course the language itself, the Arabic language, this has given to the Arabs a kind of cultural identity which survives no matter how much they are currently bombing one another in Beirut, or how Gaddafi is against – on political grounds – the feudal structures. And I also have always considered the black people as a nation – this includes the black peoples in the Diaspora – I've always had this sense of total solidarity, this sense of belonging. Additionally, I resented the fact that communication with the rest of the Blacks on the continent would have to go through the colonial sieve. We learnt first of all the literature of Europe before we even began to discover the literature of the continent and this communication problem has been due mostly to language. So it is through this that I evolved – through all these various points – quite logically to a position where I think that the black peoples should have a language of their own, quite apart from the fact that I never want to hear anybody say 'Why don't you adopt Arabic?' – I don't accept Arabic as a black African language! The Arabs happen to have inhabited a portion of the continent of Africa, but the black people exist, their culture is very specific, all their cultures are very specific, in very concrete terms, *vis-à-vis* let us say Arabic cultures. It seems to me a good idea that, since at various times in our post-colonial or even pre-colonial era we have thought in terms of an African High Command, a Union of African Countries, in addition to the fact that we have a certain contestation in Southern Africa which is very pertinent to us, specifically the black peoples over and beyond anybody else, no matter what messages of solidarity, what ideological affinities we feel for any other parts of the world, the primary struggle in South Africa is the struggle of the black peoples. In other words, culturally, politically, socially, there are *enormous* reasons why the black peoples should have a common form of communication.

I studied the various languages, analytically, that is, I don't speak Kiswahili but I know the history of Kiswahili, I know a lot of the structure, I know that it's a language very much in formation, I know that it does not belong to any nation as such right now: Eastern African nations have adopted it also, and so why don't we expand from Eastern Africa? It solves the problem of national language in countries like Nigeria where it's a very volatile subject. It's also an act of political will, if we cannot have a union of the African nations, we could at least have a language.

When you say 'We could at least have a language', presumably you mean as a means of communicating – a Yoruba would still speak Yoruba?
Absolutely. Nothing touches the indigenous languages. And anybody who likes can continue studying their French, English, Portuguese or Spanish.

So instead of a Shona speaker communicating with a Yoruba speaker through English, he –
He will use Kiswahili. It's a policy that's really so simple, so simple. Think of the useless number of subjects I've learnt at school: I studied Latin at one stage, Greek at another time. If instead of that I had studied Kiswahili, I'd be talking across the continent. I've never understood why, rationally, anybody should oppose it.

Do you see yourself as a Yoruba writer? Abiola Irele speaks of a line of development in Yoruba literature passing from Fagunwa via Tutuola to Soyinka, do you agree with this?
Well, it's obvious that I'm not an Igbo writer! The 'Nigerian' writer is a creature in formation. Obviously we're bound to end up as a hybridization. Well I'm not a Hausa writer. There is the Hausa culture, the Tiv culture – we have several cultures in Nigeria – so that makes me primarily a Yoruba writer. There's no question at all about it to my mind, I'm primarily a Yoruba writer, just as you have Occitan writers in France, Welsh writers, Scottish literature, within the same political entity. There is Gaelic literature, literature in Welsh, even when it is written in English, like the works of Powys, for instance.

When did your interest in theatre first arise? What kind of theatre?
I've been interested in theatre since I was a child. I can't come up with any dates. I participated in school plays and graduated from there to writing sketches, when I was in school and then at university.

We know about Wole Soyinka up to about the age of twelve – are we going to know about the next period of his life?
No, I think the veil of discretion must be drawn over the period after the age of innocence!

In *The Man Died* you swiftly repress the memories of a happy childhood that momentarily surface – is that the origin of *Aké*?
No, not at all. There's no way *Aké* wouldn't have come out. It's an ambience that, once you're aware it's passing, once you revisit Aké sometime, you miss certain signs, certain relationships change drastically, that were the norm when you were a child, your own personality has . . . In fact, now that you ask that question, I remember that I'd been trying to find time to write a biography of my uncle. Through that I wanted to catch some of the flavour of that period, what he represented, his times and so on, and I suppose it's from that kind of idea that *Aké* grew since I couldn't do that, but it's still a project that I might still do. It requires going through papers, talking to people. Beere (his wife) is dead now, she died some years ago, but I hope I will still write it one day. You see, it was out of a desire at least to capture something of that period.

Femi Osofisan has said that your use of space is one of the most original aspects of your theatrical activity. Would you like to talk about your use of space in theatre?
Some directors see a *text*, their primary concern is to elucidate the text by action,

to propel the innate material of the text, to project it towards the audience. When I'm directing I see myself first of all as creating images in space. The book, the text, is one thing, but the whole business of translating the text onto the stage is that one is moving to a new dimension and I think I have said that the dimension has to be strong, otherwise one might as well read the play. That dimension is more than just the inner interpretation through the actor – that is of course also important – but it's the visual sculpting of that event on stage. That dimension fascinates me a lot, ever since I've been directing.

Are your plays written with this in mind?
Some of them, yes. Not my political sketches, for instance, what I call my shot-gun sketches!

Tell me about them.
That's my favourite form of occupation actually; I build it around individuals I'm working with on stage. We improvise, a lot of things come out, it's never the same, a different thing one day to another . . . Those sketches have a kind of what I'd call a creative joy in that it's constantly being re-created, it's a permanent re-creation and finally of course it's a very direct way of speaking to the people, to my audience, certainly more direct than say denser plays like *Death and the King's Horseman*. I enjoy doing them.

Are they put on in the same places?
No, they move around a lot. The last round of these things – I do them in waves as called for by the circumstances – the last one took us to market places, market spaces, open-air university quadrangles, outside civil service offices – they come out during their coffee break or look through the windows; one took place right in front of the House of Assembly when the big rice scandal was on, when Dikko was fighting for his existence, he was the Chairman of the Presidential Task Force on Rice. That whole rice episode was just a scheme to defraud the nation of billions. I can't think of a greater crime than creating a fictitious scheme which has to do with food or health, two primary needs of humanity and society, a fictitious scheme just to siphon billions into private pockets, no benefit at all to the people who really need it, and that's what the whole rice thing was about. So we did this sketch – it's been one of my favourites – and we did it with a troupe which was not a regular troupe, there were some actor-students among them, but it was a special group that I got together and we performed in all sorts of places and finally went to Lagos outside the House of Assembly. After performing in a quadrangle near by we then piled sacks and sacks – made-up sacks to look like bags of rice – on the entrance of the House of Assembly with a banner 'To him who hath more shall be given'! That's been one of my favourites!

Tell me about the film you have just made.
Well, the film was to have been another agit-prop expression, using the medium of film, and it was something that I desperately wanted to do before the elections as pure election propaganda: its material was to have been purely all the crimes of Shagari's government during the civilian stint. When I started shooting there was a price on my head by Shagari's henchmen and they didn't even disguise it but insinuated it on television and radio, newspapers. They were foaming at the mouth because I denounced the elections on BBC and this

had a lot of repercussions in the world press. I predicted that there would be civil war or a military coup, which was all I said: there was no other possible result, no other direction, except a civil war or military coup. So when I returned and we started shooting we had to make sure we were shifting from location to location because these killer squads were really out . . . Many times in fact – we had our own supporters within the police – and the news they used to bring us was really quite chilling, but I was determined to finish that film. And then, halfway through, the coup took place, while we were shooting, and so the whole direction had to change. We could no longer come out with the message, the summons to public insurrection which is what the text originally said, we had now to make it a sort of morality tale of youthful greed and corruption. I should mention, by the way, that I'd planned this film much, much earlier, long before the elections, but just couldn't find any money for it. We knew the Shagari government would do everything in its power to suppress it, but there were at least nine states in opposition at the time, nine out of nineteen states, and we knew this film would go on their television, they would make cassettes of it, it would be shown in cinemas in those states and that would be quite enough. So that was the original idea, but I couldn't get the money and that was when I made the record *Unlimited Liability*. I was just sitting down one day and feeling so frustrated – out of the amount I needed, I think I'd got about 3000 Naira which is about 4000 dollars – and thinking what the hell are we going to do? Then I suddenly thought – we had been doing the sketches, the Guerrilla theatre was already on at the time, but they were so fraught with danger, all the time I was never really very happy at exposing these students and things were getting really wild, really, really wild: disappearances, arbitrary arrests – people just locked up for ever and you wouldn't know where they were – murder, daylight executions, people not getting home . . . The outside world had no idea what hell we were going through in that period. None whatever. Close to what was happening in El Salvador: abductions, assassinations, before the eyes of families of the opposition leaders; each day was getting more and more dangerous . . . So I was sitting down and thinking, well, I can't make this film, when I said, wait a minute, why don't I put on record a couple of the songs which we're using in these sketches? So we rushed that through. It was marvellous because there was a shortage of all sorts of things in the recording studios, granules for making records were short, there was a long queue of all the various musicians who were waiting to wax their own usual discs and the moment they heard what it was about, all of them gave me their place and that record came out, immediately, in record time, because they all said, 'No, this comes first.'

So the film itself underwent a number of changes in the course of shooting?
Yes. While we were actually editing, the Dikko event took place. So there was a political statement which the film lent itself to and I re-edited the end so that you could see that the corrupt policeman was the agent of Shagari's government and that he aided the politician-killer in getting out. So we froze a frame when money was being exchanged and inserted a postscript something like: Sometime about July 1984 a clumsy attempt was made to crate one of the guilty politicians etc. etc. and bring him back to the scene of his crime. The nation was manipulated into an orgy of patriotic rage at the failure of this attempt, but they'd forgotten the question of who let him out in the first place, and why.

Wole Soyinka

Could you tell me how you first started writing poetry, what moved you to write poetry?
Well, that's a bit of a difficult question to answer because I think from school I always scribbled some verses. I do recall that I entered the poetry competitions in the Festival of the Arts in Nigeria – I don't know which – it was conducted nationally at the time. I think I remember taking a bronze medal for a poem on a murderer's last hours. Don't ask me why . . . probably somebody got hanged around that time and I saw it in the newspaper and just pictured what his last hours were like. Now that you asked I suddenly had this flash of this poem which I hope nobody ever uncovers; I'd be horribly embarrassed – I hate all these collectors of so-called juvenilia, the Bernth Lindfors gang! So, as far as I recall I've always scribbled short stories, poems, verses, and as one grows older and more mature and more experienced I suppose one's dimensions widen and deepen.

What poets – African and non-African – do you or have you felt affinity to?
Affinity's the wrong expression. Let's just say that I've always been more fascinated by the . . . Well, I have never really enjoyed what you might call Tennysonian poetry. I found a close affinity (and I think this is due to the tradition of Yoruba poetry which some people insist is very simple and straightforward but which for me is very dense, metaphoric, allusive, also witty and mischievous: it's not *solemn* – when I use expressions like dense I don't mean solemn – but sutured with a great deal of play on words), so I do have a great feeling for poets like John Donne and the Metaphysicals . . . poetry which seems to penetrate the surface reality of things, or at least attempt to explore the not so apparent realities which are however very real, especially within my own world-view. At the same time I've enjoyed precise, very concise use of images, the Imagists, for instance, and of course I'm very, very close to Yoruba poetry: *ijala, ewi* and even the poetry of the prose language of writers like D. O. Fagunwa, whose novel I translated. Well, that just about sums it up. It's quite true that I do not find myself challenged, intellectually or even emotionally, by what I call the Tennysonian assonance of poetry.

How about Eliot?
Well, curiously enough I'm not very fond of Eliot. Even as a student I resented having to study him because his poetry doesn't move me in any way. Yes, it's true that I find his *Waste Land* to an extent – it's not difficult even for somebody who is alien to the tragedy which is captured in that poem to empathize with the mood of the poem, the regret, the deep sense of loss – I think in that sense, that's one work to which I responded. I don't share the view of most critics that he thoroughly absorbed or integrated his kind of eclectic range of alien religions. I find the intrusion of the metaphors, religions, an obtrusive kind of exotica inserted in *The Waste Land*. As a student I found myself very detached from that aspect of his poetry.

What poems and literary conventions and forms were most influential for you in your early poetry, or was it a very personal thing?
I don't know, quite frankly. I think most young men and women begin writing poetry out of their personal lives, out of their personal experience, out of their

personal emotion. The control of the medium follows, but the initial thing is instinctive response to experience, to encounters, to emotions, to emotional states of mind, correlations which strike one simultaneously as unique and – I use the expression 'correlations' deliberately – experiences which seem unique, but at the same time have a reference to one's inner experience, intuitions, and so I cannot really say that one poet or the other, some kind of poetry, influenced me. I mentioned just now the fact that I've never been impressed by Eliot's use of the oriental religions, but it's significant that when I was in prison, in the poems which came out of prison, I was drawn towards that particular terrain, so perhaps there had always been that instinct in me towards particularly the *Bhagavad Gita* which features in *A Shuttle in the Crypt* and some of the poems there. Maybe I had always sensed a way in which *I* would want to use it, but somehow Eliot's use was different. It could be the reason, but it's a purely subjective reaction and one should always mention that.

You mentioned Yoruba poetry earlier. Was that something that you grew up with or that you came to later on?
Oh no. I grew up with it. The chants of *Ijala* and other poetic genres. I remember since I was a child we had one Kilanko who was not only a musician but a poet and he used to recite poems when I was at school, in primary school. No, no, I grew up with it. We had not just raconteurs but poets, epic recitals featured continuously in our school. On prize-giving day, for instance, students would get up and recite Yoruba poetry. It was part of our way of life.

And was Fagunwa read at school?
Oh yes, absolutely! He was read at school. Even today, people still take him in their School Certificate examinations. It's a writer that is constantly set. I've been reading Fagunwa from early childhood, including pamphlets of short stories which were always lying around.

When did you actually start translating his work? At least two episodes were published in *Black Orpheus* well before the book came out.
I can't remember. It was certainly a long time ago. I'd always wanted to translate Fagunwa. I'd always felt this was a novel which should be accessible to everyone.

You often use traditional themes, figures and images, developing them in an original manner and weaving into your verse a multiplicity of cultural allusions. How do the different strands interrelate?
I should make it quite clear that I don't set out to weave it . . . If something is part and parcel of your flesh, your skin, it's inevitable. I accept this heritage, I utilize it, I mutilate it, I twist it, distort it. I act complementarily towards it. We can speak of specific metaphors. We can speak, for instance, of the figure of Ogun, because all his attributes, his idioms, his language, metaphors, poetry, all of this I *weave*. So one can talk about *concrete* situations like this. But when one starts talking about stylistics, for instance, for me that becomes the territory of the critic who's curious enough to find out where the correlations are. I don't set out consciously to set up anything.

There are certain images and themes that recur, under varying forms, throughout your work. Particularly the references to Ogun and to his archetypal journey into the abyss, reappearing elsewhere as a descent into Hades. Then there are

your four 'archetypes' in *A Shuttle in the Crypt*: Joseph, Hamlet, Gulliver and Ulysses; why these particular figures?

Well, they corresponded to certain archetypes, certain experiences, both individual and collective, which were going on in Nigeria at the time. I'm glad that you mentioned the kind of parallel between Ogun's experience and Greek mythology, for instance, because one thing that I like to emphasize, which should not be necessary but which unfortunately is made necessary by what I call the school of purism, is that as anthropologists, social anthropologists, mythologists, ethnologists have found out all over the world – the serious ones – there is a meeting point within human experience, within the collective memory of humanity, within the mythologizing attitude and inclinations of mankind. There are so many meeting points and it's foolish to deny their existence. The story of what is now known as the Oedipal complex, its expression has been tracked down not merely to Greek tradition. It's been found to be a preoccupying aspect of the human psyche in most societies. I was looking at the programme of LIFT just now, and it's interesting that there's a Chinese play which came to London not so long ago which retold the Oedipal myth through Chinese mythology – pre-existing Chinese mythology! And so, coming to Ogun, he's a recognition of a valid aspect, a continuing, a real aspect of the creative and social instinct of my own society. But I have no doubt at all it was reinforced by my discovery as a student of parallel examples in my studies of other societies. In other words, one begins by recognizing certain symbols in one's society, but one's sense of wonder and therefore one's exploitation of materials, one's inclination towards exploitation, one's sense of wonder increases by the recognition of similar . . . even while Ogun, for instance, retains his uniqueness, the fact is one's sense of wonder increases by finding parallels in Prometheus, in Gilgamesh, in the other mythologies of other societies, of the Orient, of the West, and so on and so forth. It's not a question of specificity, but of uniqueness and at the same time of complementarity. And I think that basically is why for instance we encounter these four archetypes: there's a Jewish archetype, Joseph; there is Hamlet, whose story is not in any case really English but was borrowed; there is Ulysses, the eternal wanderer (you find Ulysses in Fagunwa: what is Akara-Ogun but a Ulysses?), and so these metaphors came to me quite instinctively, naturally; but at the same time – I feel I have to emphasize this – it was necessary, while I was in prison, to try and distance myself from the immediate environment. That was also a process of sanity, to think in terms of distancing me from my reality, connecting with *other*, larger symbols.

The Ulysses archetype seemed to me to be slightly different from the other three, in the sense that it seemed very closely related to Joyce's *Ulysses*.

Yes, indeed; again, that was deliberate distancing; I did not use Fagunwa's Ulysses, for instance, Akara-Ogun.

Ulysses seems a particularly apt archetype for your work, both in terms of your experiments with time, space and language and of your using myth, like in *Ulysses*, as a kind of order on which to fit the disorder and fragmentariness and problems of contemporary life.

My use of myth . . . I wish you'd phrased that differently, without saying 'like in *Ulysses*'. Because, take Fagunwa, for instance. In what sense did he use the archetypal explorer, wanderer, seeker, quester? It was in order to organize events that are themselves chaotic and that means the whole experience of search, of quest, and that means of *life*, which tends to be pretty chaotic, to use a framework. It's the same thing with John Bunyan in *Pilgrim's Progress*. Whether it's religion which is the framework or just adventure, or whatever, one constantly uses that framework.

Yes, but to return, despite your objection, to *Ulysses*, there is also a use of myth as a way of contrasting a previous order with a present disorder, to emphasize a sense of degradation.
Yes, but if one looks into it . . . This is why I say one distorts myth anyway. A previous *order*, but . . . just how much order *was* there in the previous myth? It's a 'mythic' order: it's winnowed down through the ages, through perception, contemporary perception, and it's useful, just useful.

You have only written two novels. Is there any particular reason for this? How do you see the novel today?
Well, I'm not really a keen novelist. And I don't consider myself a novelist. The first novel happened purely by accident. In fact I used to refer to it purely as a 'happening'. I used to write short stories, by the way, which was OK. But the novel for me is a strange territory – it still is – and I turned to it at that particular time because it was not possible for me to function in the theatre. So, for me it was just a happening. Then, again, *Season of Anomy* was written at a period when it was not possible for me to function in the theatre. So I don't consider myself a novelist. And the novel form for me is not a very congenial form. Basically, I don't even like the novel. When I read prose I tend to want to read biographies, generally political biographies, political history, works of philosophy and – this will astonish you – crime, detective stories! The kind of fiction which I really enjoy is good science fiction – and the exceptional detective work like Umberto Eco's *The Name of the Rose*. But general novels and so on, contemporary novels . . . I pick up books, I browse through them very quickly because somebody says 'Oh you must read this one, you'll find it fascinating', so I read it, but generally I'm not a great novel man. I should observe that this is a recent development – perhaps no more than fifteen years – maybe less. Before that I was an assiduous devourer of the novel!

You don't espouse the view that the novel is an imported form and therefore extraneous to Africa, I imagine?
No, no, not at all! But I'll tell you this: there's an exception to what I was saying. When I was a child I *devoured* Dickens. I think there is hardly any volume of Dickens' work that I have not read. There was something that fascinated me about the kind of life he depicted and I remember that in school I read literally all Dickens' novels. I think there was a kind of exotic nature – the transitional life of Victorian England that he captured was to me so exotic. But, generally, the contemporary novel . . . I've read one or two: Rushdie, I've enjoyed, again, exceptionally, Marquez, I love his works: that's another exception. Bessie Head: I found her novels very, very gripping, fascinating, challenging, really intellectually intriguing. Then that black American woman writer, Toni Morrison, the author of *Tula, Song of Solomon*: she's a fascinating writer. Umberto Eco . . . But generally I don't read novels.

A sense of doom, of endless repetition, despite all attempts to overcome it through individual will-power or through sacrifice, seems to underlie the

actions of your characters. Yet there is also a strong sense of a need for change, through what you have described as an evolutionary kink in the circle – the Möbius strip as against the eternal cycle; and you also speak of the need to break the primal cycle even if it were of good and innocence, if necessary through violence.

Well, some people say I'm pessimistic because I recognize the eternal cycle of evil. All I say is, look at the history of mankind *right up to this moment* and what do you find? All one has to do is open the newspapers *any given day*; listen to the radio any given day, walk through the streets any given day, and you just marvel how in spite of the phenomenal strides man has made in the improvement of the quality of life, technological means, means of communication, the conquest of nature, the harnessing of the forces of nature, man till now has not really solved his perennial problem of mutual slaughter, cannibalism, cruelties, the whole unconquerable evil of power, in all societies, *all* societies, even this one. So for me that is a reality which one cannot escape. Those who want to believe that man is constantly improving, they are free to do so. For me the evidence is overwhelmingly against, but I take the position that it is again a question of struggle. One begins by acknowledging the negative, depressing reality and so one has a choice, either to lie down and die or to fight it. So therein lies what is sometimes referred to as a paradox. But for me it's the most logical, simplistic thing in the world. The very fact that you recognize the unacceptable face of human existence, that very fact means that you either commit suicide – you take your choice – or, if you don't commit suicide, you are bound to resist and to try and devise strategies or contribute towards strategies to enable humanity to make a quantum leap. Because nothing short of a quantum leap can compensate for the centuries of retrogression which human societies all over the world, I don't care where – name it – wherever, even the most so-called progressive societies, the retrogression one constantly finds in terms of the quality of human existence. That is the depressing reality. But, as I said, for me the choice is simple. Either one commits suicide or one struggles against it. And so the quantum leap for me is represented by this sudden kink, this sharp evolutionary kink in an existing, a pre-existing cycle: the Möbius kink, the Eshu kink, it has very many metaphors but it all means exactly the same thing.

Just over ten years have passed since the publication of *Ogun Abibimañ*; would you write a similar poem today?

Well, I was about to say *no* and then I recalled that I have been writing some poetry more or less in the same vein . . . not quite, because this time I merely celebrate the spirit of one human being: I'm more modest. After the betrayal of Nkomati it's highly unlikely I will write another *Ogun Abibimañ*. By the betrayal of Nkomati I'm not referring merely to the specific accord but for me the betrayal of African countries, even of the front-line states, the betrayal of the black brothers and sisters in Southern Africa, the refusal to become absolutely and unequivocally engaged in the struggle which is going on in South Africa, which is long overdue . . . It's unlikely that I will write another poem celebrating a moment of the acceptance of a challenge. It's not enough, it's no longer enough. It's terrible what has happened. The accord was shattering. But I have been celebrating the spirit of Nelson Mandela and the South African struggle; I suppose because I can't help it. I'm a very celebratory kind of person. I cling to crumbs on the revolutionary field. For me any little affirmative thing literally says 'We're still alive' and for me that is always worth celebrating.

(Rome, 24 May 1990)

There are references throughout your work to the visual and plastic arts and to painters of varying origin, from Skunder Boghossian of Ethiopia to Picasso or Francis Bacon. In fact in your 1985 essay 'Climates of Art' you connect Bacon's 'scheme of image distortion' with the 'aesthetics of movement' expressed by the traditional African mask. Could you discuss the relations between art and writing in your vision?

When people complain of what, when kind, they say is complexity and, when they want to be nasty, they say is obscurantism, deliberate complication and obscuring of one's prose, one's poetry, and demand a very linear, almost transliterating approach to composition, the transliteration of one's thoughts, my favourite answer is just to refer them back to African sculpture, which is by no means simple, which is not always realistic representation but which in fact evokes numinous tensions: tensions between the numinous world and the realistic world, tensions *within* the numinous world, however it is conceived. The tension we find in African sculpture is not linear, it does not evoke a mere uniplane concept of images of the numinous world.

You refer to the example of Francis Bacon. Well of course I use that as a kind of paralleling of the African mask in motion – I refer to the work of Dennis Duerden who very astutely points out that a number of African masks were never even conceived by the artists as the completed physical static order which we see, but that they were actually conceived *in motion*, they were actually designed as a multiple expression in relation to the dance, to the very motions which are created by those masks when they are worn. That is why we do not have what you might call galleries of masks where people go to see 'African art' on exhibition. When the festival is over, when the ceremony is over, when the ritual is over, the masks are tossed into the conservatory and are not brought out again until the next event. This alone is an index of the ontology of the masks themselves. They are different from what you might call palace art: the representation of lineages, of kings, consorts, slaves as you have in Benin bronzes, some Ife bronzes, these ones which I call the court art, classical, beautiful . . . They have their definite and distinct aesthetic value and approaches which are very different from the goals in the heads of the carvers of many of these wooden masks, the masks which we seem to be able to admire in the museums, but which are not really the originating and determining concept of those masks in the hands of the carvers. And I just used the analogy of what Francis Bacon tried to do in his painting as being the nearest way I could express the execution of those masks, their overall conception. When they are in motion it's a totally different dynamism from anything you can see in the museums of London and Paris. Now, part of my work as a director involves the fact that in addition, and as an integral part of the interpretation of a play on stage, there is also for me the sensation of carving images on stage. And again this is where my experience and my legacy meet, where the real creative impulse unifies the textual communication and where the means, the method of communication really lies.

The final poem of your latest collection, where the cremation of a worm-eaten caryatid raises the issue of the destruction and survival of art and life

in time, is surely also a reflection on the possibilities and limits of art?
That statement is not meant to be a negative one, not a pessimistic one. It indicates where act takes over from art. The artistic form is a perennial representation and reminder of certain imperatives of existence. Whether we like it or not, in terms of effecting change art does have its limitations. And I keep emphasizing that recognition of this limitation is not a negative or pessimistic view of art. For me it is a very positive one. Certain kinds of artistic production in my society are left to rot, deliberately. It's part and parcel of the persona of an art work that it is meant to vanish, to be destroyed in order to be able to reproduce itself. This is the organic nature of art.

I think we have to fasten onto the fact that some societies accept the perishability of art not as a negative thing but as a challenge, a challenge to the regenerative nature of life. The in-built perishability of art in most African societies, especially where wood-carvings are concerned, goes beyond physical perishability – the very action, as I stated earlier, of consigning to the dark rooms of the shrine a mask that has been used for a particular purpose is a recognition of that transitoriness, of the non-dominating essence and value of art. The wooden carving would be left just to perish in many societies – Yoruba societies, Igbo societies – because the next year you would have to renew it for the communal event, for the act of communal re-creation. So when it comes out the following year or two years later or ten years later, the fact that it has disappeared for some time does not – in traditional art appreciation – escalate its material value, unlike the European world where if you succeed in hiding something for a few years, when it comes out then it becomes really astronomically valued. There's some very profound difference here which for me has not been sufficiently explored. So this perambulation is just to emphasize my very deep-seated awareness that – yes – art is for many cultures a perishable commodity which represents the continuum of human productivity. It's not negative. People can look on it as wasteful, that's a problem, but it represents a certain view of art and a very important cultural perspective. It implies also that the art work itself has limitations in relation to the creative act, to the human act, the social act, the communal act which in fact sustains art. It's a complex, but at the same time very simple, logical approach to art and life which it seems to me the Western world has not been able to come to terms with.

'Mandela's Earth' is not only the title of the first section of the collection, but of the whole book. Would you like to go into your choice of this phrase as the general title for your book?
Before I do that, I want to go back to your last question. The poem 'Cremation of a Caryatid' is representative of the attitude towards art and life which I was expressing earlier. Yes, there's this work of art, and it is quite possible for little termites to eat into it and destroy it. But those termites cannot, simply cannot, because of the continuum, the philosophy of continuity that is built into both concept and execution, they simply cannot destroy the *creative essence* that produced the work of art. That caryatid *can* be destroyed. It can be destroyed by war, it can be destroyed by civil strife, it can be destroyed, as Achebe expressed it in one of his novels: when a god fails its society, they'll take it out and put it in the middle of the road and set fire to it and a substitute is created. Ultimately the will resides in human beings. It's a sad moment, a sad event that the representative of the mores, the creative essence of society has to be

banished, destroyed, sent into oblivion. This process is ritualized, the ritual is yet another dimension of the work, there's a kind of poetic sadness about it, but at the same time it's a *renewing* act, a *renewing* event that there are energies which ensure that this cycle of creativity continues.

Now, this elaboration was triggered off by your question on *Mandela's Earth*. I don't have to tell you I've been obsessed by the whole South African situation and at the centre of it all Mandela's imprisonment, because it took place at a moment when I was defining my political constituency, unconsciously. He was imprisoned at a time when my political energies were being honed towards the struggle for liberation in Southern Africa. Mandela has sort of sat in my brain for donkey years, including when I was attached to the Royal Court Theatre. My play *The Invention* was a very dark satire on the apartheid situation and there were poems I wrote during my student days: Mandela *happened* at that time and probably also assisted in honing my political sensibilities in that particular direction. Up to now I've fluctuated like – I hope – all normal human beings between a positive approach and a despairing, negative feeling generated by the betrayal of the African people by their leadership. The leaders are so suspicious of their own people that they will not mobilize society towards what for me, for three decades at least, has been the destiny of African struggle. In other words I've taken for granted that the meaning of decolonization, independence and so on was the concerted struggle towards the total liberation of black peoples, especially in Southern Africa. So by the time I started putting together the poems of *Mandela's Earth*, mostly triggered off by his refusal to accept a compromised freedom, which for me was an expression of everything I most believed in, there was the sense that whether this symbol, this caryatid, survives his ordeal or not, we cannot permit ourselves to forget the promise of renewal or even the *challenge* of renewal, which is what his incarceration has been all about. It's a lesson not merely for the struggle in South Africa, but for the rest of the African continent under heinous tyrannies beside which the white tyranny is child's play. I've just read in the papers that Mobutu has done it again: some 50 students have been massacred in Zaïre – I heard about that this morning. So this is what we're talking about, this kind of betrayal, this kind of savage treachery by our own kind.

Mandela's Earth was for me a renewal of faith, if you like, just as *Ogun Abibimañ* was a renewal of faith, a recollection of the enduring symbols of that momentary declaration of intent by Mozambique under Samora Machel. They're just periodic expressions of my refusal to be pessimistic.

Your latest book, *Isara*, is sub-titled *A Voyage Around Essay*. How did you come to write it? And where – or what – is *your* Ashtabula (your father's relation with Ashtabula and the person who introduced him to the place, Wade Cudeback, form the frame to the book itself)?

Oh, for me my Ashtabula is just right where I am at the moment! It's always been right where I've found myself most times. I don't have that kind of enduring Ashtabula beyond my typewriter, what eventually I push out of the roller. *Isara* has always been there in my head, like all works which any writer brings out. But I think one of the not so obviously acknowledged impulses to bringing out *Isara* has to do with the kind of distortion of the history of the development of the modern contemporary African intellectual by what I call the Neo-Tarzanist perspective of modern Africa, denying the existence of contact between modern Africa and the outside world. This contact goes back centuries and all experience is part of the formulation of the intellectual mind of any community. Some of these people write as if it was only when the first student went to study in England that there was any contact at all between the African world – or indeed the Red Indian world or the Papua New Guinean world – and the rest of the entire globe. It's this kind of lie, this kind of deliberate, obvious lie, for what purpose I do not understand. I don't care if the African world and its people never came into contact with anybody, including traders from the outer world. It's of no importance to me. But it happens to be a fact that they did. Why should anyone suggest that, after several centuries of contact, the entire global perception of a continent can only be in the so-called region of 'iron snakes and town-criers'? If it were so there'd be no problem. But even the newspapers of the early 1900s and before indicate very clearly that there had been this contact and it had affected both sides of the correspondence. Even the arts of diplomacy have been practised between the kings or monarchs of Africa and the outside world. This goes back quite a few centuries. Therefore today when we talk about the intelligentsia, we're talking about an intelligentsia which is not merely formed of the analytic processes of their own society, but by analytic processes which take as their grist experiences with the outside world. Reading the press snippets, the social documents, the letters of the people involved at the time makes one even angrier that anybody should have the nerve to suggest that there has been a kind of *cordon sanitaire* between the African peoples and the outside world. This is historically false. So perhaps one of the reasons why this book was written at that time, before another book – let's put it that way – has been a kind of 'Well, this material has always been there and I would have to use it sooner or later, so why not now, if only to shut the lying mouths of these people who want to regress into a non-existent kind of pristinism.' The culture of Africa has never been as 'pure' as these people try to make out – and, in any case, pure in what sense? Pure by what simplistic, narrow, uni-dimensional pattern of development, of perception? It's been constantly digesting, analysing and adjusting experiences from wherever these experiences come. So *Isara* is a piece of social history, a filial tribute, and what I hope will place that particular generation which I've known so intimately, which we all know so intimately, in its proper historical perspective and context. And then it's also a personal tribute to these people whom I knew and some of whom died before I could on a very intimate level compare notes with them. It's just something that I had to write.

The figure of the *Abiku*, or child returnee who dies, is born again, dies again and so on, is one of your metaphors for the phenomenon of creativity and it reappears, under different guises, throughout your work. Would you like to talk about it?
Each time I'm asked that question I warn that it depends on what mood I am in when I'm asked the question. Sometimes *Abiku* is a very negative thing to me. I accept and deny all responsibility for any contradiction in what I say about what *Abiku* represents to me. It depends what's been happening to me lately. To appreciate that you have to understand that I grew up with *Abiku*, not just as a metaphor but as a very physical expression of the link between the living, the unborn, the ancestral world and so on. *Abiku* was real, not just a figment of literary analysis. Some of my siblings were *Abiku*, the anxieties involved in their existence, their survival, their illnesses and so on were *Abiku*. And then of course I keep emphasizing the cruelty of the *Abiku* once they realize their own

NIGERIA

power with their parents, with their elders, how they use and abuse their power, and at the same time the kind of intelligence of the *Abiku* and their loyalty to their own group, almost like children versus the adult world. So it became a metaphor for some of the diversities of experience and society, it became a symbol for cyclic cruelty, cyclic evil, and also an expression for some of the enigma of existence, some of the insoluble aspects of existence. It became a symbol also of unwished cyclic impositions, a symbol for the unwished but recurring. *Abiku* is something you cannot totally kill off. You mark it, you scar it – you know how people scar the child, like the *Ogbanje* with the Igbo: it's a theory people swear to (and it's not just a theory) that, if you scar the *Abiku*, when the next child is born it will have those scars. You're longing for the new child as a symbol of continuity, a guarantee, a reassurance, a consolation. It's the same way as for instance in politics: there's an untenable situation and you're longing for change, you're participating in the process of change, you're looking for a re-born society, but when it eventually emerges it's got the same ugly scars, the same mark of Cain on it as the last one.

SELECTED BIBLIOGRAPHY

THEATRE
Before the Blackout (Ibadan: Orisun, 1971).
Collected Plays I (London: Oxford University Press, 1973). Contains *A Dance of the Forests, The Swamp Dwellers, The Strong Breed, The Road, The Bacchae of Euripides*.
Collected Plays II (London: Oxford University Press, 1974). Contains *The Lion and the Jewel, Kongi's Harvest, The Trials of Brother Jero, Jero's Metamorphosis, Madmen and Specialists*.
Six Plays (London: Methuen, 1984). Contains *The Trials of Brother Jero, Jero's Metamorphosis, Camwood on the Leaves, Death and the King's Horseman, Madmen and Specialists, Opera Wonyosi* and an interview with Biodun Jeyifo.
A Play of Giants (London: Methuen, 1984).
Requiem for a Futurologist (London: Rex Collings, 1985).
Childe Internationale (Ibadan: Fountain Publishers, 1987).

POETRY
Idanre and Other Poems (London: Methuen, 1967).
A Shuttle in the Crypt (London: Rex Collings and Methuen, 1972).
Ogun Abibimañ (London: Rex Collings, 1976).
Mandela's Earth (London: André Deutsch, 1989).

NOVELS
The Interpreters (London: André Deutsch, 1965).
Season of Anomy (London: Rex Collings, 1973)

BIOGRAPHIES
The Man Died. Prison Notes (London: Rex Collings, 1972).
Aké: The Years of Childhood (London: Rex Collings, 1981).
Isara. A Voyage Around 'Essay' (Ibadan: Fountain Publications, 1989).

ESSAYS
Myth, Literature and the African World (Cambridge: Cambridge University Press, 1976).
Art, Dialogue and Outrage. Essays on Literature and Culture, ed. Biodun Jeyifo (Ibadan: New Horn Press, 1988). Contains a selection of essays and lectures including hitherto unpublished material. A second volume is planned to contain a selection of Soyinka's many writings on political and social topics.

Mĩcere
Gĩthae Mũgo

One of Kenya's major cultural activists, Mĩcere Gĩthae Mũgo was educated at Kangarũ Girls' Intermediate School, at the Alliance Girls' High School, at Limuru Girls' School (where she was the first African student to be admitted into an all-white school in colonial Kenya), and at the Universities of Makerere (Uganda), Nairobi (Kenya) and New Brunswick (Canada). At the Alliance High School and at Makerere she wrote and acted in plays and received the best actress award at the Uganda Drama Festival. At Festac '77 she played the part of the Woman in *The Trial of Dedan Kĩmathi*, the play she had co-authored with Ngũgĩ wa Thiong'o. Senior Lecturer and then Associate Professor in the Literature Department of the University of Nairobi, she was also Dean of the Faculty of Arts until forced into exile in 1982. She spent her first two years in exile as a Visiting Professor at the University of St Lawrence (USA). She now teaches at the University of Zimbabwe. Poems by Mĩcere Gĩthae Mũgo have been published in *An Introduction to East African Poetry*, ed. Jonathan Kariara and Ellen Kitonga (Nairobi: Oxford University Press, 1976), 115–18; *Growing Up with Poetry*, ed. D. Rubadiri (London: Heinemann, 1989); *Is That the New Moon*, ed. Wendy Cope (London: Lion Teen Tracks, 1989) and in a number of journals as well as in her early collection, *Daughter of My People Sing* (1976).

8

Mĩcere Gĩthae Mũgo

The interview was held in London (August 1984). Extracts have been published in Italian in Rinascita, *XLII, 25 (6 July 1985), p. 21.*

Could you talk to me about the production of *The Trial of Dedan Kĩmathi* that the Wazalendo players are working on at present here in London? From what I have heard, it is not just going to be put on at the Africa Centre, but will be taken to community centres, to areas with a concentration of working-class people and of the unemployed, and to areas with a high concentration of black people, especially black women. The intention is to get it to people who do not ordinarily go to the theatre, but who will now be able not only to see the play but participate in it directly through a system of open rehearsals. All this in Britain, not in Kenya. Won't its whole scope change?

This raises the whole issue of the relevance the play has for a British audience or an Irish audience or a Scottish audience or a black audience or whatever. The general thrust of the play is anti-imperialist. We have numerous examples of imperialism here against the various classes of people, economically, politically and so on. Then when you compound the whole problem with race, with the minority groups, you can see how it all becomes relevant.

But beyond that we recognize – and both Ngũgĩ and myself recognized this when we were writing the play – that it was the ruling classes in Britain that in fact collaborated, for political and economic motives, in the colonization of Kenya and in entrenching this hold on the Kenyan people. We do realize that it wasn't the ordinary British people, the workers, the miners and whatever, who actually came and colonized Kenya. And we know that in the same way as we colonized people were given a very distorted history of ourselves – a history that showed imperialism as something benevolent, as something that brought progress, as something that brought civilization, as something that brought Christianity in order to take away darkness and so on – the same lies, the same distortions were fed to exploited people here in Britain. So the history they know of Kenya and British involvement in Kenya is as upside-down for the majority of them as it has been for us colonized people. We want them to see the real actors and actresses on the Kenyan scene: the liberators, the women, the men, the children who fought in that liberation war, and to appreciate the fact that from a historical perspective the oppressed here need to be in solidarity with them in their vision to liberate themselves.

So what finally emerges may be a very different play from the original one. But the original *Trial of Dedan Kīmathi* already had a possibility for expansion or adaptation in it. The characters tended to be very symbolic; I find it significant, for example, that you gave most of them type names: the Boy, the Girl, the Woman . . .
You are absolutely right. In fact I think this is what art should be – a creation that possesses the kind of richness and elasticity that relates to other realities, as opposed to being provincial, or restricted to a place, or to an era in history, that other people cannot identify with, embrace. So, one of the advantages of symbolism is that it transports a given work of art to a plane beyond the present, beyond the obvious. I am making the point that if one is evoking a vision that incorporates humanity – not humanity in a loose sense, but a humanity we have solidarity with because it is struggling, as we are, to liberate itself – one has to write in such a way that the artistic piece can speak to all strugglers in Africa, in Britain, in the Caribbean or wherever else you like. We actually deliberately tried to do this in the play. And it has been performed in South Africa, in Soweto, and also in Zimbabwe, Zambia and Nigeria. But I want to emphasize the point about the play's collective thrust and vision. As you may realize, the drama is in fact structured and written in such a way that you have no choice but to depend on cooperative effort. First of all, even though the play centres on Kīmathi as the guerilla leader of the anti-colonial and anti-imperialist armed struggle, a 'Kīmathi' cannot play alone without some of the most minor of the characters. Some of the scenes, the movements, would make absolutely no meaning without the presence of people who actually say nothing but occupy the stage, sometimes as mimers, other times as singers and dancers and other times as mere members of the crowds. You know, the sheer people volume of the cast really creates a spirit of collective involvement and participation. Take the rehearsal on Saturday. We were dealing with people who hadn't seen the script before but, when we came to the crowd scenes and the crowd's responses, everyone became so animated, so involved that it was like something we had been rehearsing for a long, long time.

With your emphasis on self-reliance and on collective organization, you're really continuing the experience Ngũgi had at Kamīrīīthū I suppose . . .
We are also very lucky to have a co-director who believes in the same principles as us – Dan Cohen, who has done very extensive studies in theatre and drama. He's most enthusiastic about the idea of taking the play to the community, to the people, because he has been very much into this idea of promoting community theatre, street theatre, group theatre, collective productions and so on. Right now the play is his number one commitment. He insisted from the very beginning that he would be very, very disappointed if we were just creating a theatre effort that would be seen at the Africa Centre and nowhere else. So he's absolutely in line with our spirit.

112

You're talking about a production that is being prepared in Britain, in relation, partly, to problems rising in this country. Would it proceed along similar lines in Africa?

Let me first of all describe the experience we had with this play when it was originally produced in Nairobi, Kenya, because I feel that the role it played at a particular stage in our country in 1976 is quite significant. The drama was one of the two choices that Kenya as a nation took to the World Festival of Black Arts in Lagos, Festac '77 (the other play was Francis Imbuga's *Betrayal in the City*).

Now what happened during the Kenyan production was that as soon as the masses, ordinary women and men, particularly those from working-class sections in urban areas such as Nairobi, Kisumu, Mombasa and so on heard about the play, they actually got onto buses or hired buses and other public vehicles, to come and see the performances. So, they converted the Nairobi National Theatre – a very elitist place – into a people's community theatre centre. When they came to the booking office and were told the tickets had been sold out, they said, 'You can tell that to someone else. How dare you take our play, reproduce us on stage, take our hero, Kĩmathi, take our history and now exclude us from participating in the dramatization of this history by telling us that the tickets have been bought out? We are going to see it somehow.' You see, they had travelled long distances: some of them overnight, all the way from places like Mombasa and Kisumu; others had come from Meru, Eldoret, Nyeri and so on. So they said, 'We are storming in; we are seeing this play.' During one of the shows, the director of the play and its co-authors had to be called, and we had to allow them into the already packed auditorium. We let them sit on the steps, along the aisles, wherever they could find space. I'm telling you, they sat to the end. Then they flooded the front of the theatre, singing and dancing pieces from the play. Some then demanded to see us again and talk to us, asking: 'How, how did you know what Kĩmathi was like? He was exactly as you have shown him. Even the character who played his part looked like him!'

So their identification with the play's ideological and political message aside, artistically, I think they really enjoyed it. The great thing about art is that it can re-create situations, experiences, history and a people's reality so that they relive past moments with a new freshness. When this is done effectively – with empathy and vision – the people who know the re-created history and background can recognize themselves in it: their sisters, their brothers and friends. The comments that we received from Mau Mau ex-combatants made us realize that as a written and performed piece *The Trial of Dedan Kĩmathi* had functioned as a reflective mirror to the audience that really mattered – the heroes and heroines of our history. This was most flattering to us.

But, in Kenya, progressive theatre has been like this. Let us take the Schools' and Colleges' Drama Festivals, for instance. They were supposed to be fora for competition between educational institutions in performed drama, with cups, shields and certificates awarded; but they broke loose of this hold under the guidance of, above all others, Wasambo Were. At the time I'm thinking about – the late '70s and early '80s – he was Chief Inspector of Schools in Kenya. He decided to make a touring theatre troupe, following National Theatre performances, so that the three winning plays would be taken to the masses around the country. He went even beyond that to embrace audiences from the grassroots. He organized the festivals in such a way that the plays entered for the national festivals were first of all performed at location level, then at district level, provincial level and, finally, they came to Nairobi. After Nairobi the winning entries ended up being taken back to the people, thus completing the cycle.

Then, of course, you mentioned the example of Kamīrīīthū. Well, there have been other 'Kamīrīīthūs' in less conspicuous places that people haven't heard much about. I think that, for a long time, in the hands of politically enlightened educators, theatre has been an artistic as well as a political weapon for the education, re-education and conscientization of our peoples in Kenya. This has been the case especially during recent years. You should see some of the plays that schoolgirls and schoolboys write for the Drama Festival. Looking at the efforts re-kindles one's faith in the youth of this country. Some of them have even moulded and shaped a lot of our orature, the stories we were told by our mothers and grandmothers, turning them into drama through which they make modern, present-day statements. And the high quality of the art created in making these statements has been something to celebrate. I think they have shaped drama into an artistic mode or genre that will no longer tolerate being made to sit on a shelf, to be occasionally read, looked at and then shut up again. They have injected drama with the action and dynamism that go with performed art.

The other side of the coin is that, under colonialism and neo-colonialism, theatre has been used by the dominating classes to undermine the people and their self-assertion.

I'd like us to go back to the earlier stages of theatrical activity in East Africa. Could you say something about your experiences at university, about the travelling theatre, which had already started at Makerere back in the '60s, if I'm not mistaken?

Yes, Makerere had a very strong and rich tradition in drama. The tradition made us look up to Shakespeare, classical drama, Western theatre traditions, but also encouraged us to explore with African theatre, including composition and creative writing. At Makerere I was a member of the Drama Club, Creative Writing Club, the Free Travelling Theatre and so on. The idea of the Free Travelling Theatre was given a lot of momentum by David Cook and Margaret Macpherson as well of course as a lot of students who were involved in it. Dramatists such as Rebeka Njaū, Jonathan Kariara, Robert Serumaga, Rose Mbowa, John Ruganda and others of us were, at some stage or other, a part of this tradition. Obviously, some of its trends were quite bourgeois and elitist, but so were the general educational goals we were made to pursue. We more than survived them!

Once the discovery had been made of removing the theatre from Kampala, from the capital city and the seat of higher learning, taking it to the people, it took on a different form. As we were saying earlier, once a play is enacted and people are involved in shaping it, remoulding it, reinterpreting it, it becomes something new. What really happens is that it grows. It becomes a collective asset. Sometimes it becomes too huge for even the author(ess) to handle, because the way he/she conceived it is overtaken by the process of re-creating it for the stage.

Now this travelling theatre tradition generated from Makerere also became a part of the University of Nairobi's theatre history later on – in the '60s. I think that the Nairobi University Free Travelling Theatre made an even greater impact within the Kenyan context, where the dominating theatre was very elitist, very colonialist, centred around the Donovan Maule Theatre and the National Theatre. Under colonialism and neo-colonialism, the leading educational institutions took their queue from these and from Shakespeare. So the University Free Travelling Theatre took drama to the villages and towns. Thousands of people would come and watch. In turn, the students found they were enjoying performing in the countryside more than in Nairobi because of the welcome and involvement they experienced there. Here again, I am convinced that drama is *nothing* unless there is rapport between the performers on stage, and the audience. In fact the audience can change and shape the mood (the mode even) of the play because of their response to and involvement in it as they clap, ululate, join in the singing and dancing, etc. During the pre-Festac production of *The Trial of Dedan Kīmathi*, members of the audience did just this. So, with the Free Travelling Theatre, performance in the open air would give birth to a huge 'cast' of 300, 400 and more people because all the villagers used to join in and even the local drunkard would sometimes pitch in, providing further free entertainment to the crowd. This theatre created a very important tradition of the youth back to their own communities. We found that the students themselves became very enthusiastic about this. It helped, as well, to shape that idea of the university as a part of the community, thus undermining its usual ivory tower image. Involved drama students used to feel rather special during, say, a graduation ceremony when the Free Travelling Theatre would be mentioned as an example demonstrating that the university need not be an ivory tower but a service institution for the people.

The drama festivals you were speaking about before have been very much clamped down on by the authorities, haven't they? Has this not suffocated much of the creative effort?
In fact what they have done is to send these kids exploring so much at the stylistic level that they have come up with aesthetically excellent pieces because they've had to look for that image, that metaphor, that idiom, that symbol, that figurative expression etc. that incubates their political message so that the statement registers with subtlety. And, as they experiment with symbolism, they are not only circumventing censorship but producing artistic creations defying limitations of time, of history, of place and whatever; and the authorities have really panicked because of this.

So drama is a very dynamic genre for exploring tensions and conflicts. Much more so than poetry, fiction and the novel. It is also a genre through which one can reach the masses immediately and urgently. The political, artistic message of a powerful drama can be communicated in one, two or three hours. This is not the case, say, with a novel where one needs reading skills, leisure and conducive facilities to go through the book – sometimes needing a week to do so.

Is all this a new phenomenon or is it connected with the oral traditions?
No, it's not a new phenomenon at all. If you look at our theatre within orature it assumes a very immediate, spontaneous and participatory style. Take a situation like a marriage ceremony where a participant may suddenly be required to stand up and combine song, dance and performance to pay tribute to the bride-to-be, the bridegroom and so on. What such a person is being challenged to do is to respond promptly, impromptu and, moreover,

artistically. And, mind you, there are other people sitting around who make up the 'audience', judging how well the performer does it, how well he/she uses body language, spoken language, the voice, the eyes and so much else. It's very demanding. Or take a funeral situation: an old man in Luo country, or a young man who has just died. His age-mate will stand up and begin reciting poetry about what a great warrior the deceased was, or what a great farmer . . . Then another person gets inspired by this statement and stands up, making his own little dramatic performance. Sometimes drama was in the form of mock fights, following a war: that was real drama. With all the excitement and dramatization of the incidents that had happened. What these people are really doing is re-creating history, reliving experiences, bringing the events from the field to the people in the village who may not have partaken in given social events. This way they too become participants. This way historical and cultural experiences become communal. Those are just a few examples, but there are a whole lot more, especially when you go to children's play-songs, or to the whole area of dance. Within orature or within a traditional African set-up it becomes very divisive to separate dance, music and drama.

What I am trying to say is that all the techniques we are employing today in order to use drama as a vehicle of communication and conscientization in social development, whether through body language, mime or whatever, are being borrowed from an orature set-up. And when we speak of orature we do well not to speak of it in the past tense, for this is the art our people are still consuming in the rural areas, in the villages and in the working-class environment of our cities. Again, the definition of our African orature theatre has always defied boundaries that would make it be contained within a given house or room; it defies the idea of monied people being the exclusive audience because they can come and buy expensive tickets that reserve them the front seats. Orature theatre is very community-conscious: it depends on that to excel and to continue.

I think that this is what progressive theatre traditions are trying to do today – to be part of the class struggle by rooting themselves within the communities of those struggling for economic and political freedom. Just as some of the orature drama has focused on our rites of passage – the milestones in life that are dramatized as part of our social functions – so revolutionary theatre will focus on the milestones of our history of struggle for justice and human development.

Today the phenomenon of street theatre – a form of orature theatre – is becoming a common sight in European and North American metropolitan set-ups. Some critics have refused to categorize orature theatre as drama. We need to research into the African origins of this theatre, going back to antiquity. Not many of us have done this. One person who went into some depth on this was Joe de Graft. He really did a lot of studying to understand the exact origins of African drama. Yes, drama has been part and parcel of our existence and it has that meaning for our ordinary men and women. This is why the Kamīrīīthū experiment worked out so successfully, because you're dealing with possibilities that are almost natural, with people so conversant with drama as a mode of expression that it comes almost naturally to them. It is a form of art that they appreciate and so they involve themselves immediately, without any problems. I think this should be a very clear message to the artist in Africa. We should really exploit this mode in order to reach our people more. It can be used for literacy campaigns, for cutting down ethnic barriers, crashing the economic conditions that have been imposed on us. I think that any socialist education should explore all this very, very seriously.

Drama was also used a great deal among the Mau Mau fighters in the forest to pass messages, or to call committees. When the fighters found their morale going low they would have a group enact a historical scene in which people were strengthened by what took place, just so as to uplift their dampened spirits. Kīmathi himself was a very good dramatist. He used to set up little dramas when he was a schoolboy and in the forest too. The tribute we are paying to him in the book is not just imagined, it's actually historical. So drama has been used on the battlefield; it has been used as part of the teaching process; it has been a part of the play method through which children learn; it has been used for social functions. And it has also been used *formally* as something that is *performed* and that people come and watch.

Tell me briefly about yourself, your background, education, writing – how you came to start writing.
As a child, I used to be very shy – an introvert, to some extent, and was never comfortable in big groups or crowds. So, I tended to be the kind of child who sits in a corner, reading. Books became my friends. This interest in reading stimulated interest in writing. I would write short poems and stories just for the enjoyment of it. I also enjoyed memory work – which we often got in plenty in the form of assignments from our teachers, especially in intermediate school. It was at Kangarū Girls' Intermediate School in Embu, during the Emergency, when the combined interests in reading, memorizing passages and writing urged me on to the stage. I came to enjoy verse-speaking and elocution competitions. Ultimately, this led to my involvement in drama. At that time, we used to perform Bible drama, Christmas plays and Western children's favourites such as *Snow White, Cinderella* and so on. It was a very colonial English diet, but it awakened our talents in theatre. I have, therefore, been involved in drama since the age of eight. After intermediate school, I went to the Alliance Girls' High School, Kikuyu. My interests in writing and drama deepened here. I was a member of the Creative Writers' Club which was at one time patronized by the dramatist Rebeka Njaū, then a teacher at the school. I wrote poems for my boarding house, Burns (Alliance tended to be very Scottish!) and was pen-named by appreciative fellow-Burners the house's 'poet-laureate'. I was a top competitor on all the school's verse-speaking and elocution contests. I also took part in all major school drama performances. Some of the roles I remember playing are: Androcles in *Androcles and the Lion*, Lady Macbeth in *Macbeth*, one of the leading characters in *School for Scandal* and the rest of that kind of theatre.

This was during the Emergency, you say. What were your personal experiences of this period?
I had been sent to Kangarū, one of the most outstanding government intermediate schools of the time (on merit, I should point out), because it had boarding facilities for girls. A lot of day schools were either closed at the time or extremely exposed, under liberation war conditions. Most of the teachers at Kangarū were white and the majority of them hated the very word Mau Mau. The school was on the slopes of Mount Kenya, or Kīrīnyaga, one of the headquarters of the Mau Mau combatants, under Field Marshal Dedan Kīmathi. Any time that there was a battle between Mau Mau freedom fighters and

occupying colonialist forces, some of the teachers would also create a war situation with us children in the classroom. Sometimes we would be forced to go and view the corpses of murdered combatants. The sight was often intolerable – bloated bodies covered with flies, sprawling guts, disintegrating flesh, etc. – And as for the stench! I would be unable to eat food after that. In fact I used to throw up. But we would be forced to eat the food. And as for the food! In those days of scarcity and rationing, the maize and beans would be infested with weevils. I hated it. Up to this day, I cannot stand the sight of a dead body, or a weevil in food. I have nightmares from looking at a dead body and, for this reason, funerals are a torture for me.

I was one of the youngest children in the school then. And I suppose that, like many children who grow under colonial violence, the hardships we went through taught us to be tough, even as it left psychological scars on our lives.

Presumably your schooling presented you largely with British literary models. How did you react to them? Which authors did you prefer? How did all this interact with the culture of your home?
Our English and Literature Studies were, definitely, well-seasoned English diets. Outside the classroom, of course, we even excelled in country dancing or Scottish country dancing. Remember, a school like Kangarū was a kind of junior preparatory institution for would-be future leaders, the fortunate one per cent of whom were expected to make their way to secondary schools such as Alliance, Maseno, Limuru, etc., designated for the training of a collaborating African class of elites to serve the colonial system. So, we had to be fed on British models. We studied Shakespeare almost religiously, memorizing long passages from *Henry V* and the rest. We read Kipling, Jane Austen, Emily Brontë, Wordsworth, Keats, John Bunyan, Milton, Chaucer and so on. Mind you, here I am including the diet subscribed at Limuru Girls' School where I went for A-levels.

For some reason, I really enjoyed the histories and tragedies of Shakespeare – not the comedies. Today, I marvel at the fact that we never questioned Shakespeare's deification of the ruling class, or his marginalization of the masses either as gullible crowds or as jesters. We had enough intelligence to do so, but we were, ideologically, under the captivity of colonial educational propaganda.

I also liked the Romantic poets. Wordsworth, Keats, Burns and Blake were some of my favourites. There was something about their rebellious spirit against the evils of industrialization that moved me. Of course now, some of their pessimism, mysticism and limited critical realist visions make me quite uncomfortable.

Colonialist education fed us with the idea that we were special, privileged people, who must set an example to the rest out there in the villages. At the same time we were also taught to be good Christians. A part of the discipline that we were taught in these schools, however, has been a lucky inheritance. Responsibility, hard work, thrift, a strong stand by one's 'principles' (many of which now carry question marks) were fed into us and have come in handy as we have learnt to use them in the process of re-educating ourselves.

The attempt to alienate us from our African roots did not wholly succeed. Some of us were brainwashed into wanting to be like our colonial agents; others of us became all the more curious to discover those roots.

When did you become aware of the existence of Black Literature?
Partly at Alliance Girls' High School through the library, partly at Limuru Girls' School, again through private reading, but mostly at Makerere, where we were introduced to prominent writers such as Chinua Achebe and Wole Soyinka. From then onwards I became an avid reader of Black Literature. While doing my Masters and PhD degrees in New Brunswick, Canada, I took courses in African American Literature, African Caribbean Literature and Indian Literature.

I clearly remember my introduction to the African American heritage. I was in the school sanatorium with a bad attack of the flu when the headmistress came to see me, bringing copies of Wright's *Native Son*, *Black Boy* and Trevor Huddleston's *Naught For Your Comfort*. I could not put any of the books down. Later on I looked for books by James Baldwin and Ralph Ellison. From then on I became a part-time student of African American Literature which was not offered on the colonial syllabus.

My first-hand, full-scale experience of racism was at Limuru Girls' School where it is my understanding I was the first African to be admitted into a white high school in Kenya's colonial history. I was a keen sportswoman and so easily made it into the school first eleven in the hockey team, netball team and so on. But whenever we were in the school bus, travelling to and from the matches, I would find myself occupying a little island, as the other girls would ensure that they sat as far away from me as possible. This happened in a lot of other areas of my school life. I found positive, dignified ways of dealing with these islands of hurt and loneliness. Reading was one way. African Literature and African American Literature particularly spoke clearly and passionately through that loneliness. Strangely, armed with one of these books, I felt so much strength that I simply defied the isolation and was left feeling triumphant. I felt proud, every inch, for being an African.

How has being a woman affected your writing?
Women writers are still marginalized up to this day and it is a contradiction that all educators and promoters of literature need to address. In my case, I have found the responsibilities of being a mother and a single parent – especially since going into exile – quite overwhelming. Quite deliberately, I have decided to concentrate my efforts and energies on bringing up my two daughters and on keeping at the top of my academic career, through research, teaching and publication. In between these challenges, I have tried to put in some creative writing. Now that my daughters are fourteen and sixteen, I am finding quite a bit of space to work on my creative writing. My ambition right now – dream rather – is to strike a financial position that would enable me to work part-time professionally and write for the rest of the time. As I say, it is a dream!

My awareness as a woman goes back to my childhood upbringing. There were ten children in the family – seven girls and three boys. I grew up in a household where my parents insisted on absolute equal rights between boys and girls. My parents and my father, in particular, lived way ahead of their times in their championing of women's rights, as far back as the '40s and '50s. Rather wealthy at the time, they also taught us to be independent of their wealth and to use our heads as well as hands to make something of ourselves. They had more than a dozen farm hands and domestic workers, but we were not allowed to have our chores done by them. In fact we were made to work with them on the farm and around the home. We used to be infuriated by this. Now I realize how correct my parents were in these policies.

I have a lot of admiration for my parents and owe the beginnings of my awareness in what I articulate as a woman in my writings to them. My father died in 1983 when I was in exile in the United States. He had agreed to let me write a book, having dialogue with him, on these issues and on his stint as a Senior Chief during the Emergency – a collaborative role that betrayed the very principles he had nurtured us on as children.

In these days of re-awakening, in terms of women's rights, I see my role as a woman writer as being that of assuming sides with oppressed women from among the peasants and workers, in their struggles to liberate themselves and fellow oppressed humankind from the shackles of imperialism and neo-colonialism. It is with this commitment in mind that Ngũgĩ and I tried, in *The Trial of Dedan Kĩmathi*, to highlight the contribution by women to the anti-colonial, anti-imperialist struggle, as central participants in the Mau Mau liberation war. Under neo-colonialism, the women continue to occupy the front-line in the continuing war to defeat imperialism. This unflinching participation continues to inspire me as a woman, as a writer, as a political activist, as a professional worker and as a mother.

SELECTED BIBLIOGRAPHY

POETRY
Daughter of My People Sing (Nairobi: East African Literature Bureau, 1976).

THEATRE
The Long Illness of Ex-Chief Kiti (Nairobi: East African Literature Bureau, 1976). Previously published in a shorter version in *The Fiddlehead*, 90 (1971), pp. 3–37. Also contains a radio play, *Disillusioned*, pp. 62–82.
(With Ngũgĩ wa Thiong'o) *The Trial of Dedan Kĩmathi* (London: Heinemann, 1977).

ESSAYS AND CRITICISM
Visions of Africa: the Fiction of Chinua Achebe, Margaret Lawrence, Elspeth Huxley and Ngũgĩ wa Thiong'o (Nairobi: Kenya Literature Bureau, 1978).
'Written literature and the black image' in *Teaching of African Literature in Schools*, ed. E. Gachukia and S. K. Akivaga (Nairobi: Kenya Literature Bureau, 1978), pp. 30–9.
'The "Saviors" and "Messiahs" of Wole Soyinka's Drama', in *Teaching of African Literature in Schools*, Vol. 1, ed. E. Gachukia and S. K. Akivaga (Nairobi: Kenya Literature Bureau, 1978), pp. 139–48.
'The relationship between African and African-American literature as utilitarian art: a theoretical formulation' in *Global Dimensions of the African Diaspora*, ed. Joseph E. Harris (Washington, DC: Howard University Press, 1982), pp. 85–93.
'Literature for primary schools', *Insight*, LXXV, 2 (1985).
'Women and books in Africa: a question of survival', *Journal of Humanities* (Zomba, Malawi) I, 1 (April 1987), pp. 91–100 (first presented as keynote address to 1985 Writers' Workshop, 1985 Zimbabwe International Book Fair).
'Towards a definition of African orature aesthetics', *Third World Book Review*, II, 3 (1987), pp. 40–1.

Ngūgī wa Thiong'o

Born at Kamīrīīthū, Limuru, in 1938, Ngūgī wa Thiong'o was educated at Kamaandura Mission School and at Maanguuū, one of the Gīkūyū Independent and Karinga Schools Association schools, before going on to the Alliance High School and thence to Makerere University College in Uganda, where he read English (concentrating particularly on the work of Lawrence and Conrad) and composed his first stories, two novels and a play. The turning point of his intellectual development came however at the University of Leeds, where he encountered the work of Marx and Fanon and began researching into Caribbean literature. And it was at Leeds that he composed his third novel, *A Grain of Wheat*. On his return to Kenya he began teaching at the University of Nairobi, became the editor of *Zuka: A Journal of East African Creative Writing* and changed his name from James Ngugi to his traditional Gīkūyū name of Ngūgī wa Thiong'o. In 1972 he became head of the Department of Literature (since 1968 he had been engaged in an ultimately successful attempt to reject the primacy of English literature and culture in university literary studies and establish the centrality of Africa). In 1977 the play he had co-authored with Mīcere Gīthae Mūgo, *The Trial of Dedan Kīmathi*, was presented at Festac '77 in Lagos.

After publishing his fourth novel, Ngūgī's involvement in the Community Centre of Kamīrīīthu led to the production of a play co-scripted in Gīkūyū with Ngūgī wa Mīrīī and thence to his detention in the maximum security prison of Kamītī, an experience he recounts in his 'prison diary', *Detained*. Kamīrīīthū and its aftermath convinced him of the need to adopt Gīkūyū for all his future creative writing, starting with his prison novel, *Caitaani Mūtharaba-inī*, which he himself later translated into English (*Devil on the Cross*), and including, up to the time of writing, a second Gīkūyū play, *Maitū Njugīra*, and the novel *Matigari ma Njirūūngi*. In the preface to his latest essay collection, Ngūgī declares that even in the field of explanatory prose he will from now on be writing in Gīkūyū.

In exile in Europe since 1982, Ngūgī has taken up a new interest, that of filming, and has also continued publishing children's stories.

9

Ngũgĩ
wa Thiong'o

The interview consists of discussions and interviews carried out at the Heinemann Educational Books offices in London (July 1983), at the English Studies Department of Rome University (May 1984), and again in London (September 1989). Extracts from the earliest interview have appeared in Italian in Rinascita, *XL, 37 (23 September 1983), pp. 27–8.*

Although you are best known for your novels, your plays have had particular importance in the development of your position as a writer and of course in your life itself. Would you like to talk about this?
Well my primary interest is obviously the novel, but I have also been interested in theatre. Or rather I have been drawn into theatre, unwillingly, sometimes, but now it is one of my major preoccupations. I started writing plays in the '60s and some of my early plays, including *The Black Hermit*, were written when I was a student at Makerere University, but up to 1977 the plays I had written or the plays I had collaborated on with other writers, like the one I wrote with Mĩcere Mũgo called *The Trial of Dedan Kĩmathi*, were all written in the English language. But in 1977 I started working with peasants and workers at Kamĩrĩĩthũ Community Education and Cultural Centre. Initially I was invited by the peasants to work there to help, along with other people, in the development of adult literacy and culture in the village, with theatre obviously being at the centre of the cultural activities. But I had never before really confronted the issue of language directly until I worked with that community, so the question arose: theatre, but theatre in what language?

The process of answering that question in theory and practice changed my life. For one thing, when a friend of mine called Ngũgĩ wa Mĩrĩĩ and I drafted the first play in Gĩkũyũ language called *Ngaahika Ndeenda* (*I Will Marry When I Want*) for that community, we found that they knew the language much better than we did, so it was a kind of revelation to us, this process of having to learn our language anew. Then when we came to write about the history of the people we realized the people knew their history *much* better than we did for they had been participants in that history, the history of the struggle against British colonialism. Again, working in a collective spirit among the peasants and factory workers was very crucial in my development, really *seeing* the results that can be produced by people putting their resources together so that each person could contribute whatever little or big talent he had in a common pool, which produced fantastic results. The play became very successful, with peasants and workers coming from miles and miles to see this play which was being performed at an open-air theatre built by the peasants of the village themselves. But the Kenyan regime stopped the public performance of the play in 1977 and I myself was arrested and detained for a year at a maximum security prison for the whole of 1977–8.

In 1981, we once again tried to revive the theatre and the same group from the same village tried to perform *Maitū Njugīra* or *Mother Sing For Me*, scripted by myself. This is a kind of musical drama really, celebrating the struggles of Kenyan workers in the '30s: Kenyan workers who were struggling against very repressive labour laws. Now this play, this musical drama, was rehearsed in November–December of 1981 and also January and part February of 1982. But once again the peasants, the theatre group from Kamīrīīthū, were not allowed to perform, even though this time they were going to perform at the Kenya National Theatre in Nairobi. What they did was interesting because they moved to the university premises and continued with their rehearsals, but these rehearsals were public so that about 10,000 people fortunately were able to see them, but these rehearsals too were stopped. Now the regime did something that was even more frightening. On March 11 they came to our village, de-registered Kamīrīīthu Community Theatre and Cultural Centre, banned *all* theatre activities in the village and on the following day, very early in the morning, they brought three truckloads of armed policemen and razed the whole open-air theatre to the ground. So the theatre which was built with so much effort and love in 1977 is now no more, thanks to the armed policemen of the Kenyan neo-colonial regime.

This was done openly?
Openly, yes. I'm talking about 12 March 1982. But this was the beginning of the current cultural repression in Kenya. Many university lecturers were later detained including many members of the opposition in Kenya. One, for instance, was Ali Amin Mazrui, who had his play *Cry For Justice* performed at the University of Nairobi in May. Two or three weeks later he was arrested and put in detention without trial. Others have been put in prison on trumped-up charges. So you can see that, though my primary interest has been the novel, my interest in the theatre has so far been the one that has really changed my life and therefore now I am inevitably more and more committed to theatre.

So this is why you chose the theatre as a medium of expression?
In a sense I did not choose theatre, but theatre chose me: I have never sat down to write a play in the same way that I have often sat down to write a novel. I've always written plays as a result of some kind of request, so there's always been some kind of communal demand for me to present a script and this was particularly clear in 1977 when I even thought I had given up on theatre. In 1977 there was this demand from the peasants of the village for that kind of script or

outline of script in which I collaborated with Ngũgĩ wa Mĩrĩĩ. Theatre is very much a communal effort because even if you want to write a script it still needs a director, it still needs actors and, finally, it still needs an audience. Now, in a Kenyan type situation, theatre has another dimension which I think is quite important and this is its capacity for immediate communication. Once you're involved in theatre then you see the kind of impact that it can make and, when you see the total group involvement in the whole project, it's like nothing else I know of apart from maybe actual struggle, but in ordinary life theatre gives you a special kind of joy and that's why people who go into theatre don't want to leave it, although it has also a lot of headaches. I'm sure it's this communal involvement as well as this capacity for theatre to make some kind of immediate impact so that you're communicating fairly directly and immediately, that draws me to it. But there's a very big difference between the writing of *The Black Hermit* in the '60s and the writing and composition of *I Will Marry When I Want* in the '70s. In the scripting of *I Will Marry When I Want* there was much greater communal involvement: whereas in 1962 I could write a script and present it to the actors and the actors would go on stage trying to memorize each line as written in the script, with *I Will Marry When I Want* the people themselves were involved in the development of the script.

When we did the first outline of the play, Ngũgĩ wa Mĩrĩĩ and I, we took it back to the village and, between April, May and roughly June, people were reading the script and adding to it, commenting here and there and so on, for instance in the use of language. Because of the school system Ngũgĩ wa Mĩrĩĩ and I had been used to conceptualizing thoughts in English, but the people had been using their language all their lives, so they knew it much better than we did and they sometimes found our use of language was rather defective in places. The old men and women, for instance, would tell us that if you want an old man to speak with dignity he uses this kind of imagery or this kind of proverb and so on.

When we came to rehearsals of the play, again, this was done in the open and the spectators were as much directors as the formal directors: each person was commenting on whatever was happening on the stage as we were rehearsing. In fact I remember one actor who was recruited because of the audience. There was one actor who was very thin and tall and he was trying to portray a rich man in Kenya. Now most rich people in Kenya develop what Kenyans call 'public opinion': they are very fat, they develop very big tummies and these tummies are called public opinions because they put their noses or their stomach-noses into other people's affairs. Now, this person was very thin and somehow he was not quite able to portray 'public opinion' in the right way, so there was one person in the audience who became very angry and said 'No, look, those people, they walk like *this* . . .' And he did it so well that the people who were watching him gave him a kind of ovation and so he had to continue playing that role. He was recruited into the play by the spectators.

So there was a lot of communal involvement in *I Will Marry When I Want* and I can say that the script which has been translated into English was really the result of that cooperative effort, so there is a sense in which you can say Ngũgĩ wa Mĩrĩĩ and I were merely the coordinators or editors. But this was even clearer when I came to script *Mother Sing For Me*. *Mother Sing For Me* was also based on songs and dances from different nationalities in Kenya. Now, I only know two languages in Kenya, so there was no way in which I, as an author, could possibly have been able to incorporate songs and dances from nearly all the nationalities from Kenya unless there was a lot of other people's involvement. So in *Mother Sing For Me* there was even greater and more obvious involvement of many, many people even before the outline of the script was presented to the actors. Again, in the course of rehearsals they added to the script and in fact the script which I now have is a result of all the improvements and additions done during the rehearsal stage of *Mother Sing For Me*. So in *Mother Sing For Me* I was even more of a coordinator than in *I Will Marry When I Want*.

You said during your talk on theatre that dramatic form is fairly unimportant to you. Surely your use of song and dance and mime is a choice of form: it's not naturalistic and that's a very important choice of form, isn't it?
What I said was that form by itself, in other words the formal elements, are unimportant *by themselves*. If the play were based merely on formal elements and if it were possible to have that kind of play, it wouldn't really be interesting, but the reason why the people were able to identify with the play was because of the other aspect of form: content. Formal elements are the external manifestation of the real dramatic content which is in the idea – the tension, the dialectical tension in the idea. If this marries with an appropriate form then it becomes explosive. I'm not saying that formal elements are not important, since these are in fact what distinguishes one kind of theatre from another, but I'm saying that what gives it its primary importance is in fact the content and that when we're looking at theatre and drama we're looking at that tension in the idea. That's where the real drama is, but the formal elements obviously are very important.

Do you write in verse or in prose, or do you follow a kind of rhythm?
All my plays tend to alternate between verse and prose, but it's not really a planned thing, it just comes out in the process of writing. In the play I collaborated in with Ngũgĩ wa Mĩriĩ, *I Will Marry When I Want*, there is a lot of verse form, the dialogue is in verse form. In the play I collaborated in with Mĩcere Mũgo, *The Trial of Dedan Kĩmathi*, written in the English language, you find a mixture of both prose and verse, but *I Will Marry When I Want* is mostly in verse form. *Mother Sing For Me* is in verse form, but here I was much more conscious of playing around with elements of language. In the course of writing, I arranged the composition in verse form and I played around with internal rhymes. I enjoyed myself a great deal playing around with the language, but the actors were not even aware that what they were saying was actually rhyming all the time.

To turn to *Devil on the Cross*, there must be specific linguistic problems when you write a novel in a language that's only beginning to be used for written literature. It can't have been easy for you . . . How do you as a writer feel personally about the English language? There must be a certain ambiguity in your relationship towards it . . .
Of course it was not easy. Even the conditions in which I came to write *Devil on the Cross* were not easy. Linguistically it was not easy: there are so many unanswered problems in writing in African languages. For one the orthography is not often very fixed. So you find that there may be one or two or even three ways of writing the same word and often you are not quite sure which word to choose or how to write that word in a way that would mean you'd be

understood by your readers. The other thing is obviously that we have no actual tradition to fall back upon. When you write an English novel or a novel in the English language you tend to assume the whole body of novels and novel writing that has gone before you; you don't have the same kind of tradition when you are writing in an African language. So all these problems are really there. In fact it was when I started writing a novel in Gĩkũyũ language that I came to realize the importance of certain words I used to read in T. S. Eliot, I think *The Four Quartets*, I can't really remember, where he says something about words not being able to stay in one place. You handle this word and you find it'll slip through your fingers: words slide and crack and do all sorts of funny things.

Writing in Gĩkũyũ language I came to realize the importance and implications of those words even more, because I could write one sentence or one paragraph in the evening thinking it was saying one thing and in the morning when I came to read it I found it saying the opposite, depending on how one read the paragraph. The challenge for the writer is so to write that when a reader comes to read at least he can move in the direction intended – or probably intended – by the writer.

All these are interesting questions which I think face many writers when they are operating in their own languages and it's part of the excitement and challenge of utilizing these languages that have not much in the way of modern literatures written in them.

Now the English language. I think I used to have complexes about it when I was writing in the language. But now those complexes are really not there because I have found I can now see the English language like any other language. Now I'm fascinated in it as I would be fascinated in French or Italian or in other African languages. It's just one language among several but I don't feel any loyalty to it one way or another. So in fact confronting the issue of my own language has solved my relationship to the English language or any other languages all over the world. For me this language is now a language like any other. It is important because of the culture it has produced, it is important as a means of communication between the English-speaking peoples or those who understand the language, but I don't feel it dominates me now as a writer in the way it used to when I was writing in it.

Looking back at the two versions of *Devil on the Cross*, is the English version just a translation or is it an adaptation that differs from the Gĩkũyũ original?
No, it's a translation. In other words I told myself that I had to do a translation *as* a translation. I had a few problems of course, but I learnt a lot in trying to translate the novel into English. I've insisted with my publishers that any publisher interested in the book has to do it from the Gĩkũyũ original, not, definitely not, from the English translation. So for instance there's a Swedish edition of the book and it was a direct translation from the Gĩkũyũ. In fact the Swedish edition came out at about the same time as the English translation. That means that from now onwards Gĩkũyũ language will have a direct dialogue with other languages and other cultures without the mediation of the English language. It also means that African languages, through books being translated from one language into another, can begin to have a dialogue. I can visualize a situation where a novel written in a Kenyan language could find translation in Yoruba or Igbo or Hausa in Nigeria and vice versa, so that for the first time the Yoruba language and culture or Hausa language and culture will

be having direct dialogue with Kenyan languages and cultures. So I see enormous possibilities for the growth of our cultures through the mutual rendering of each other's work into each other's languages.

What particular problems did you find translating *Caitaani Mūtharaba-inī* and *Ngaahika Ndeenda* into English?
I Will Marry When I Want was a joint effort between me and my co-author Ngũgĩ wa Mĩrĩĩ, so that made it easier. I did *Caitaani Mūtharaba-inī* on my own, but the problems were the same. The translation made me first of all re-evaluate the whole tendency of African writers using English or French or Portuguese to portray characters who would of course never speak those languages. Now, there has been a tendency in such literature, that elsewhere I've called Afro-European literature, to make those characters talk English or French as if they were really speaking an African language. In other words there has been out of necessity the tendency to want to make a reader feel that what he's hearing is a genuinely African peasant really genuinely speaking an African language with all its rhythms of speech and imagery. But the contradiction is that that peasant or worker is actually speaking English or French or Portuguese in the novel. Sometimes in so doing there's a tendency of creating not necessarily naïve characters but characters whose expressions would sometimes sound naïve because some of the writers would try to render the syntax of the African speech directly into English or French or Portuguese.

When I translated *Devil on the Cross*, in the first half I was working as if I was writing a novel in English. That is, I tried to see if I was rendering the feel of their speech into English and so on. And then, in the middle, I just realized that this was wrong. Because anybody who really wants to feel the rhythm of speech and syntax and so on can learn the Gĩkũyũ language. I don't need to prove any more that that character is really speaking an African language, that that character is really indeed an African peasant. If one needs that, he can as I said learn Gĩkũyũ and read the novel in the original. So what I thought was important was to try and get the equivalence in English; it was not necessary to make a reader feel the rhythms of speech of an African language. The novel had to feel natural to an English reader in the same way that when I read a French novel in translation or a Russian novel in translation it is not the Frenchness of the language or the Russianness of the language that I am looking for. All that counts is the rendering into English the essence of the Russian experience or the French experience in that novel. If I was doing the translation of the novel again I'd probably make a much better job than I did. I know some of my Gĩkũyũ readers who had read the Gĩkũyũ original and now have read the English translation have complained deeply about the loss of certain things in the English translation.

In *Detained* you say that a novel is 'the work of many hands and many tongues'. You have already explained how this applies in your theatre, but in the novel the collective aspect is presumably indirect. Would you say your theatrical experience is likely to influence your novel writing?
Obviously the different art forms interact. That is, what one gains from theatre can apply for instance when it comes to dramatic representation of characters, particularly when they're talking to each other. I think drama can help the novelist to avoid long explanatory passages and often help him in dramatizing action in the novel as opposed to explaining, for instance, the emotions. As for

the novel being the work of many hands, I felt this very strongly particularly in prison where in writing *Caitaani Mũtharaba-inĩ* or *Devil on the Cross* I had obviously to rely on the other detainees and warders. And then I realized that the same collective tendency obviously is there, in the outer society. It's only that one is not so keenly aware of it because there are so many things happening around the writer in ordinary society. It's quite clear to me that there's a way in which the novelist is also a kind of editor: he gets different bits of information from people, different bits of stories about people's lives from different people, and all he does really is give all those stories a form or an outline. But I do agree with you of course that the collective nature of novel writing is a bit more indirect than with a play where people can sit round a table and keep on adding bits and pieces or where people can actually improvise or add to the play as they perform on the stage.

You particularly appreciate the communicative possibilities offered by theatre. But I know the original Gĩkũyũ version of *Devil on the Cross* also reached people directly, through readings in bars, in . . .
Yes, it was fantastic. In a sense you can say that even *Devil on the Cross* was a development of my theatrical involvement, because what happened was that when I was arrested in 1977 and taken to prison at Kamĩtĩ Maximum Security Prison I decided that the only way I could show defiance and have a way of ensuring my own survival was attempting to write in that very language which had been the basis of my present predicament and so I set myself the task of writing a novel in the Gĩkũyũ language. So *Devil on the Cross*, written on toilet paper in prison, was the result of my attempt to connect myself with the very cultural activities I was involved in with the peasants and workers at Kamĩrĩĩthũ and which found their expression in the writing and performance of *I Will Marry When I Want*. Now when I came out of prison in 1978 after Kenyatta died and all political prisoners were given an amnesty – though this proved only to be temporary – I prepared the novel for publication, so both the novel and the play were published in 1980 in the Gĩkũyũ language. The publishers had thought they would publish only a few thousand copies of each, hoping to sell them over a period of two, three, four or five years. But in fact the first editions of each of the works were snapped up within two or three weeks of publication and within the year, that is, between April and December 1980, they had done three printings of the play and of the novel, each printing being 5,000 copies, which was a record for them for any novel or play written in any language for sales over the same period of time. Now the reception of the novel and the play was really fantastic because they – particularly the novel – were read in buses, in *matatũs*, ordinary taxis; they were read in homes; workers grouped together during the lunch hour or whenever they had their own time to rest and would get one of their literate members to read for them. So in fact the novel was appropriated by the people and made part and parcel of their oral tradition.

The oral tradition is also present – very strongly – in the novel itself, in the proverbs and fables and also in the figure of the narrator. Why is your narrator a *gĩcaandĩ* player? And why a prophet of justice – what kind of prophet are you referring to?
Gĩcaandĩ is a complex form of poetry among the Gĩkũyũ people. It's very difficult and those who really knew it were very highly cultured. They knew the language *very* well, as well as the culture in which that language developed.

Often they used to hold competitions among themselves, weaving words here and there, weaving in riddles and proverbs, and whoever would win by making the other unable to respond to a particular puzzle would win a gourd, the kind of instrument used by the *gīcaandī* poets and singers.

The gourds used to have writings on them. These *gīcaandī* artists had in fact invented a form of writing like the Egyptian hieroglyphics. It seems they represented some of the important statements with symbols on their gourds, so the whole story sometimes, or maybe the middle part of the story, was already inscribed on their gourd, so they had a hieroglyphic form of writing which circulated only within that circle of society artists. Unfortunately many of these *gīcaandī* artists have died, there must be very few still remaining. So by using the *gīcaandī* artist as the narrator I was broadly speaking paying homage to that very, very important tradition in Gīkūyū literature.

Why prophet of justice? Because the singer and the poet were very highly respected in Gīkūyū society and they were seen as prophets, their words were listened to very, very keenly and what they had to say was important. In other words people took notice of what they had to say about so many problems in the land, about the morality of the different people or about the good life as opposed to the bad life, that kind of thing. So the singer, the poet, the man of words was often seen as a prophet. That's why again this *gīcaandī* artist in the novel is both a poet-singer as well as a prophet who would know the truth and narrate the truth.

You have always used a lot of biblical language and symbolism in your works and this is true also of *Devil on the Cross*. Could you explain this?
That's a very important question. The answers to it can only be found within a historical context. Christianity was part and parcel of the impact of imperialism in Africa and for a long time the Bible was the only reading material available to most literate Africans, so quite a number of literate Africans would probably be acquainted with the Bible and stories in the Bible. Even today in many neo-colonial regimes as in Kenya, the church and the bar are the only two venues available for people's entertainment, particularly on Sundays. In our village, for instance, you find a church being erected every other week, in a village which doesn't even have a nursery school or a primary school. In other words, the Bible is part and parcel of that heritage, so to use it or to refer to it you are also referring to a common body of knowledge, a body of knowledge you can assume you are sharing with your audience and that's why I use the Bible quite a lot, or biblical sayings, not because I share in any belief in the Bible, or in the sanctity of the Bible. It's just simply as a common body of knowledge I can share with my audience, and the same is true when I'm writing in Gīkūyū language, I use the Bible quite a lot.

When and how did your writing for children start, how does it fit in with your other work, what sort of stories, characters and themes are dominant?
I've always been interested in writing for children, partly, I must say, influenced by having children, and you find that in most societies in Africa there is very little reading material for children. Of course there are plenty of stories in the oral tradition, but in a book form, or between two covers, there are very few story books or novels or even books about general information. I also had this need, but I never really came to doing anything about it until I came from prison – prison seems to have been a watershed in my life. So I really started

writing for children in 1981 I think – 1981 or 1982 – and I wrote three books for children, ordinary stories, as part of a projected ten books which deal with the adventures of one character, Njamba Nene, just before and during the armed struggle for independence in Kenya, the armed struggle which was led by the Kenya Land and Freedom Army or Mau Mau. So the hero is engaged in different activities and adventures which will, I hope, give any child different aspects of the struggle for independence, through the eyes of this particular boy, or through the activities of this particular boy. Now I have a problem because when one writes for children the reactions from the readers are very important, but the fact is that the books were published when I was away, so I have no feel at all of how they have been received. I have no feedback at all.

You didn't try them out on your own children as you were writing them?
Yes, I did try them on my children as I wrote them, but of course it's different when you try them on your own children. When you're reading to them you'll be adding one or two little explanations and stopping to add this or take out that. So that is really the missing factor in my new venture in writing for children and that is really why I can't tell you very much about them.

Are your books for children on sale in Kenya?
Yes they are. One came out in September 1982 and the other one came out in December 1983. The first one is called *Njamba Nene na Mbaathi i Mathagu* and it simply means Njamba Nene and the flying bus (or the bus with wings). The second one is called *Bathitoora ya Njamba Nene*, Njamba Nene's pistol (or gun) and the third one is called *Njamba Nene na Cibū Kĩng'ang'i* or Njamba Nene and Chief Crocodile. The books are being translated into English by Wangũi wa Goro.

What do you feel is your identity as a writer? Do you consider yourself a Gĩkũyũ writer, a Kenyan writer or an African writer?
I can only tell you my practice as a writer. Basically as a writer I am interested in human relationships and the quality of human relationships and indeed the quality of human life. So I am interested in exploring all those social forces that prevent the realization of a more humane quality of human life and human relationship. In our case this is imperialism and its distorting effects, including its distortion of people's capacity to evaluate themselves in relation to their environment, both natural and social. That's the perspective from which I write. As a writer I feel at one first and foremost with Kenyan people who are struggling against neo-colonial oppression and repression, I feel at one with Kenyan people as they struggle against imperialism, in this case an imperialism led by the United States of America. Although there are other Western imperialist interests in Africa, particularly British, West German, French and Italian to a certain extent, the main imperialist interests in Kenya are led by the USA and this is shown by the fact that the USA has military facilities on Kenyan soil. In my view, no president, no party, no leader has the right to commit a people's territory for use by another foreign military power. In other words I oppose the USA having bases on the Kenyan soil and I support Kenyan people when they oppose that kind of external domination. Now, to the extent that Kenyan people are struggling against imperialist domination aided by the small ruling class, I feel that those Kenyan people are in the same situation as all other African people struggling against imperialism and in the same way I feel

that African people struggling against imperialism and for national independence and democracy are in the same position as all Third World peoples from South America, from Southeast Asia, struggling against the same phenomenon. And I feel that those people in the Third World – whether from Africa, South America or Asia – struggling against imperialism are in the same battle as, let's say, European peoples struggling against the system of exploitation in their own countries. So in that sense I feel that the struggle of Kenyan people, African people, Third World peoples, is not in contradiction with the democratic forces of peace in Europe today. That is my identity. I belong to Kenyan people, African people, Third World people, all peoples struggling against economic exploitation and social oppression, those in the world struggling for human dignity.

Much of what you have said about language and literature is true also or has been true in the recent past for another literature of African origin, Afro-American literature. Do you see any connections in your own work, in your practical political and literary struggle, with Afro-American writers and their literature?
My own journey towards where I am today has been through all sorts of places. I went to Makerere University College in Uganda where I studied English literature in its traditional form from the times of Shakespeare to just before the Second World War. But I was hungering for a different kind of literature. I started reading African literature which so excited me because I could identify with the assumptions, the background, the characters, the problems. So I started reading Achebe, Abrahams and so on. But I also started reading West Indian writers like George Lamming, so that when later I wanted to do more work in literature I concentrated on Caribbean literature. Again, I could recognize the world of Caribbean literature very well: it's the same world that I knew, the same world dominated by slavery and imperialism in its colonial and neo-colonial stages, and of course the struggles of those people against those different stages of social oppression. I also looked at Afro-American literature and, when later I went to the University of Nairobi in 1967 and in the '70s, one of the struggles at the University of Nairobi was in fact the struggle to introduce a new kind of syllabus for the study of literature in Kenya, a syllabus which would have oral literature at the centre, then written African literature from East Africa, from Africa and from the Caribbean, from Afro-America and so on, and then the literature of Europe, provided it was available in English translation. So the Afro-American literature has been part and parcel of my growing or developing consciousness. But now I'm interested in the whole interaction between the cultures of the Kenyan peoples and the cultures of other African peoples and the cultures of Third World peoples, and then the connection between the democratic struggles and cultures of Third World peoples and the democratic humanist content of the culture of European peoples and so on. Because the democratic content in the humanist tradition of the great literature of Western people is absolutely in harmony with the literature and culture of struggle in Africa, Asia and South America.

(London, 20 September 1989)

At the beginning of *Decolonising the Mind*, you say this is going to be your 'farewell' to the use of English even in explanatory prose, not only in literature. Is this still your position?

Yes, it's still my position. It just means that I shall be using Gĩkũyũ mainly, like some people operate in English, in French, in Chinese . . .

In the chapter on fiction in *Decolonising the Mind* you talk about your research for an appropriate form and an appropriate content for what was to become *Devil on the Cross*, emphasizing particularly the importance of orature in this process. Reading *Matigari* one feels there has been a similar kind of development, is this so?
Yes. *Matigari* is based very much on orature, particularly the narrative techniques and certain assumptions about time and space, or perhaps not so much assumptions as attitudes to time and space in oral narratives where often time and space are fairly flexible. I like this idea of being able to move freely in time and space.

Reading *Matigari* I kept thinking back to some of your previous works. It seemed almost as if you were voluntarily recalling characters, incidents and themes that had appeared before. Was this a conscious strategy?
No, I was not aware of that. I suppose you're right in the sense that there's an attempt at summing up experiences arising from the previous attempts. But then in every writer's work there are echoes of previous literary texts.

I was wondering if you were trying to sum them up and bring them forward in a new development.
Not necessarily. I was much more aware of the need to exploit the oral forms of narrative. In *Matigari* even the narrative tone is supposed to be very much like an oral tale. I wanted to write a tale that could do the work of *Devil on the Cross* or *Petals of Blood* in terms of multiple references, without necessarily having the same kind of narrative voices. I wanted to make it refer to different moments in time and space while having a very clear narrative continuity.

Something that struck me particularly was that, in comparison with the characters of your previous works, Matigari seems to be much more openly and much more explicitly a kind of Christ figure, a Messiah figure. You actually state this, whereas previously similar analogies are left more implicit.
I think it arises from this attempt at multiple references within a simple narrative, these multiple echoes of different experiences. The biblical myth is there; the notion of birth, death and resurrection. There are allusions to the Last Supper, Christ and his disciples. But there are also references to many other things, for instance: to the natural cycles of birth and death and germination. Also seasons.

Another echo is that of Dedan Kĩmathi and the legends surrounding him . . .
Yes, the making of a legend, myth-making. I'm interested in how myths grow, how the human imagination captures the essence of things in terms of myths, of heroes and hero-worship and all that.

To take up on some of the characters in the book, the female figure seems considerably less important than in most of your previous works.

Yes, Matigari is all-consuming. In a sense both the woman and the boy are really different aspects of Matigari, and Matigari is different aspects of the woman and the boy. They are all part of one another. You could say Gũthera is Matigari, and

Matigari is Gŭthera, and Gŭthera is Ngarŭro wa Kĩrĩro or Mŭriŭki, any way you like. I just got three figures who could be father and daughter or man and wife and child, or brothers and sisters. They're just different suggestions, there's no attempt at having romantic idealizations or anything. They are echoes. I know many of my readers have been looking for Wanja in Matigari, but Matigari is not like that at all. Matigari is a collective figure, his particularities are echoes of different facets of our history. There is one scene where he meets John Boy outside the house and John Boy asks who he is. And, in order to explain who he is, Matigari has to go into history and say he has been there even before the times of the Portuguese in the sixteenth century. John Boy says he doesn't want history, but Matigari *is* also history, of course.

One of the most intriguing symbols in the novel is the 'riderless horse'; could you say something about it? Or do you want to leave it to the reader's imagination (at the beginning you invite the reader to use his imagination and apply the novel to his own situation)?
It keeps cropping up. The novel opens with memories of the hunt and it ends with Matigari being hunted in the same way. No, I've no idea what it means. Do you know what it means? It could be anything!

SELECTED BIBLIOGRAPHY

NOVELS
Weep Not, Child (London: Heinemann, 1964).
The River Between (London: Heinemann, 1965).
A Grain of Wheat (London: Heinemann, 1967).
Petals of Blood (London: Heinemann, 1977).
Caitaani Mŭtharaba-inĩ (Nairobi: Heinemann Kenya, 1980). Specially commended by the Noma Award Committee in 1981. English edition, translated by the author, *Devil on the Cross* (London: Heinemann, 1982).
Matigari ma Njirŭŭngi (Nairobi: Heinemann Kenya, 1987). English edition, translated by Wangŭi wa Goro, *Matigari* (Oxford and Nairobi: Heinemann, 1989).

SHORT STORIES
Secret Lives and Other Stories (London: Heinemann, and Westport, Conn.: Lawrence Hill, 1975).

THEATRE
The Black Hermit (London: Heinemann, 1968).
This Time Tomorrow (Nairobi: East African Literature Bureau, 1970). Contains *The Rebels, The Wound in the Heart* and *This Time Tomorrow*.
(With Mĩcere Githae Mŭgo), *The Trial of Dedan Kĩmathi* (Nairobi: Heinemann Kenya, 1976).
(With Ngŭgĩ wa Mĩrĩĩ), *Ngaahika Ndeenda* (Nairobi: Heinemann Kenya, 1980. English edition, *I Will Marry When I Want* (London: Heinemann, 1982).

DIARY
Detained: A Writer's Prison Diary (London: Heinemann, 1981).

ESSAYS
Homecoming: Essays on African and Caribbean Literature, Culture and Politics (London: Heinemann, 1972).
Writers in Politics. Essays (London: Heinemann, 1981).

Barrel of a Pen: Resistance to Repression in Neo-Colonial Kenya (Trenton: Africa World Press, 1983).
Decolonising the Mind. The Politics of Language in African Literature (London: James Currey; Nairobi: Heinemann Kenya; Portsmouth, NH: Heinemann, Harare: Zimbabwe Publishing House, 1986).

CHILDREN'S STORIES

Njamba Nene na Mbaathi i Mathagu (Nairobi: Heinemann Kenya, 1982). Received Honourable Mention at the 1983 Noma Award. English edition, *Njamba Nene and the Flying Bus*, translated by Wanguĩ wa Goro (Nairobi: Heinemann Kenya, 1986).
Bathitoora ya Njamba Nene (Nairobi: Heinemann Kenya, 1983). English edition, *Njamba Nene's Pistol*, translated by Wangũi wa Goro (Nairobi: Heinemann Kenya, 1986).

Mazisi Kunene

The tradition of the great Zulu poets, from the praise singers of the Zulu
kings to writers such as B. W. Vilakazi, is carried forward and renewed
in the powerful, visionary poetry of Mazisi Kunene. With its epic
proportions and tone, it has been a central influence for many African
authors, both in its diction and imagery and in the concepts it majes-
tically unfolds. Born in Durban in 1930, Kunene was educated in South
Africa, studying Zulu and History at the University of Natal, and at the
School of Oriental and African Studies in London, after going into exile
in 1959. A founder member of the anti-apartheid movement, he ran the
London office of the ANC as the UK and European representative. He
has also been director of education for the South African United Front
and director of finance for the ANC (1972). He has taught at the Universities of Iowa, where he was head of African Studies, Stanford and
California, Los Angeles.

10

Mazisi Kunene

The interview, which originally appeared in Commonwealth *(Dijon), X, 2 (Spring 1988), pp. 34–42, was carried out in Naples in July 1986 during the Italian Communist Youth Federation's Africa Festival, where the author had talked about his work and participated in a round table discussion with Wole Soyinka and Zégoua Gbessi Nokan.*

Could you tell me something about how you first came to write poetry?
Oh, that's a difficult question! It just happened – there's no explanation because it just happened. My home was on a hill or mountain overlooking the ocean, a very spectacular place, so I used to look at the sun as it came out of the ocean and it was so fantastic. I didn't know what to do about it, it just troubled me. And then it just came, it just happened, there was no plan. I must have been about eight or nine years old. When I wrote the poem, I took it to school in my exercise book and a man, who was head teacher then, saw it and said 'Oh, this is poetry, this is good!' I didn't know it was poetry and I was a bit embarrassed of course. I couldn't say anything, but I was pleased, I suppose. And from then on I just kept on writing. Yes, there's no explanation . . . but should there be an explanation? Does a person start to write for something?

Was this early poetry in Zulu or in English?
In Zulu. I never write in English. I only translate into it.

Yet your poetry reads as beautiful poetry in English. I was wondering if what reaches the reader as a complete and self-sufficient poem in English is different in any way from your original poems in Zulu? Do you have to not just translate Zulu words, but also maybe change something in the images as you translate them?
Not so much the images, but I have to change something because sometimes the

Zulu version is too exotic to be understood in English. Sometimes I play a game of translating Shakespeare into Zulu in my mind and it sounds quite silly. It wouldn't sound as good in Zulu as it sounds in English. So I have to do a lot of reorganizing. That's why I hate translating. It's a painful process. But fortunately there's a girl from Spain who is also interested in this translation, so she is very patient, she sits there for hours, just hours, listening to some of my attempts to translate from Zulu into English. It helped me to translate Zulu into English through her, but she's gone now. I don't know if the process is quicker if I translate from Zulu into English without an intermediary, if I just do it myself . . . I think it helps, aesthetically, it helps to have an intermediary: there is a kind of control as it were. The English that was spoken in our schools was the English of the missionaries, who were not really the best English speakers. At best they were readers of Wordsworth, Shelley, etc. The Romantic poets are easy to read without one having to go through the effort of understanding the message.

So you were actually taught in English at school?
I was taught in English at high school and Zulu at junior high school.

But was the literature you were taught mostly English literature?
There was no literature really. The literature that I knew, I was taught at home by my parents. Both of my parents came from very big clans and valued their positions as coming from those important clans. My mother was from the Ngcobo family, which is a big family of the Zulu nation, whereas my father came from the Swazi royal clan so there was a kind of conflict. My mother would say 'Pueh, this is not really Zulu' and my father would put it in his own way! So there was a kind of very deep critique of how you put things in a language. Literature was very important: it was not just literature for its own sake, it was history, politics, the philosophy of society and everything. So through history and through literature they were training their own children about various aspects of life including ethics.

When did this take place, in the evenings?
Not just in the evening, all the time. When I started writing, my father bought me a small table, a folding table, so that I could go round the house. In the morning I could write on one side, facing the sun – because I like the sun – then move and face the other way, always following the sun. Sometimes my father would ask me to read and it was a very intimidating experience because he was of the royal clan and he was very stern. He was strong. He didn't talk much, he didn't say very much, but I would know if he liked the poem or if he didn't like it, whereas my mother would say quite directly 'No, no, no, you don't put it that way!'

So your father and mother were probably the primary influences on your work?
Without doubt, yes.

And through them, the oral culture of your people?
I don't know what you mean by oral culture. Even now I still doubt if it is a good idea to have decided to put literature in the esoteric form of writing. In some ways I think it's disastrous for literature. It makes literature accessible

only to a certain group of people, the literati and the critics, whereas the performance of literature as I have seen it is very different. There is an immediate criticism of the performer, or the person who creates literature is aware of an active audience and therefore cannot just say flippant things. The performer has to be very serious and has to be concerned about significant events in society. And then I really do think that in the future, strange as it may sound, literature will be spoken, because as television becomes more and more dominant people will want to hear and see rather than read. Then the cassettes and all those sorts of things will tend to make the spoken word much more dominant. There is an affectation, I suppose, in those societies who have adopted the writing of literature, which makes them feel that literature that is not written is wrong. There are different literatures – the literature that is written and the literature that is spoken. There are different kinds of mental discipline involved when one is writing them. I sometimes speak the literature as I am writing it and try to experiment, to see if it's better spoken than written. It's *different*. Unfortunately the tendency has been to study oral literature – I prefer to call it the literature that is spoken – as if it will one day evolve into a written literature, instead of studying it as itself. I hope, for instance, that as I write my epics nobody will read them: they will use them, use episodes for plays, for musical compositions, poetic pieces, etc.

And so in fact recover the performance aspect of spoken literature: not just the words that are spoken but the presence of the person who is speaking them. Traditionally, I suppose, the utterance of the poem was only part of the whole, together with music, movement . . .
Yes, you have to turn the word into music. It's not the same if you say the words or if you sing them. As one is performing one is singing-speaking. Then one must add a dance of course, musical accompaniment, response from the audience. One must add to this a variety of dramatic movements including mime, imitation, and other vast combinations of actions. One has to dramatize what one is speaking about. Written literature is not the same; here one must be both an actor and a creator of the poem. Some poets are not great as actors, so it helps sometimes to have some actor to perform the literature. I hate to read, for instance, especially in Europe, because there you are reading to audiences that are sober and sitting down. They listen and then clap their hands routinely, which is unfortunate. I would prefer to perform to people who are not so sane, who are *engaged*, even drunk! Yes . . . because then there is an involvement.

When did you leave South Africa?
In 1959. Many centuries ago!

How did you come to the decision to leave? Or were you forced into it?
It was both. I was teaching in Lesotho, at the university. I heard that I had been given a scholarship to go to England. I didn't want to go. First of all, I was tired of school; besides I didn't see the point of going to England when I was an African. A lot of things were happening then, in South Africa. While I was in Lesotho they publicized that I had been given a scholarship in the paper and I was too embarrassed to refuse. I thought I would spoil the chances of others if I refused. At that time going to England was a political act. Canon Collins, the man who for many years had championed the causes of Africa – he was canon

at St Paul's and created Defence and Aid, Christian Action – had been to South Africa. They had said 'Come and see for yourself, you keep on criticizing us . . .', so he went and saw and said 'I don't like it still!' So I couldn't refuse this scholarship, so I went. But then also the ANC told me I must go there and start the boycott movement. So I went and started the movement with a friend of mine who is dead now, Tennyson Makiwane.

Was most of your published poetry written after you left South Africa?
I am writing all the time. I was writing in South Africa. It's like a disease – it *is* a disease, a terrible disease for me to write because it is uncontrolled. It's a terrible thing, a terrible thing. It's like somebody else is writing. It's not me, it's somebody else, only *using* me. And sometimes I get exhausted. What I am trying to explain is that I am writing all the time. I never really bothered about publishing, but somebody used to come to me every Sunday and I got very bored with his coming every Sunday afternoon, so I thought to myself, 'What can I do with this person to occupy him?' and then I thought – he was an English speaker – maybe I could occupy him with translating, make him do something useful! So I published my *Zulu Poems* from that activity. I made a selection but I don't even know from what or from where, that's why I can't really answer your question, there are a lot of them, I just picked at random. When people started praising them I was very angry; I said 'Well, these people, they are very patronizing. I knew these poems were not masterpieces; they were just some poems; it was not my best work.' So I thought 'Let me translate the epics to make them quiet!' So I translated *Shaka – Shaka* I had thought about when I was in high school – but it was different, the legend tended to mix with the historical fact, so I changed it. I changed what I had written, so what I translated was the final poem. I think the *Anthem* was written mainly outside of South Africa.

What is the relationship between your *Shaka* and some of the other Shakas, Thomas Mofolo's, for example?
My *Shaka* is more historical. Mofolo's is just myth; it's just a lot of tales. All that stuff about the witchdoctor, the diviner and so on . . . it didn't happen. Shaka actually hated diviners: he lined them up one day and said 'Someone has tried to bewitch me by putting blood on my house, you must tell me who did it.' They all chose a lot of people, some among his friends, until finally, late in the afternoon, one of the diviners said 'No, I think I know who did it, *you* did it!' and Shaka said 'All right, yes I did, and as for you bunch of diviners, look how many people you would have killed for nothing!' He was very practical. I think Mofolo's *Chaka* was very much influenced by the missionaries; I've been told it was revised many times because of missionary pressure. They didn't want the original Shaka to be a hero, they wanted him to be a man of darkness as against their man of light. They wanted him to be a man who sold his soul to the devil.

How did you reconstruct the story of Shaka; what sources did you use?
Many sources: my family, for a start, especially my great, great grandmother who lived a long time and told many stories about that period. When Shaka's nephew was king she was still a young girl and she knew many things. Other sources too, of course. The story of Shaka is current in the society. Of course I made my own interpretations which I based on my understanding of the society, what it would accept, what it would not accept, its organization . . .

For instance, they say Shaka was a tyrant – that's quite ridiculous. He had to be controlled by the council – he was only a young fellow – and the council tradition was very strong. You cannot rule, if you are a king, without the council. And it's not only the council representing the different districts, but also the family council which was very strong. You cannot override it, you have to compromise and make your point through argument, you have to win the council over. So there are lots of things that he couldn't have done, it's impossible. Also if you're organizing an army, in ten years, taking an army of about 500 people and turning it into an army of 90,000–100,000 disciplined people, you need to do a lot of training in discipline to change things, switch the cards around. Shaka made a lot of changes, but he had to give reasons for what he was doing. And the fact that he himself was a leader who was involved in the fighting did a lot to convince people, because at the time he came into power there was a lot of corruption and the other rulers were content to collect the loot without risking their lives fighting. Shaka was different. He reorganized the army, the court, and the customs. He was a participant, which really makes him a leader rather than someone who was just sitting as an observer of his own experiment. So my *Shaka* is more authentic, definitely.

Shaka has become a kind of symbol for Africa: he appears again and again throughout the different literatures . . .
Yes, there's no question that he was a most unusual man, a genius, both a military genius and a political genius. When he came into power he was maybe about twenty-two and already he had been fighting in the wars, he had made the Mthethwa Empire safe from all kinds of raiders and he had acquired a big reputation. When he came into power he was young and when he died he must have been in his early thirties. His brothers conspired against him. They felt that they didn't want to risk their lives, they wanted to live a nice aristocratic life, an idea which would have been disastrous because that time was not the period to sit down. The British were coming in and the Boers were moving in. Shaka had by then started studying the British method of fighting – with guns and so on – and found weaknesses in the gun in that you have to reload it. He felt it was not quick enough and you couldn't use it in the rain!

How did *Anthem of the Decades* come into being?
There are two ways of looking at myth. The Western way and especially the British way has been to think of myth as true or false and come to the conclusion that it is false. This is the way I think they systematically destroyed their own rich culture. I don't think the people who create myth think of it as true or false, rather there are two levels of myth. There is the level of cosmology, the understanding of the world order, how the world order is organized, and that level is systematic and abstract. Since it is abstract it is very difficult for the ordinary person to understand it. So the thinker reduces it into a story and as a story it becomes a mythology. And that's why it lasts a long time. It encompasses the world order as it is seen and experienced by the people. Of course an ordinary person believes it; I mean it is just like the story of the Bible, it becomes a sacred document which cannot be questioned. But the more intelligent – it's not so much intelligence as a question of power – the rulers, the aristocracy know that it is only partly true. What they then do is to use it either to elevate themselves through the belief system, or incorporate themselves into the belief system, or else to patronize – in a good sense – the intellectual development of the society.

The myth in *Anthem* has two levels. There is the idea that at first God thought 'Oh, let human beings live forever'. He sent a chameleon to convey this message but later changed his mind and decided humans must die. That's a very simple story. However, when you look into the symbolic meaning, you realize that the chameleon is very slow and all the qualities it has are qualities of cosmic order: slow movement, ability to change itself according to its different creative moods. It has the ability to see in all directions. At the same time, the chameleon is slow, it looks 'old', wise and timeless. It has got fingers, like human fingers. This is a very accurate symbol of the idea of permanence, the permanence of things. In Africa, if you are too fast people think there is something wrong with you. You have to be 'slow': slowness means reflection, respect and reverence. It's very important to have a symbol which represents all these factors and the chameleon is the best symbol. The chameleon as a symbol of the cosmos is found not only in southern Africa but throughout Africa. In ancient Egypt, for example, the chameleon is depicted as the eye of the universe, of equilibrium. So, in opposition to the chameleon it is logical that the lizard, the salamander, which has got speed and is ugly, should symbolize death. The salamander can only see in one direction: it is the messenger which does not stop to think, does not reflect, but just goes in one direction. Speed has always symbolized death to Africans. When the first missionaries came, people thought: 'These people are talking too fast, they will be the death of us!' The missionaries didn't know this kind of respect, of reverence by sitting down, of waiting to be greeted. They'd just say 'Hello. How are you? I greet you in the name of the Lord!' and people would say 'This man is dangerous, he is talking too fast, he doesn't greet properly.' They equated them with the lizard and they were right of course! So *Anthem of the Decades* encompasses these philosophies. Its symbols represent very interesting, very profound ideas which are at the core of the African thought systems. I'm writing five epics now that are based on the myths and legends. What is interesting is to interpret this mythology, understand the central meaning, not just the mythic statement, but the meaning.

Could you explain the title of your most recent collection, *The Ancestors and the Sacred Mountain*?
These are my ancestors, of course, and the sacred mountains . . . well, they were the kings of Swaziland, so they were buried in the mountains. But originally there were two books, one called *The Ancestors* and the other called *The Sacred Mountains*. Heinemann selected from both and put them together.

What is the relation between your poetry and your political commitment?
There is no separation in the first place because the writing is only a vehicle of ideas. The person who is active politically, who is engaged politically or socially is the one who comes first, he's the most important, and the instrument that that person uses is of course the instrument that is available. In this case the instrument is poetry. It's both. I am involved – it's inevitable because I come from an involved family which historically was involved – it's logical, there is no point at which I think 'I must be involved in politics', it's just normal. The white minority government is troublesome. This must just come to an end, I thought as I grew up. As for poetry it is just *somebody* who is ever troubling me . . . There are a lot of publishers who want my poems and edit them for publication. As I'm reading them I am amazed myself by these ideas, they're

incredible. They are of course not my ideas. In my normal condition I could not think of these ideas: they are too many, too strange. So I am astounded by these poems. I read them for my own self expansion. I think I'm lucky. I used to think that as I was writing all the time I might not ever have the good fortune of reading what I had written, but now I am able to read some of the things. As I read them they seem not things that *I* have written, they are things that *she* has written because I think that the highest creative powers are female. Sometimes I used to get concerned because if you have written something and it is many years after, you wonder if it is good, and if it is not so good, then you wonder if the whole collection is as bad as the few you read. But I am lucky because as I read, the poems are amazing, absolutely incredible.

Do you rewrite your poems at all?

Not much. After I've written I don't want to see them. I feel drained by the poems so I don't want to see them, I don't want to read them. To edit the poems was a big effort for me. It's only because people keep on saying they want my poems. So it is in a way in response to that kind of demand that I look at them again. The poems are very strange, their ideas are really quite strange. Some do not have a consistent theme, they are just combinations of ideas, but the totality of the ideas is enough to make a systematic meaning, a powerful impression. But they are strange. You see, when I look at a root, I can say 'OK, that's a root, describe the root of that plant', but these are not things like that, they are things that become fingers, they assume their own logic and they are strange to me because the logic they have assumed is not a logic I would normally think of, it's too esoteric. It corresponds, as an idea, to the thing itself, but it's too distant to have been thought about. If I say 'root . . . fingers', well, there is a connection there, but some of these things are too strange, too different.

After I had finished some of these volumes, the Department asked me to submit what I had been doing in the past two years. I submitted the volumes and they calculated there were 5,000 poems and they said it was not possible for a human to write so many poems in such a short period. They thought I was falsifying my record but actually it was only a small portion of what I had written.

Once just recently I was writing a puppet play (I had been asked by the Theatre Department at UCLA) and I had never written one. I was in Senegal, writing the play. It pretty much wrote itself, so in the end I was thinking I must not hurry with it because I'd be too eager to finish it, so I left it and asked whatever powers or forces . . . and they said 'Go to Africa', so I went out to ask the earth and said 'What do I do now to finish, what should I do?' I was seeing all the characters in real life. There is a part in which a decision has to be made to create human beings. This task is given to a god or a goddess (we don't know which because the creative principle is neither male nor female, it is both), a hunchback goddess. And when I was in the street, buying some tapes, I saw this woman, a tall, very tall woman, bent over, walking with a stick, looking this way and that, and I said '*That* is the goddess', but I said it to myself, without saying anything to the fellow who was with me, it was too strong then. But I told him the next day that I saw the goddess, without telling him where and when. He said, 'I saw her too.' When I asked him where, he said she was crossing the street and of course it was the woman. It was very strange, I don't know whether I was transmitting my thoughts to him. Anyway, in the play, she is pulling out from her hunchback images of forms, human beings, different forms, different shapes, different types. She does not like all the forms, so she claps her hands and annihilates the forms which she does not like. Many forms appear and she gets to a point where she says 'Yes, if an ant could walk . . .' and she gets very excited, so she pulls out an ant and the ant is walking and there are two ants. So she introduces them to the gods as the human beings and the gods are disgusted. The ants dance around – she is making them dance – and the gods are disgusted: 'An ant! Is this all the human being is . . .?' Then she claps her hands backwards and they stop dancing. Then they take off the masks to show the human form and the gods are absolutely amazed: they say 'It's incredible!' They look at the human form and it is very beautiful and they all sing the anthem of the gods. As they sing, the human beings, the human twins move towards the earth on stage.

The earth is a terrible place. Even the gods are frightened of it, they don't want to go there and one of the gods actually opposes the creation of humanity. He says 'What's the point? This creature is neither an animal nor a god, it's just foetal, it's a foetus!' Which is true! I mean, human beings are foetal, animals are much better, they have got their own clothes, they can sleep anywhere. That's just one of the episodes, but I don't want to tell you the whole story.

What I was trying to say was that when I had finished the play it was something else, something outside of me. It had created itself. I was deeply moved by this thing: I knew I had created some great piece of work. It *is* great. It only needs someone who has got hands – some people have no hands – to bring it out, to make it into a film or an animation or a mask play. They are going to produce it at UCLA in the fall. But I would really like a Japanese team to make it. The Americans said I needed to reorganize it for the American audience because 'You make theatre to make money and in your play there are not enough conflicts'. I know that in the Aristotelian system it is said that conflict is essential, but it's not central in the African system, rather the reconciliation of opposites. Resolution of conflict is, itself, inspiring; it depends on the depth of the solution. So they said, 'You must have some spectacle', but spectacle by itself does not make great drama . . . But maybe the American audience could be civilized, introduced to some ideas, not just 'bang! bang!' The American attitude to Africa is very old-fashioned. They cannot equate it with an idea system, they can only think of it in terms of 'Give us something ghoulish, something African!' Whereas the Japanese producers have respect for different cultures, especially African cultures.

How do you continue to write in Zulu when you have not been in your country for such a long time and your work cannot be – or at least has not been – published in Zulu and read by a Zulu-speaking public?
You see, I am chosen. I know it. Being chosen is not always a good thing. It is what you call a sacred mark, it is put on your forehead. So it is not possible for me to lose the ability of language in the first place. In the second place, there are two of us. There is one who is listening and the one who is writing. In all these years I have been my own audience: I can say 'Ah, that is not so good . . . that is good . . . that is great!' and I can celebrate. I know when a thing is great, when it's fantastic. And some people say 'What an egoistic man!' but they don't see that I am not referring to myself; I am referring to *him* – or *her* – and this is incredible. So all these years I have been my own audience, which is best, I think, because one of the things that has killed many African writers is cheap

fame. They write maybe two or three novels or two or three plays or one or two
books of poetry and they become famous and they die, because in that fame it's
the audience which then controls what they will do next. Fortunately for me, as
I am chosen, I am also chosen to be silent, not to talk and not to be spoken to.
Now, at this moment, I am about to talk. After all these years I am going to
talk. Never mind about those other things, they're just a drop in the ocean,
nothing. The time has come, it's going to come out now in flood, it's going to
explode . . .

**But are you not troubled by the thought that your work is not being read by
your people back in South Africa?**
It has not troubled me. In all these years it has been necessary for me to write,
only write, so it has not troubled me. But now it is they who are sending
messages and saying we want you to get it out. Just the other day I met a man
from a factory – a factory worker – and he said 'We want your poems.' I was
amazed. Poetry is a luxury that people working under those conditions sometimes cannot afford. The time has come, I feel it because I am ready to open.
Sometimes I get depressed because it is too much. Do I worry about people not
reading me in the original? I used to worry a bit, not so much for them, but
because I did not know how he – or she – would be received. But now I know,
she is ahead of everything, so when she speaks, keep your ear on the ground
and you will hear her.

SELECTED BIBLIOGRAPHY

POETRY
Zulu Poems (London: André Deutsch; and New York: Africana Publishing Corpora-
tion, 1970).
Emperor Shaka the Great: a Zulu Epic (London: Heinemann, 1979).
Anthem of the Decades. A Zulu Epic (London: Heinemann, 1981).
The Ancestors and the Sacred Mountain (London: Heinemann, 1982).
Nine recent poems are included in *From South Africa, New Writing, Photographs and
Art*, ed. David Bunn and Jane Taylor, special number of *Triquarterly*, LXIX (Spring/
Summer 1987), pp. 323–33.

ESSAYS
'South African oral traditions', in *Aspects of South African Literature*, ed. C. Heywood
(London: Heinemann; and New York: Africana Publishing Corporation, 1976),
pp. 24–41.
'The Relevance of African cosmological systems to African literature today', *African
Literature Today*, 11, (London: Heinemann, 1980), pp. 190–205.

Njabulo Ndebele

'An act of knowledge through self-confrontation' is how Njabulo
Ndebele describes his notion of an art whose value lies in 'inventiveness
of treatment, in sharpness of insight and in the deepening of consciousness'. Calling for 'a new formal articulation' for the material life of Africa
in order to 'enlarge intellectual interest and expand the possibilities of the
imagination', and for an engagement with the 'complex totality of life',
the author's 1984 Noma Award acceptance speech provides a manifesto
for recent African writing.

Born in 1948 at Western township, Johannesburg, and brought up
mainly in Charterston location, the setting of many of his stories,
Njabulo Simakahle Ndebele graduated in English and Philosophy at the
University of Botswana, Lesotho and Swaziland, going on to read for an
MA at Cambridge and a PhD at the University of Denver. During the
Black Consciousness period he edited the student literary journal,
Expression, and was recognized as one of the Movement's leading
literary theoreticians. Better known today for his short stories and criti-
cism, he began by writing poetry, published in the anthology *To Whom
It May Concern* (1973) and in journals such as *The Classic*, *The Purple
Renoster*, *Izwi* and *Staffrider*. Founder of the Congress of South African
Writers, head of the English Department at the University of Roma,
Lesotho, he has now returned to South Africa and is head of Department
at the University of the Witwatersrand, Division of African Literature.

11

Njabulo Ndebele

The interview took place in Rome (3 October 1987), during a seminar on 'The New African Literatures'.

Could you talk about your early years, your family environment, your first conscious encounter with literature?
I was born on 4 July 1948, in Johannesburg, in what was then the Western Native Township: it has since been occupied by what are called 'coloured' people. I think the last of the African people moved out around 1960 or so. It was very ironic because we moved to the town of Nigel in 1952 which is about 33 miles east of Johannesburg. The township there – that is the African section – was called Charterston location. That is where I grew up and went to school and that is the setting of my stories in *Fools*. The irony that I was referring to is that from about the late '60s we were moved to a new location called Dudusa – which has been very much in the news in South Africa during the last few years, it was one of the 'hot spots' – because our township was also given over to the so-called 'coloured' people. So I have a very practical, concrete experience of being part of these Government resettlement schemes.

Relatively speaking, mine was a very sedate family environment. My father was a teacher and my mother was a registered nurse, so I had a relatively trouble-free childhood. It was a fairly comfortable environment with plenty of books in the house, plenty of music, plenty of culture. At that time professional people – the teacher and the nurse in my case – still commanded a lot of respect and had a tremendous leadership impact on the communities. In my township we didn't have either a doctor or a lawyer, so the most influential people were teachers, nurses and priests and what you'd call 'Board members' who were part and parcel of the civic structures. For that reason I got used to a lot of people coming into my home for this and that, so we were never closed off from the community. This is one of the problems about the new policy that

147

the South African Government is busy about: trying to create a middle class. They did not foresee a situation where they might need to do so, so what they did was to bunch everybody in the townships, with the result that we did not as it were develop a middle-class consciousness that would totally shut out other people. So that enabled us to live in a socially rich environment. I had access to the world of the mind and to the world of music in my family, but at the same time there were the social contacts within the township, so one had a bit of everything. It was that kind of environment.

Very early in my life I became aware that my father had been a writer, a playwright, and had published what was the first published Zulu play in South Africa. So that went a long way towards making me aware of the possibilities of becoming a writer. My sister was a very talented musician. She had a fine voice and was a good actress, but it was not possible for her to exploit her talents because in the townships being an actress or a singer was not regarded as a worthwhile profession: there was supposed to be something socially wrong with people who did these things; it was a tainted profession. You enjoyed listening to music and singers as long as you did not become one of them! I suppose also it's not entirely true to say that it was socially tainted. I think it was a middle-class view: my father saying 'You must have a profession.' My sister went on to do nursing. But I always look back and think she would have been a very successful musician. My younger brother is a talented artist, but again I was the only one who made it because writing – in which I took a lot of interest from a very early stage – goes hand in hand with education, so I could go further, read books and acquire more education and become better at writing. So in a sense I made it because my profession was closely allied to education and advancement.

Was it a multi-lingual environment?
Yes it was, a very multi-lingual environment. I grew up speaking several languages: Zulu, which was my own; Xhosa, which was the predominant language in Church for hymns and everything; Sesotho . . . In the township churches the sermon was always translated. If the priest who was giving the sermon was Zulu-speaking someone would come up to translate, if he was Sesotho-speaking the same: it goes on all the time, even in concerts, in the halls there was always a translator. So on average everybody in the Johannesburg area can speak at least four languages. Now that I'm more conscious of the value of this I enjoy flipping from one language to another. Sometimes you discover that the person you're talking to in another language actually speaks the same language you do, but you only discover it later!

Was your schooling in English?
Initially, from kindergarten right up to Standard Six, the schooling is in the mother tongue, but from around Standard Four English is beginning to be used a lot, till from Form One onwards it's entirely in English. I think, to be more accurate, the first three years of school are entirely in the mother tongue and then the rest of the years the medium of instruction begins to be English and then of course you have to learn Afrikaans. So we were learning three languages as we went along.

And at home you spoke Zulu?
Yes, we spoke Zulu, but with a mixture of languages: English would crop up all the time, particularly from the parents. Then the reading materials, the

magazines – I grew up reading *Drum, Bona, Zonk* and others like *Africa South, Classic* and *Sketch* that were lying around in the house since my father subscribed to them – and the newspapers, the *Star*, the *Rand Daily Mail*, these were all in English, so my practice in English took place informally inside the house. Then the world outside: advertising was almost invariably in English. Only recently do we now have advertising sometimes in Zulu, sometimes in Sesotho, depending where you are. What I'm trying to say is that the whole world around us was dominated by English. I didn't really choose to write in English, it was force of circumstance. In fact I started writing in Zulu, but I abandoned it because all the people who fired my imagination, the poets I discovered on my own – Dylan Thomas, W. H. Auden, Louis MacNeice or the Second World War poets and others like Wilfred Owen, several others: even Dante, who I read ponderously in English translation (I was very young, but I kept going and he really fascinated me) – I read in English. My poetic imagination was influenced by much of the reading I did and there was no similar fascinating imaginative world that I was exposed to in my own language. There wasn't that degree of experimentation and play with ideas and language reinforced by extensive study in the schools: there was none of that. So you just find yourself writing in one language rather than another simply because it seems to offer more in terms of what your imagination is ready to absorb at a particular point.

Were you exposed at all to writing by African authors?
Yes, definitely, through the magazines. In *Africa South* for instance you'd come across the odd short story; the writings of Nat Nakasa, of Zeke Mphahlele and others like Lewis Nkosi who wrote in *Drum* magazine I read while I was doing my secondary school years. My father also had a lot of banned books that were hidden away somewhere, so I was able to read Nkrumah's autobiography and several writings of a political nature by West Indians. I read also Peter Abrahams: *Wild Conquest* and *Tell Freedom*. There was a book called *Splendid Sunday* I remember, also *Down Second Avenue*, Harry Bloom's *Episode* . . .

You actually started writing poetry, didn't you? I mean, you were well known as a poet before your stories began to appear.
Yes that's right. I was known as a poet, though I also wrote and produced several plays when I was at school. I've been searching for those manuscripts, but I must have lost them. I wrote a lot of plays when I was at school in Swaziland, but basically I wrote a lot of poetry.

How about when you went to university?
I still continued to write poetry, but that is where I started to write fiction. I was fascinated by this book called *We Killed Mangy Dog* by Honwana. Most of my published work deals with the theme of childhood, so when I came across Honwana's collection, particularly the main story, 'We Killed Mangy Dog', I was really fascinated. I edited a magazine called *Expression* from the University of Lesotho, which we sent all over the world to other universities, and I wrote a story for it modelled on 'We Killed Mangy Dog' and from that time onwards – around 1970, 1971 – of course I continued to write poetry, but I became more fascinated by fictional form because it allowed me a lot of room to explore things in a more explicit manner and to examine relationships more

fully between individuals and communities than I ever could with poetry. I felt poetry was somewhat an insulating medium. It begins from the inside and I felt that I needed a form that would prompt me to grapple with objective reality a lot more explicitly. It's always very difficult to talk about why you choose one form rather than another. It's difficult to reduce it to a series of rules. But in general I found that the fictional form helped me more.

It has been said that the short story – like the poem – is popular with South African writers because they need a very immediate mode of expression. This seems to be connected with another commonplace about writing in South Africa: its allegedly 'journalistic' tendency. But much of the writing that comes out of South Africa is also very fine literature. How do you feel about this, and about the short story particularly?
I think there is possibly a more acceptable sociological reason for it. In my view most African writers who write in English had the problem of breaking into the white world. All the established magazines were white-owned. So there was the idea at a certain point that it was unthinkable that a black person could write a novel or a story, hence the growth of writing for newspapers. Judging by the difficulty people like Sol Plaatje had publishing their work, the climate was not acceptable for novel-writing by Blacks, while it was tolerable to accept short pieces. So we go back to Dhlomo who was publishing in *Sjambok* very early in the 1920s right up to the 1930s. Then many people started writing short stories for the newspapers like *The Bantu World*. Then came *Drum* and magazines like *Africa South* and *New Age* and *Zonk* and *Bona*, so the short form became the dominant form.

People who write short stories now write them because other people had been writing them before: it has become a tradition. I think that is the main reason why the short story became so prominent. It has less to do with the feeling that we are too angry so that we don't have time to contemplate the kind of leisure that is required for writing. My major reason is that people who write in African languages for publishing houses controlled by and large by Afrikaners and aimed mostly at the school market were free to write novels, so there are very, very few short stories written in the indigenous languages: people go for novels all the time. And we can't say these people were less bitter than those who wrote in English, or that they suffered less, or that the pressures on them were less. So I feel an explanation in terms of availability of publishing outlets is a much more acceptable reason for the dominance of the short story, at least in English. But the situation is changing now, because again there are publishing houses who are more willing to accept novels. More novels have been produced in the last ten years than from the beginning of the century. I haven't got the figures, but certainly since 1976 novels are beginning to come out more and more. I expect that to continue and I want to make a contribution to it.

You say 'since 1976'. Is 1976 a kind of watershed in the development of South African writing?
Yes. These things tend to be measured by the major political upheavals, but it actually began some time before with the Black Consciousness Movement. One of the things that the Black Consciousness Movement gave expression to was the sense that people must set up their own organizations, their own artists' groups and so on, just as the students had broken away from NUSAS and

formed their own black organization. So there was a flourishing of these all over the country. Attempts were made to organize trade unions, to organize doctors to come together, black social workers, black taxi-owners . . . Even the writers formed various cultural groups within the townships. It was the time of oral poetry: the most famous group was the Medupe cultural group. They used to recite their poems to the background of drums and singing and dancing. There was a lot of that and there was great interest in poetry at the time. So when 1976 shook the world there was already in the townships a cultural base for the expression of the popular political sentiment symbolized by the events of 1976: the structure was already there. A similar thing took place with regard to drama. There was a lot of activity, particularly around the Gibson Kente thing, so when the events of 1976 came they already found a cultural foundation and this simply continued up to today.

Of course this was given even greater impetus by the coming of *Staffrider* magazine. If you look at the early issues you find that the policy was that there was really no editor as such. You had cultural groups all over the country and each group would make its own selection of publishable manuscripts and send them to Ravan Press. It was a very grassroots, mass-based editorial policy. These cultural groups were already in place and *Staffrider* had to give a sort of organized voice to all of them. The thing about *Staffrider* was how it was able to bring together both experienced and new, unknown writers. People like Nadine Gordimer and Sipho Sepamla contributed, as well as some of the unknown voices: that was the fascinating thing about *Staffrider*. So when the novels came – *Amandla*, Sipho Sepamla's, Mbulelo Mzamane's, my own *Fools*, and of course Wally Serote's – I think again they were merely part and parcel of that development whose roots were firmly in place. I would like to regard 1976 as a political expression that merely gave further impetus to what was already in place in less formal ways.

How do the productions of the '70s and the Black Consciousness mood relate to the period immediately preceding it? I'm thinking of the poetry of Brutus and Nortje, for instance, which was presumably unavailable to most people.
That is true; there was a sort of gap. It's true in most cases, though not in mine. There was a big gap and this gap is very unfortunate. It's one of the tragedies of apartheid because people are always re-inventing the wheel. Writing problems that may have been solved forty years ago are still being grappled with because our forebears were not studied in the schools. There was no cultural tradition of criticism and so on. It's always fascinating to read the essays of H. I. E. Dhlomo; suddenly you come across something that was written in the '30s and you think that you just discovered it! You think this is an original idea and you find that somebody thought about it and wrote about it very carefully in the '30s. So there was definitely a big gap and it's going to take a while to bridge it. A concerted effort should be undertaken within the context of the new attempt to come up with an alternative system of education in the townships. But definitely there was a gap and with it I think we come back again to the problems of apartheid.

The poetry of Dennis Brutus and others like him is really the poetry of highly literate people. Much of the poetry that comes out of *Staffrider* is the poetry of people who are not very educated and still have a long way to go in reading and mastering the language, so you can see the gap already even at that level. By and large those who were a lot more educated and aware of the tradition like people like Miriam Tlali, who enjoyed I think a solid education (under the joint matriculation board which was a very demanding matriculation examination – most of the people who have gone through it really had a grilling), so that there again there is the link between education and literary production. So I agree, there was a great gap.

What sort of connections were there between the Black Consciousness Movement and the Afro-American movements?
To my recollection there was very little actual physical contact. There may have been a lot of influence, in the sense that there are similarities between the Black American experience and the South African experience. Most people who were articulate spokesmen of the Black Consciousness movement would have been aware of the writings and the activities of Stokely Carmichael, Bobby Seal, Malcolm X and those people. Most people would have been aware of those things. But it is influence rather than direct contact and not determining in any case.

One of the striking things about much Black South African writing is the confluence of different art forms: the part played by visual arts, graphics and photographs, in the magazines, or the presence in many novels and short stories of music and singing. The impression one derives from all this is of great artistic vitality. I suppose it may come from the jazz experience.
What you're talking about is basically an urban influence, but it's also a very complex urban influence, because within that influence is also a strong folktale tradition which most of us have absorbed, folktale and also the praise poem which is very rhythmical, very repetitive, with various forms of repetition. One of the requirements in the primary school was that we had to memorize one of the praise poems of the big kings. So we knew these things by heart and we could rattle off several stories; the folktale stories we used to tell when we were in the townships too. So that tradition is still there.

Because there is still this interrelationship between town and country?
Yes, but also, in addition to that, there is still this very vibrant oral culture in the townships themselves and it assumes similar forms except that the content will be different. So you find that kind of thing in the novels. I would say it is a reflection of that complex.

To return to your own writing, there is obviously a strong autobiographical element in it, but I imagine this is very much transformed through fiction. What is the relation between autobiography and fiction in your stories?
I have been at great pains to explain this relationship, because what I have taken out of my experience is really the form rather than the content. The fact that the father of the main characters in the stories is a teacher and the mother is a nurse; in one story the children are two, whereas in my family we were actually three: these are little things, but actually it's mainly the quality of experience in a middle-class African family. It is really that rather than the things that actually happen. I'll give you an example. Take the story of 'The Music of the Violin'. We were just talking with some friends and somebody came up with this story of some children in the townships who have middle-class African parents and are harassed by them. It never happened to me, but it fascinated me and I took that up and wrote about it. What writers rightly fear

is that it will be thought that all that happened in the stories is actually there. I think there always is something of the writer's life in whatever he writes, but it's always mediated by other things. So there is a lot that is fiction and as I said the form of experience is autobiographical.

Let me conclude by saying that I think the relation between the two is a necessary one because you have got to inject into your fiction a certain genuineness of experience, otherwise there is a risk of artificiality. So what one goes through, what one feels, what I feel as I go down the streets of Rome and I meet Italians for the first time and I respond to them, I think that the quality of that experience can enable me to write a story set in Rome totally out of my mind, totally coming out of my imagination but yet coming out of my experiences. I think it's an unavoidable relationship.

Perhaps at this point I should pick up on something that you mentioned earlier, but which we didn't go into. You talked about the tendency for South African writers to be accused of reporting. I think that is the crux of the matter: more often than not people do not see the relationship between autobiography and fiction, they do not realize that when you are writing fiction, if you are an artist, there is an inherent element of distortion. It is through that distortion in fact that you get at the reality. I think this reporting problem is related to the tradition that Black South African writers have developed of writing for newspapers and magazines, so that the tendency to be dominated by the medium of the newspaper in which you are reporting things tends to be very great. In addition to that is the fact that some writers have commented on (Lewis Nkosi for instance): that more often than not in South Africa the reality of oppression is more powerful than the words. Some of the things that happen are mind-boggling. The massive movement of people from one part of the country to another and the suffering it entails: bulldozers bringing down houses, policemen setting houses on fire, kicking children. It's the sort of thing that belongs to fiction to a very large extent, so when you actually see it there you are rendered powerless. And at the same time you have got to say something about it, so you end up reproducing it.

Let me give you an example. My last story is called 'Death of a Son' and it was my first attempt to write an overtly political story – in addition to 'Fools', I mean. There is this woman who is a journalist, whose husband is working for a German multinational company. A young couple who are doing very well. Their son – a baby really – is killed by a policeman who was shooting at random as they have been doing in the townships over the past few years. So there is that terrible thing. The policemen, the soldiers, once they discover the body of the child who has been killed, take the body away and it has to be bought back for the burial. So it is that sort of thing. Now things like that happen. But how do you deal with them? I chose to change the focus of emphasis away from the actual death of the child, away from the horror of the seizure of the corpse and its disappearance and the effort to get it back. I moved away from these things to how this horrible event had affected the marriage, the relationship between the man and the woman, how it revealed their weaknesses to them. At the end I tried to bring them together into a much more intimate marriage based on a real knowledge of who they are and what their possibilities are, what their weaknesses are, what their strengths are, so that at the end of it all they come out triumphant rather than totally overcome by the horror, the powerlessness, the politics and so on. Their relationship is reinforced and they are as it were reborn.

It seems to me that we need to take a greater interest in how the spectacle affects the individuals. Politically there is a similar dimension to this matter in that what apartheid has done has been to reduce the capacity of the oppressed to understand the mechanisms of oppression by bombarding them with horror. You look at the horror and your mind is completely preoccupied with it. You do not find time to understand the horror and how it actually comes about. When you see someone being bundled into a police van, this is what absorbs you and not what it is that leads to this man's being bundled into the van; who these policemen are; what it is that is behind them, making the decisions for them to do this; what the connections are between the police and commerce and industry or the connections between politics and commerce. These things are left outside of the spectacle, because the spectacle reduces the capacity of awareness and consciousness. The mind is completely consumed by the horrible drama before us.

Part of the attempt then in 'Fools' and in the other story I was telling you about is to say this thing then is bad, it's horrible, but we've always known it's horrible. The thing to do is to understand how it actually affects us, more and more. In that way we can develop the capacity to deal with it the way it really ought to be dealt with through as inclusive an understanding as possible of all the factors that go into creating it. That I think is the problem essentially with 'reporting' as opposed to producing fiction. It is a difficult thing for most people to understand, but I think most people who try to write suffer from it and are aware of it to various degrees. It's a question of how they can develop the capacity to deal with it.

I have tried in most of the workshops I have had for young writers to get down to this problem because I think it's crucial. In all of them I have spent a lot of time on character development because I think that is the thing in relation to any given incident. We explore the incident in terms of how it affects communities, how it affects relationships between people because that is what we have to understand, a lot more than the spectacle we have witnessed.

Earlier you said that in *Fools* and also in some of your poetry the protagonists were mainly children or adolescents. Why this focus on childhood?
I think it's very difficult to rationalize what one might call an instinctive, imaginative preference. I have always been fascinated by children, by the sufferings of children. I remember one poem that I wrote: I'd just seen a horrible thing, a woman who was totally drunk in a shebeen. The child was trying to get her breast to suckle and she was just lying there . . . There were flies all over the place. It's scenes like these that excite my sense of indignation and, I suppose, compassion. I've seen many: I was just giving you one little example. Later, much later in my life, I was reading Johnson, I think it was, Johnson or Boswell. Somewhere he says you measure the success of a civilization by how it treats its young and its aged. You measure the extent of its sensibilities, its compassion, its values through how it takes care of its weak. And now in South Africa children are actually being detained and tortured. That, for me, more than any other thing indicates the nature of the South African problem, that basically people who are in power have no alternative vision to what is now reproducing itself, beyond what they can control.

I have children of my own and very often you do something or say something to a child and later because they are looking at the world around them they throw it back at you. Maybe they are playing and someone is the father and someone is the mother and there your utterance comes back exactly as you said it and you realize what an oaf you have been. What I have attempted to do therefore is to get this innocent but deeply ironic point of view. The children reflect the adult world exactly as it is without intending to be judgemental on it, yet the fact that they throw it back like that is a drama of recognition. So I wanted to explore this point of view to its fullest: how children's fears interact with the adult world – with the fears of the adult world – and how very often children reflect it back better than any adult ever could. So I was looking for that genuineness of reflection, that innocence. I think it is possibly also a point of view that assists one in coming to terms with the relationship between reportage and fiction. There you have the children saying their bit, throwing the world back exactly as it is but in a way that is devastating in its silent judgements. So there's a moral to it as well as the potential I recognized later on from the point of view of technique, when I felt one could capitalize on this interest in children by turning it into a technical victory. So I think when I look back that that is possibly why my interest in children was so intense. Later on I merely wanted to make greater use of this interest by putting it to good technical ends.

I am now going away from that and writing about adults. The novel I am working on is about a completely adult world and I felt that I needed to do this in order to get away and consolidate my own voice. But my interest still remains. I'm also writing a children's novel, which I hope to complete before the end of this year. I started writing it about two years ago, but I got bogged down with voice again, certain parts were not really well imagined and I needed to give myself more time to let the imagination flow more naturally. So I think my interest in children is an abiding one, I think it will continue to remain for a long, long time, well into the future. This means I may be writing specifically for them as well as engaging in various kinds of social action on their behalf. But I also need to explore other worlds.

You are a founder member of the South African Writers' Congress, how did it start?
It started off about a year or two ago as what was called the Writers' Forum. It was felt that writers in South Africa had to come together from different political persuasions and talk about their problems. It was supposed to be non-political with people coming from different persuasions, but after a period of time people began to feel that the times are too demanding for us to engage in leisurely talk that is seen not to lead to a concrete set of objectives. So it was felt that the Writers' Forum should be turned into a Writers' Association with specified objectives and activities to meet those objectives. Not everybody agreed, but I think the majority of the writers who were consulted felt that we as writers had got to take a definite stand in the light of the broad mass-based democratic movement that is sweeping the country. The organization was subsequently formed after a conference in July this year. About 150 people, representing about 80 different writers' groups came together at that conference, at the end of which we established the Congress of South African Writers.

We recognize the leadership of the mass-based democratic movement in South Africa and want to be part of it and be in a position to assist in the promotion of a free and democratic South Africa. Anyone who shares these goals can join the movement. We also believe that the indigenous languages have to be developed and promoted as far as possible, and that the reproduction of work by writers and artists must be consciously worked at through conferences, workshops and seminars. We want to operate – as far as possible – at grassroots level. We have divided the country into regions and our intention is that in each region there must be several branches, with each branch enjoying a certain amount of autonomy in relation to the regional centre and the region itself enjoying a lot of autonomy in relation to the national body. So that we are really emulating what is already taking place at the political level through the idea of street committees and things of that sort. This is to ensure that as many writers as possible throughout the country at the grassroots level participate. And we also hope to establish links with writers' associations throughout the world whose views are close to ours. That in a nutshell is what the Congress is about.

What is COSAW's position on the cultural boycott?
This is a matter that is currently under review. We feel that we've got to respond to the demands of change as the struggle unfolds. There are cultural groups that have left the country to perform overseas and they have been boycotted because people didn't know who they were. Also, as far as people going to South Africa is concerned, we have worked ourselves into a corner where the people who have a monopoly of expressing their views are ones that the Government generally agrees with, so they come and go without any problems. We feel that if we want Terry Eagleton, say, to come and address academics and writers in South Africa it should be possible for us to have him, without it being felt that he's breaking the boycott. So the whole thing is under review. My feeling is that it will be more flexible, but the fundamental idea still remains. People who are likely to come to South Africa and lend legitimacy to the regime either by word or deed should be discouraged from doing so. So we are looking for a suitable mechanism. I think the cultural boycott should be put in its proper perspective. It's merely a means to an end and is one among many others. Perhaps too much time and too many words should not be spent on it, but for the moment we support the demand that sports people should not come because the Afrikaners do need them, but this doesn't affect genuine scholars who come. I think our future position is likely to be more creative.

Could you explain COSAW's view of the language question?
The Congress's position on this is that to insist that African languages should be left alone because that would mean supporting apartheid is to give in too much to the oppressor. To promote African languages at the same time as the Government is promoting them is to recognize that we are promoting them from two different positions, in the same way as SASO (South African Students' Organization) developed out of the very universities that were established for Blacks only according to the apartheid policy. We feel that a positive attitude should be adopted. Since millions of people speak those languages it should be possible for us to translate a lot of good material, which is not banned in English, to make it available to as many people as possible. It should be possible also to wrest away from the Afrikaner publishing houses the monopoly in the publishing of work in those languages and to encourage the production of mature, progressive writing for adults. Most of what is produced now is for schools and children and is on very restricted and basically very reactionary themes: of people going from the rural areas to the cities and coming back because the city is bad, returning to their own bantustans and

living happily ever after. I think there is a growing recognition that this should be a contested terrain. So it's in the field of publishing, of themes and styles and making the languages alive today in the world of the twentieth century and to encourage writers – against the kind of thing I was talking about earlier on when I described how I was *driven* towards English – to feel equally that they can either write in English or in an African language without their choice being determined by the market possibilities. So I think those are the overriding considerations.

There is an interesting dimension to this which is the role of Afrikaans itself. Our position is that you can't blame people for speaking a language. It's not the language, it's the political role it occupies in society that needs to be altered. There was a very articulate plea from the Western Cape, where you have the so-called Coloureds, for whom this is a mother tongue. I think the future of the Afrikaans tongue is in the hands of this community. There are poems and novels that have been written in Afrikaans challenging the system and carrying the same kind of vision that can be found in good works of art written in English. We want to make it known that this is a recognized aspect of our struggle because of our belief that all the languages of Southern Africa are the heritage of everybody. I think there is an increasingly mature acceptance of that situation. After all it is one of the ways by which we have to demonstrate that in talking about a new South Africa we really mean we are going away totally from the constricted vision of apartheid and that we recognize that every culture in South Africa has the right to project its progressive aspects as a contribution to the overall struggle.

SELECTED BIBLIOGRAPHY

SHORT STORIES
Fools and Other Stories (Johannesburg: Ravan Press, 1983). Winner of the 1984 Noma Award.
'Death of a Son', in *From South Africa, New Writing, Photographs and Art*, ed. David Bunn and Jane Taylor (special number of *Triquarterly*, LXIX, Spring/Summer 1987), pp. 32–40.

ESSAYS
'The rediscovery of the ordinary. Some new writings in South African fiction', *Journal of Southern African Studies*, XII (1986), pp. 143–57.
'Turkish tales and some thoughts on South African Fiction', *Staffrider*, VI, 1 (1984), pp. 24–5, 42–8.
Actors and interpreters: popular culture and progressive formalism (Sol Plaatje Memorial Lecture) (Mafeking: University of Bophuthatswana, 1984), Mimeo.
'The mechanisms of survival', *The Guardian* (12 September 1984), p. 11; *Staffrider*, VI, 2 (1985), pp. 39–40, and elsewhere (Noma Award acceptance speech).
'The English language and social change in South Africa' (keynote address delivered at the Jubilee Conference of the English Academy of Southern Africa, 4–6 September 1986), in *From South Africa, New Writing, Photographs and Art*, ed. David Bunn and Jane Taylor (special number of *Triquarterly*, LXIX, Spring/Summer 1987), pp. 217–35.
'The writers' movement in South Africa', *Research in African Literatures*, XX, 3 (Fall 1989), pp. 412–21.

Essop Patel

Made up of the 'fragmentary', divided images of his country, but also of the 'unbroken music of intimacy' and the universality, openness and freedom of sea and sky, Essop Patel's compositions are 'poetry of human consciousness', created by an author who sees himself ultimately as 'a field-hand who must use his pen to cultivate the colourful world of loving'. The only writer among those interviewed to come from an originally non-African family, Essop Patel is a third-generation South African. He was born in Germiston, Transvaal, in 1943, and educated at Germiston and later at Ladysmith. He then departed for Europe, where he stayed eleven years. After doing a variety of jobs he eventually read for an Honours Law degree. On returning to South Africa Patel was articled to a legal firm in Johannesburg, which he abandoned after a brief spell. He entered into a business venture which proved unsuccessful. Subsequently he read for a postgraduate law degree at the University of the Witwatersrand. Essop Patel is a practising advocate in South Africa and Botswana, currently concentrating on human rights and public interest legal matters besides writing poetry and editing anthologies.

While in London, the author began working on what was to become *The World of Nat Nakasa: selected writing of the late Nat Nakasa* (Johannesburg: Ravan Press and Bateleur Press, 1975), later republished in a new, expanded paperback edition as *The World of Nat Nakasa* (Braamfontein: Ravan Press, 1985). He also edited *The World of Can Themba: selected writing of the late Can Themba* (Braamfontein: Ravan Press, 1985) and *The Return of the Amasi Bird: black South African poetry 1891–1981* (Johannesburg: Ravan Press, 1982), with Tim Couzens, and participated in the preparation of another poetry anthology, *Exiles Within* (Johannesburg: Writers' Forum, 1986). The author has re-edited *When the Scavengers Come*, contemporary short stories by black South African writers, for publication by Longmans UK. He is presently co-editing a collection of post-Soweto short stories and an anthology of Namibian poetry.

12

Essop Patel

The interview took place in London, at SOAS (7 September 1989), during the author's visit to Britain to attend the ACLALS Conference at the University of Kent and to do background research for a poem.

Perhaps we should begin with the beginning . . . Would you rather discuss your 'beginnings' in relation to your poetry or to your life?
I'd rather talk about neither, but let's begin with the latter . . . I was born near a gold-mine dump in Germiston. I was born in a room at the back of my grandfather's shop, since in those days there were no luxuries such as nursing homes for Africans, Coloureds and Indians – the people of colour – so we were born in backyards and hovels. During my childhood I spent many school holidays at my grandparents' home, often on a fig tree by the loo. I also explored the ridges and contours of the gold-mine dumps and I was fascinated by the headlamps of the miners emerging from the darkness of the earth covered in yellow dust.

My father, a congenial soul, inherited a modest shop in Van Reenen, which is on the border of Natal and the Orange Free State, along the Drakensberg mountain range. Van Reenen is a little village set in one of the most scenic parts of South Africa. My paternal grandfather, at the age of thirteen, came to South Africa. He worked in Johannesburg as a dish-washer. After having learned the local languages he graduated as a hawker selling goods on the streets of the Golden City. He returned to India – the return of the prodigal son, I presume – and married my grandmother. She was much older than him. Much later in life he established his own business in Van Reenen which my father inherited. Although my father disliked being a shopkeeper he had no choice, being the only son, but to join his father. My mother is a humble Muslim, a deeply religious but fairly open-minded person. She came to South Africa as a child from one of the farming villages in India: my ancestral roots return to the paddy fields and sugar cane plantations.

My first taste of schooling was in Germiston location. It was a sprawling ghetto of all hues of human beings, popularly known as 'Jamtown'. Later the bulldozers of apartheid dismembered an entire interwoven community and eradicated 'Jamtown' from the face of this earth. I remember the Defiance Campaign march in 'Jamtown'. It was led by the late Patrick Duncan, the son of the first Governor General of South Africa. He was then a member of the Liberal Party but later became the first white member of the Pan-Africanist Congress. Naïve as I was at the tender age of nine I really believed that the Defiance Campaign would overthrow Malan's apartheid regime. But that did not happen. It is not happening yet! What happened was that I was politicized. I became aware that I lived in a divided country and that black people had no rights. Elsewhere a child is socialized at a tender age, but in South Africa a child of colour is politicized whilst he is sucking lollies.

Later I was transferred to Ladysmith to continue with my schooling. Ladysmith was terribly colonial in contrast to 'Jamtown'. My brothers, sisters and I were boarding with my parents' friends. We lived in the midst of the Indian community and every fourth night we went home to Van Reenen. It was in this tiny village that I explored the green, lush hills, cool mountain stream, and collected ferns from the black soil. It made me aware of the splendour and beauty of my country. When I was in high school life became frustrating because one was trapped in a web of apartheid. There was no hope of freedom and I was not immune from racial discrimination. The Whites called us 'Coolies', the Coloureds referred to us as 'Charras' and the Africans called us 'Emakulaas'. Racial abuse is an aspect of South African life. The Indian population is equally guilty of racial abuse. No one is blameless.

I realized that within a year or so I would have no choice but to enrol at an exclusively Indian university college on an island in the Indian Ocean not far from Durban. But I had other ambitions. So I boarded a flight from Johannesburg via Salisbury (Harare), Entebbe, Khartoum, Malta and on to Luxemburg, and eventually arrived in London. For several years I worked in London, from a Wimpy Bar in Norwood to clearing tables at the Dale Cafeteria in Hyde Park; from a wash house in Kennington to a spice factory in London Bridge. Later I worked as a clerk in the City and finally ended up in the foreign exchange of Thomas Cook's in the West End. One day I said 'No, life does not stop here' and began to think of acquiring a degree and possibly one day to return to South Africa. During these formative years in London I saw the windows of the world open and broaden my world view. Although I came from a racially divided country, where colour was (and is) the criterion, I realized that in fact the human race was a single entity.

It was in London I met the late Nat Nakasa. He was *en route* to New York on an exit permit. We met for a cup of tea at the Lyon's Corner House (which used to be just opposite South Africa House). During our conversation he asked 'What happens to a person's writings when he's dead?' I was unable to respond to his rather cryptic question at the time, but after his death I became interested in the man and quite often wondered what actually prompted him to choose exile and why he elected to take his own life. I came upon old editions of *Drum* at the British Museum Library, and more material at the Collingdale Newspaper Library. I compiled a so-called manuscript, with no intention of publishing it but purely for my own interest in finding out about a South African writer who could not return to his country, to his people. I think alienation killed Nat.

When I returned to South Africa, Peter Randall was in the process of establishing Ravan Press. At the time I was looking for some material pertaining to South Africa's oppressive laws. We spoke about the need of an indigenous publication house to promote local literature. A few days later I handed Peter my so-called manuscript of Nakasa's writings. He and Lionel Abrahams agreed to jointly publish *The World of Nat Nakasa*. On reflection I realized that it was not what I really intended, but it was expedient for that particular moment. The subsequent paperback edition, which is also the second impression, is a substantially revised edition. Nat Nakasa was essentially a journalist, but in the archives of the University of Witwatersrand library, of all places, I discovered Nat's one and only short story, 'First Love', which had been submitted to PEN and was rejected. Subsequently I motivated Tim Couzens that we should co-edit a collection of South African black poetry. Many people then believed that black poetry was either in exile or began with Oswald Mtshali's *Cowhide Drum*. We believed that there was a substantial volume of black poetry written in English which had never been anthologized, so . . . Our endeavours resulted in the publication of *The Return of the Amasi Bird*.

When did you first read Nat Nakasa's work?
In the '60s I read Nat Nakasa's pieces in the *Drum* magazine, as well as other bits and pieces. Being at school and being young, journalistic writing wasn't considered serious because we were all living through the same tension and agonies, and it was simply news. But on a later reading of Nat Nakasa I discovered that what he wrote in his satirical and punching style of journalism constituted a historic document. It was a testimony of how people lived and were forced to live. I am one of the firm believers that a substantial volume of South African writing – including drama – has been lost over the years. The publication of *The World of Nat Nakasa* was my humble contribution to rescue a part of South African black literature before it was totally forgotten or lost for ever. When I returned to South Africa I also discovered there was a vast gap between my generation and the writers of the '50s – Eskia Mphahlele, Can Themba and others who had gone into exile and most of them were either listed persons or their works were banned. Simply a few smuggled copies were circulated among those who had some access to banned literature.

Subsequently I also compiled and edited Can Themba's writings. Heinemann had published *The Will To Die*, which I first read in London when it was published. Then I thought, 'Well, it's a good collection', but much later on, re-reading a smuggled copy, I discovered that there were gaps, omissions. Many stories were not included; some of his best journalistic pieces were omitted and odd bits of poetry were left out. So I decided to work towards compiling a comprehensive collection, which was published as *The World of Can Themba*. Don't ask me what's 'the world of' next . . .! Or whose world is next. In between, I kept on writing my own poems.

When did you start writing poetry?
I started writing poetry when I was in London . . .

Not as a child, not while you were at school?
Well, I recollect that I wrote two poems whilst I was at school. One was modelled on William Wordsworth's 'Upon Westminster Bridge' – this was a stylistic effort. It was not a serious effort and it was never published. Whilst at

school I had this desire to write, but growing up in South Africa was a frustrating experience and the creative craft was an indulgence which was not encouraged at school. Being the second eldest in a family of nine and desiring *to get away* from an oppressive society meant that I had to persuade my parents that I wanted to leave home. It was not the easiest task when one came from a conservative community in a divided South Africa. Ultimately I succeeded in *getting out* to discover 'a new world', particularly in London, where I came into close contact with South African exiles and met people from other parts of the world. I also had the opportunity of reading widely, especially reading what I wanted to read and not something I was told to read . . . I started putting pen to paper in London. If you look closely at *The Bullet and the Bronze Lady* you will find some of the poems were written in London. When I returned to South Africa I also discovered the development of the whole Black Consciousness Movement, spearheaded by Steve Biko.

When did you return exactly?
In '73. They started in '68 – the Movement lasted roughly from '68 to '76–7, so I think I was midway. I had not read what Steve Biko and others were writing, but I soon discovered that my thinking on Black Consciousness went beyond theirs for the simple reason that I had had the advantage of reading widely and *freely* Black Consciousness literature from the United States and Obi Egbuna, the Nigerian writer who wrote *Destroy This Temple* which was published here. One of the thoughts that I had about Black Consciousness was that once you have discovered your identity and once you have become assertive, where does one go psychologically and politically? Once I have discovered myself – discovered my identity as a human being, no longer as non-White or non-European – and once I have acknowledged my humanity and am capable of asserting my being then I must move beyond colour, race, creed, gender, etc. by elevating my consciousness to a *higher level* because as a 'black' person I do not operate *in vacuo* but I act and interact with other human beings whatever their colour, creed, etc. may be. Once I have discovered my humanity and acknowledged your humanity, then obviously we must raise ourselves to the level of *human consciousness* and at that point race, colour, creed and gender etc. become insignificant non-issues. At this point of time in our history I think that Black Consciousness as an ideological weapon has served its purpose in South Africa and it is really time to move on to the planes of *human consciousness*. One should not be 'shackled' by Black Consciousness because it is not an all-embracing and an all-time ideology. What one should do is to use it as a stepping stone. Once you have discovered yourself you ought to go beyond that to the level of *human consciousness* because one has a further duty to liberate the die-hard racist, if that is ever possible.

This brings me to the point of my Hannetjie poems. They are satirical; they are a dig at the Afrikaner, who is trapped in a white cage. The one thing about the Afrikaners is that they have a reasonably good sense of humour and they have the capacity to laugh at themselves. I was rather surprised when two Honours students at the Rand Afrikaans University elected to comment on the Hannetjie poems.

When did you first think up Hannetjie – or perhaps meet her?
Many people believe there is a real Hannetjie. But I must confess she is a poetic conception. I will tell you what triggered the conception of Hannetjie. My

cousin clandestinely married an Afrikaner lass. Ah! In local jingoism a coolie married to a Boer – an Indian married to a white woman – this was heresy! It was before the repeal of the Mixed Marriages prohibitions and the Immorality Act. The former prohibited inter-racial marriages and the latter criminalized sexual liaisons across the colour line. Not to attract the attention of the police he set up his love nest across the road from the Hillbrow Police Station! On one occasion my cousin and his Afrikaner wife came to the office together with a very naïve Afrikaner lass. We had an office in the predominantly Indian suburb of Fordsburg in Johannesburg, and their sheer presence must have raised eyebrows and perhaps set many a tongue on a wild gossip along the juicy grape vine. Downstairs there was an Indian café, typically called the Taj Mahal. Somebody in the office ordered some samosas for tea (samosas in South Africa are often referred to as the *'Driehoek koelie koek'*: *Driehoek* simply means three corners; *koelie* is the derogatory epithet for Indians; *koek* is just cake). Well, this Afrikaner lass sat there consuming hot and spicy Indian delights. It certainly brought a shade of redness to her erstwhile pale complexion. She was such a simple person that she really believed – having been brought up in the confines of an Afrikaner community – that all other racial groups including Indians were inferior beings. Her naïvety, her simple-mindedness not only fascinated me but astounded me. Here was a white matriculant on the threshold of university admission who believed that Neil Armstrong's lunar landing was a Russian conspiracy simply to subvert wholesome Christian dogma and that television was the devil incarnate. Here was an Afrikaner enjoying every bit of Indian delicacy and yet firmly believing that she could not bear the thought of having an Indian neighbour. The irony was that her best friend was secretly married to an Indian.

Then I asked her what did her father do. She said that he worked on the railways. So in one of my poems I exploited that mentality by referring to Hannetjie's *'spoorweg mentality'* – meaning railway lines mentality. I realized that here I had discovered a creature, a human being who represented Afrikanerdom in all its bigoted manifestations. I feel sorry for the Afrikaner youth because their future will be relegated to shame. They will for ever be insecure if there are no psychological transformations in South Africa – what a pity!

About this time Vorster was expounding the policy of 'détente' with selected African states, but there was no 'détente' between Blacks and Whites in the country. My first poem in the Hannetjie series was 'Hannetjie goes to a party', where she was conceived and conceptualized as a human being. Stephen Gray reproduced three Hannetjie poems from *They Came at Dawn* in his anthology of modern South African poetry. From time to time Benjy Francis, the director of Afrika Cultural Centre, has nagged me to script a stage play around the character of Hannetjie. I wish I had time to undertake such an assignment.

Hannetjie relaxed while she was put away with some moth balls. She emerged when the new constitutional dispensation conceived the tricameral parliament consisting of the House of Assembly for the Whites, the House of Representatives for the Coloureds and the House of Delegates for the Indians. The Africans were left 'houseless'. The so-called Indian House of Delegates is an ongoing circus with some very comical characters who are supposed to be honourable members of parliament. The level of debate in the 'House of D' is incredibly puerile. The first so-called Prime Minister of the Indian community, a one-time Latin master, has a record of shady dealings which were the subject of an enquiry by the James Commission. This chamber of duds has provided theatrical material for Seira Essa's play *The James Commission*. Out of this milieu I conceived the liaison between Hannetjie and the Rajah.

The 'Hannetjie-et-Rajah' poems are not only a satirical exposure of political collaboration between the government and the sell-outs but also an attack on the short-sightedness of a very small minority not only within the Indian community but also the Coloured community and some Africans who are willing to work with the apartheid regime for their personal gains and benefits.

I have recently considered turning Hannetjie into a braless, briefless radical and possibly later a revolutionary. But for now she is plotting somewhere in my recesses. Eventually I am hoping to give Hannetjie the ultimate identity of a South African. In the process of political and social changes, the Afrikaner who has travelled along the *spoorweg* must finally cross the junction of liberation. That is when Hannetjie will possibly liberate herself from the shackles of her upbringing.

How does her language come into this?
I am interested in the development of the English language and fascinated by regional patois. South Africa is a large country and across the land patois varies from region to region. Let us take Indians. The highest concentration of Indians in South Africa is in the so-called 'samosa triangle' of Natal which is the area bounded by Durban, Pietermaritzburg and Stanger. Most of them are great grandchildren of the Indian indentured labourers who were brought to work on the sugar plantations by the British. They have virtually developed a patois of their own. Those of us who live in the hinterland find it difficult to comprehend the patois of the coastal Indians which is coupled with a peculiar accent. The Indians in the Transvaal have a different patois which is consistent with the general patois in the province and it is shared with the Coloureds and Africans as well as the Whites. When you move down to the Western Cape . . . there is a melodious patois, it has a fantastic rhythmic lilt. Alex La Guma and James Matthews have successfully captured it in their writings.

Farouk Asvat, Mafika Gwala, Achmat Dangor, Sipho Sepamla and myself are contemporary patois poets. Our use of patois varies according to our style and regional associations. I have essentially experimented in patois, with the intent of developing the English language through its 'creolization' or 'hybridization'.

How about Adam Small? Do you consider him part of all this?
Adam Small writes in the patois of the Coloured community of the Cape peninsula. His language is predominantly Afrikaans, peppered with a certain amount of English diction flavoured by local usage. Small is essentially an Afrikaans writer using an Afrikaans-based patois whilst we are essentially English writers doing the same but from a different vantage point. Ours is English-structured patois. Adam Small is recognized for having successfully captured the Afrikaans patois of the Coloured people. His writing became acceptable whereas some of us have been criticized for experimenting with language. Our objective is to make poetry alive by developing the patois.

It is rather interesting that South Africa is such a blinkered country that even in its development of literature until recently the traditionalist believed that good literature is literature written in the traditional mould. Some believe it must be developed within the Eurocentric tradition. My argument is that we are living in a multi-cultural and multi-language society where a variety of nuances have a bearing upon the development of a South African English. The majority of the Blacks as well as Whites have elected to articulate their aspirations in the English language. It would be rather artificial for red-blooded South African, Black or White, to vocalise himself or herself in the blue-blooded Queen's English. I have chosen to experiment with the English language that comes from the grassroots.

I believe that the English language is enriched by the diversity of the people of the Third World. It is no longer an insular language but a universal one. Modern English is essentially an English of cross-cultural pollination. In recent years in South Africa there has been some degree of acceptance not only of the development but also the experimentation of patois in literature. The usage of patois in South Africa can be traced back to Andrew Geddes Bain's *Kaitje Kekkelbek*, or *Life among the Hottentots* and Frederic Brooks' *Nature's Logic, or Isaak van Batavia's Plea for his Manhood – a True Story* in the 1820s. Writing in any patois certainly demands mastery of the craft of poetry and a profound knowledge of the language. It is essential to write poetry of excellence be it in patois or otherwise. Excellent poetry demands creative hard labour and thought, if not it slips into writing slogans – that is dangerous.

Structurally, there seems to be a progression from *They Came at Dawn*, which is a collection of poems, to *The Bullet and the Bronze Lady*, which is divided into five distinct sections. But some very early poems are also included in the second collection . . .

These poems are very personal and very private and I deliberately omitted them from previous collections. When I was much younger I felt that they would not have any meaning for the public. On second thought I realized that generally people have shared experiences and therefore I included them in *The Bullet and the Bronze Lady*. The first volume *They Came at Dawn* was a deliberately selected collection at a particular time from a whole lot of poems which I'd written over a period of time. Some of these poems were read on various occasions. Professor Zeke Mphahlele read them and advised me how to compile a balanced volume. Benjy Francis of the Afrika Cultural Centre introduced my poetry to James Matthews of BLAC Publication House. James indicated his interest in publishing a volume of my poems which lead to the publishing of this first volume.

By then some of my poems were already published in *The Classic, New Classic, Staffrider, Ophir* and some of the major anthologies of South African poetry, and from time to time I was preoccupied in writing and re-writing the 'fragments'. At this time, Ramadaan Suliman, an actor at the Afrika Cultural Centre, regularly visited me on Fridays for lunch. Whilst browsing around he discovered the 'fragments' on my desk and requested that I permit him to read it. After a week or so he suggested that the Centre could workshop a performance around the 'fragments' and that I should consider consenting to such a project. I agreed. The manuscript of the 'fragments' was passed on to Bhekizizwe Peterson, who is now a lecturer at Wits. Bheki produced the first performance script which was then conveyed to Benjy Francis for workshopping with a group of actors. It was at one of the workshops that Bheki, Benjy and myself produced the final performance script. About the same time the Afrika Cultural Centre was invited to the Third World and Radical Book Fair in London to stage one of their productions. They decided to stage 'The Mountain of Volcano'. To back the stage performance the Centre decided to publish the performance script. I suggested that they should include the poems in the publication. So we inserted all the 'fragments' including some of my earlier poems, for example 'Take My Bruised Hand, My Dark Rose', which is a very old poem. The Afrika Cultural Centre published 'Fragments in the Sun' with the performance script of 'The Mountain of Volcano'. It was performed here in London, in Birmingham and other venues in this country, as well as at the Market Theatre in Johannesburg. The volume was published during the first state of emergency and in some quarters it was regarded as 'subversive'. Therefore it was not widely circulated inside South Africa. I have considered submitting it to an overseas publisher, perhaps in Africa or in this country.

Why do you call them fragments?
For two reasons: firstly they constitute a variety of fragmented images of different aspects from South African life, from destruction of communities to homelessness; from bannings and incarcerations to deaths in detention, etc. . . . Secondly they reflect divergent and different intensities of South African reality: anger, bitterness, hope, passion, love . . . After having written all the fragments, I then inserted a final piece of hope – an epilogue so to say – the 'New Dawn'. It pre-empts the beginning of another poem. The 'New Dawn' does not only enlighten the present but also casts a glance into the historical past and provides a glimpse into the future.

I'm interested in the titles of your collections. Could you discuss them briefly?
Let's begin with *They Came at Dawn*. The title of this collection is from a poem to Don Mattera. In South Africa when one is raided it is seldom during the day. It happens between one minute past zero hour and the early hours of twilight. So it was simply that they came in the early hours of the morning. Presumably they feel that during that hour one is least receptive and they can obtain the necessary information or evidence when one has just tumbled out of bed at the unexpected knock. One neither has the time nor the opportunity to conceal prohibited or banned objects or escape from the intruders since one is unprepared for such an unexpected invasion of one's privacy.

Fragments in the Sun: the refrain 'in the sun' is certainly South Africa. 'In the sun' the stark reality of South African life and living is nakedly exposed. For example, you can drive through one part of Johannesburg where you will see the most beautiful houses with lush green gardens and crystal clear swimming pools and then proceed a few kilometres – 'in the sun' – and you will observe a sprawling shanty community living in the most inhumane and degrading conditions. Always, 'in the sun' you can see this contrast. But when darkness enfolds over South Africa it hides the sharp contrasts of the haves and have-nots under the starry sky. But then again under the cover of darkness we conspire, plan, prepare and agitate the coming of the 'dawn'. Earlier you asked why 'fragments': simply because most of these poems come as fragmentary images.

The title of *The Bullet and the Bronze Lady* is derived from the conjugation of two poems: the one is 'Bullet' and the other is 'Bronze Lady'.

'Bullet' is a poem that primarily deals with the weapon of death. The irony is that South Africa is one of the richest countries as far as mineral wealth is concerned, but it still has the need to produce and stockpile an arsenal of armoury to kill. Yes, indeed, other countries also find the need to produce nuclear weapons not only to destroy others but possibly for their own self-destruction. Perhaps it is not so ironical that South Africa is the largest bullet in the arsenal of the Western world. It has been effectively used to destabilize the front-line states and to perpetuate the oppression of the Blacks so that the Western world continues to enjoy the glittering returns from their investments in South Africa.

Then quite often I have wondered what would happen to the armament industry around the world if people ceased to make bullets. Certainly people must have an incredibly perverted psychology to create armament knowing that it is to be used for killing others. 'Bullet' is my anti-nuclear armament poem also, against trigger-happy people as well as against the lunatic gunmen walking around in Dallas or in Pretoria. I do not know whether that makes me a pacifist in the typical British sense – a subscriber to the peace pledge movement or a CND supporter – perhaps it does, but then I think we have a beautiful world around us and we need to save it from destruction.

The 'Bronze Lady' . . . Do you really want to know what triggered this poem? The 'Bullet' is basically my political protest poem. 'Bronze Lady' is primarily a social comment on the destructive aspects of inter-personal relations . . . I have written another bronze lady poem which is in *They Came at Dawn*, it is the 'Bronze Lady of Vrededorp'. Perhaps you are wondering why the colour bronze? Let me tell you that in this world the hue of human shades varies from white to black and within that spectrum there are beautiful complexions. I believe one day there will be a proliferation, a fusion of those human shades and it is going to be part of the real solution to the complex racial problems. Alas! An Optimist!

Psychologically people of South Africa in the new dawn ought to be 'bronze' people. That does not necessarily imply a common pigmentation. There has been a political phobia – largely based upon indoctrination and disinformation – that when liberation comes the white man is going to be dumped in the sea, the Indians jettisoned back to the sub-continent of India, the Coloured people, not knowing where to go, will aimlessly meander possibly in the Karoo and the Blacks will end up dismembering the beautiful landscape of South Africa according to their ethnic affiliations. This is the greatest lie perpetrated by the advocates of apartheid. For the sake of humanity that falsehood has to be relegated to the garbage can. In fact it is incumbent upon us to harmonize our lives in such a manner that in the post-apartheid South Africa the colour 'bronze' ought to symbolize unity in nationhood and diversity in thought. It is also the image of my hope of what I perceive will make racial discrimination a totally irrelevant issue because in post-apartheid South Africa people will be people.

But the 'Bronze Lady' – the poem – is about social oppression. In the volume it follows a poem titled 'On a Wednesday' which deals with divorces: at a certain point in my professional career I was briefed literally with hundreds of divorce suits. Quite often I found myself at a problematic crossroads realizing that I was dealing with a human being whose private life has ruptured and whose interrelationship with another has reached the edge of a desperate precipice. There was I, an advocate, unsympathetically leading evidence of some very personal and private aspects of a person's life in a public chamber. Formally the marital relationship is simply dissolved by a decree of divorce. But after that one steps out into the sunshine, out of the sombre wooden panelled court room. At that moment one need not even say 'Good luck for the future'.

The advocate returns to his chambers and the latest divorcee simply gets lost in a stream of pedestrians. The tragedy is that we invariably overlook the fact that we are dealing with a human being who is in need of compassion beyond that decree of divorce.

Once there was a person who simply wanted to talk, talk about her suffering, about her agonies, about her pain. She spoke and the poem 'Bronze Lady' is a biography of that person. Most of the people whose divorces I have handled came from the Coloured community, there have been very few Indians or Africans and possibly no more than three or four white persons. The colour bronze also personifies a person of the Coloured community. A divorcee quite often returns to the ghetto of hopelessness with little future and perhaps a loveless predicament. In some cases the divorcee is victimized by his/her family, in other cases rejected by friends, and most of them end up leading very, very lonely lives. They have no family support systems to restore their well-being. I ask myself the question: 'Are we so careless that we can treat human beings in terms of legal cases, see them through their pleadings and then at the end of it all we mark our briefs with a fee and return to our abodes without ever thinking about the social predicaments of others?' But here was somebody who just wanted to talk. She was like Coleridge's Ancient Mariner and I was the Wedding Guest so I had to listen to her story of pain and suffering. I hope that at the end of it she felt somewhat rescued. Perhaps by simply talking in her moment of utter loneliness she may have felt consoled.

We are so concerned about the political situation that quite often we forget or simply overlook the social dilemmas and predicaments of others who have to endure pain, loneliness, etc., etc. I wanted this collection to be broad . . . beyond politics. I also wished to extricate myself from the 'enforced' tag of being just a protest poet. I hope this collection proved that I am capable of writing social poetry and even love poems. It is not enough just simply being a protest poet. I think those of us who have been labelled 'protest poets' have served our relevant purposes at a certain point in history and it is time for others to do their protest bit. I believe that there must also be some universal relevance to our poetry. Hopefully 'Bronze Lady' is one of those poems which would be relevant, maybe some woman suffering utter loneliness in the United States or South America or India could identify with it. I hope so. Certainly I firmly believe that our struggle is no smaller and no greater than that of the Palestinians or the people in Nicaragua. And for that reason I wrote poems like 'Sister of Dawn' and 'Sand in the Eleventh Hour Glass': these are all-embracing Third World poems I hope, although poetically somewhat optimistic at the end . . .

A lot of your poetry is optimistic at the end, isn't it?
I believe in hope! I find myself in a ghetto of pessimism and I have to live there . . . So I survive by hoping. I don't subscribe to the fallacy that we can achieve nothing until somebody gives it to us on a platter. Part of the struggle is that there is hope. If it is possible I'd like to bring the people of the world closer together through my poetry. Whether I achieve that or not, that's another matter, but it is worth the effort.

How about the subtitles?
The first group are political poems but to some these are 'protest poems'. I detest the label 'protest poetry' because I don't write protest poems. I write

about a particular historical and political moment. So the 'Song of the River' is the ever-flowing and ever-changing political situation. At no point of time is anything static. There's a current, there is a counter current and another current and that signifies that wherever the song is you're going to have a sad song, you're going to have perhaps a folk song or a love song and possibly even a happy song . . .

'Poetic Miscarriage' deals with the series of patois poetry. I've questioned myself about this. Am I not merely misusing poetic licence? The expression 'poetic miscarriage' actually appears in a prose poem on 'Hannetjie's poetic miscarriage'. Hence the miscarriage. But then I've also realized more recently that it exists not only in South Africa or the Caribbean but even in England – leaving aside for a moment the black or Asian British or English writings, but let's go back to the Cockney jungle: that is where you could develop really indigenous patois in English literature. Good examples would be Bill Norton's *Alfie*, and Nell Dunn's *Up the Junction*; then we have the movement of Beat poetry from the Liverpudlian poets. I'm fascinated by this whole area of patois literature in the English world, not only in South Africa but elsewhere. I don't believe any longer that it's poetic miscarriage. Perhaps it's a poetic *carriage*, drawing the English language further towards universality.

'Scream Silently': these words appear in 'Bronze Lady' and are used as a sub-title here. That section of poems deals with lives of people like in 'Lunch Hour Poem', or situations, like 'Desecrated on a Street Corner', which is about rape. Quite often we are really negative and callous. When somebody's screaming we don't hear it and that scream itself becomes doubly silent: to the screamer and to the person who turns a deaf ear.

'En Route' are poems from outside South Africa. They may be poems written from my travels, my observations outside my country. I had an experience whilst flying from Karachi to Teheran – this was before the Ayatollah's days – and looking down I saw the Baluchistan desert: part of it is in Pakistan and the other portion is in Iran. On the map you see a neat dotted line dividing the desert between two countries, but from the sky there's no division: it's man who has created his own divisions unfortunately.

The 'Crucible of Darkness' are subtle love poems. So I suppose that will convey that I'm not just a political creature; I hope so.

That comes through in all three collections, doesn't it? Perhaps particularly through the presence of the sea, which dominates this last section of *The Bullet and the Bronze Lady*, but is also present in your earlier work.
I'm fascinated by the imagery of the sea, the sky . . . I have an explanation for this. The only canopy, the universal canopy above all of us is the sky. Nobody can see geographical divisions above us; we cannot say this is the South African sky or this is the British sky . . . If you get onto a raft or on a boat you simply say there is the sky; it belongs to all of us. But people are selfish so they say this is *my* country or this is *my* land. I have the strong desire to see mankind as one. When I meet people they always say 'You're an Indian; where do you come from?' I say 'I'm human and I come from South Africa.' Recently I read a poem by the Russian poet, Yevtushenko. He makes a profound statement: 'I'm a racist.' Say that and someone is likely to hit you over the head, but in the next line Yevtushenko explains that his race is the human race, and I consider that to be a superbly provocative statement. So we don't have to pander to nationalities and nations. We can create cross-cultural acceptance of the human race,

exchange our ideas and ideals. The sea . . . it has its own sense of freedom. Being in the South African predicament I suppose I need a sense of freedom of movement and freedom of expression.

You were talking about barriers: avoiding barriers, breaking down barriers, not seeing barriers. This preoccupation is apparent throughout your poetry, in the way, for instance, natural imagery seems to slide into a human situation or into a social situation and back again, sounds slip into other sounds and words into similar sounding words, sight into sound and vice versa. I want to ask you about the presence of visual art in your poetry.

First let me give you a very trivial answer: perhaps I should never have been a lawyer, perhaps I should have been a writer, possibly, full-time and a painter part-time! I think the real answer is that through art we can advance the horizons of people and through art form we can communicate messages. I remember being in Palestine when I saw a painting by Salman Mansur, 'Carry On'. An old man walking through the old city of Jerusalem carrying Al'Aqsa mosque on his shoulders. Salman Mansur is Muslim. Jerusalem is the city where Christ was crucified. When I first saw the painting I perceived that the old man seemed to be carrying the weight of our burdens through life. I lived in Jerusalem in the Palestinian quarters, on the Mount of Olives. With my wife and sons we walked down the hill to go to the old city. One of the things that struck me was 'Am I not walking along the same path trodden by Christ?' I went back to look at the painting again and the old man who is portrayed as a Muslim carrying Al'Aqsa which is the third holiest Muslim mosque. If you peel the metaphorical layer off the painting, you will see that it's not only the old man carrying Al'Aqsa but Christ carrying the cross, women carrying the burden of their children, the fisherman in Smithfield Market carrying his fish. It's something that came through very strongly and vividly in a flash. A friend commented that perhaps I also attempted to superimpose the imagery of Christ carrying the cross in my poem 'Carrying Al'Aqsa'. And the Arabic word *samid* means 'steadfast' or 'hold on'. Perhaps we all need to hold on . . .

The other poem is 'Gathering Crimson Lilies'. You walk into London's art galleries and somebody is there admiring a painting and you stand a few paces behind that person. Suddenly in a flash you observe the person standing in front of the painting is superimposed and submerged onto the painting. The person is fused into the painting. The person is part of the painting.

While in Britain you have been researching into old collections of San writing and into the history of the Malay slaves. What was this for?

It's a new poem that I'm working on which goes back into South African history. I start with the Khoi and the San people and the arrival of the Dutch settlers and the bringing of the slaves. The poem works at three levels: three time frames are juxtaposed so that the past, the present and the future are fused together. It's a surreal poem. Let me give you an example – the arrival of a young pioneering settler onto the South African soil. His entourage is welcomed by certain modern-day characters of contemporary history: Malan, Vorster, Botha . . . So different historical figures from the past and present meet at a single point in time. I'm also introducing Khoisan language into the poem. One part of the poem resembles a newspaper page from a *Khoisan Chronicle* or maybe a *Khoisan Guardian*. It is written in newspaper columns and gives news about the Khoisan National Congress which is summoning a rally against the arrival of the settler dictators!

I am engaged in a poetic experiment. Basically the idea is to have the poem in four parts: first the Cape Town piece: the Khoisan country; the arrival of the Dutch settlers; the introduction of slaves who became known as the Malays, but should correctly be called the Cape Muslims. In the Cape Archives the records of the slaves indicate that most of them came from the Malabar coast of India or from the Bay of Bengal region. Very few came from the Malaysian archipelago. The next part deals with the English and the Zulus and the introduction of indented Indians in Durban. The third deals with the Transvaal: the discovery of gold, the scramble for it by the Europeans and through that a series of confrontations between the Boers and the English. The fourth is much more contemporary. It is paradoxically set in Bloemfontein, in the traditional Afrikaner heartland. It was in the very same city that the African National Congress was inaugurated. The focal point of the rebel and the rebellion, the oppressor, the oppressed and the oppression is centralized. At this stage these are ideas, but ultimately the four parts of the poem must form a South African tapestry.

Will you provide a glossary?
One of the considerations regarding the new poem throbbing in my recesses is that it will not only have a glossary, but explanatory notes relevant to history. It's a new experimentation in South African poetry.

Is this going to be your version of the collective epic you say is constituted by the poems of *Return of the Amasi Bird?*
At this stage I haven't decided whether it's going to be epic . . . It's not, certainly, going to be *fragments*. It's intended to be a series of poems which will link up relatively easily. Whether I write it as one single poem or in four parts with one title will depend on the development of the poem as a whole. But it's hard labour, because I am actually having to do research not only into history but into geography and into language development in South Africa. There isn't very much research on regional language development. So I have to listen to people, walking around with a tape recorder on street corners and recording their conversations. But the difficulty is to attempt to transcribe people's patois with the correct diction.

I gather you're preparing a new edition of *The Return of the Amasi Bird?*
No, it's not a new edition of *Return of the Amasi Bird*. We are waiting until 1991 when we will perhaps amplify the collection by including poems from this decade. What I'm preparing, hopefully for external publication, is an anthology of approximately twenty poets who've emerged over the last two decades in South Africa and have made an impact, some more than others. One of these is Peter Horn who is a lecturer at the University of Cape Town.

Would you say there have been many changes in the kind of poetry that has been developing recently?
You can talk about the development of poetry at three levels in South Africa. One I would call internalized poetry, what a writer writes about himself, or about things like the giraffe and cities: very personalized, internalized poems.
Then there's the externalized poetry which is poetry of consciousness, social, political and human consciousness, and is often labelled as 'protest poetry'. A fairer term would be political poetry, but I think even that is not so fair. It is poetry that intends to carry a message, though. From that group of poets one or

two are making the effort to make their poems more universal rather than parochial. What we need to do is to look at our poetry again; review it critically, objectively, and ask ourselves the question: are we making a contribution to Third World literature or are we just making a contribution to South African poetry? I would like to be part of the former, to go beyond the borders of South Africa. The greatest thing about literature is that it defies borders. It's like my sea and the sky: no borders, no divisions.

Then there's the fresh developing poetry in South Africa: emerging, aspiring young poets, young writers, even short-story writers . . . It's a new generation. They are confronted by new political challenges and they complement the history of this present period to a certain extent. To that group also belongs the emergence of more women writers which is a healthy contribution to the development of South African literature as a whole. Two people I can immediately think of are Ingrid de Koch – she's just had her first collection published – and Mavis Smallburger, though very little of her work has been published other than in local anthologies, broadsheets and small magazines. Ah! There is another, Gcina Mhlope. She's an actress, but she's written some very fine poems as well.

Then there is 'worker poetry' and we also need to look at oral or voice poetry. So we're beginning to see new developments in South Africa. We're not in a static situation politically or poetically. There are fresh challenges ahead of us in the development of truly South African poetry. Our literature has been compartmentalized into black South African literature and South African literature, which refers to the white writers' contribution. It is an unfortunate division and for this the blame largely rests on the academics. The thrust and ethos should be towards a national literature – but we are on our way towards that goal.

SELECTED BIBLIOGRAPHY

POETRY
They Came at Dawn (Athlone: BLAC Publishing House, 1980).
Fragments in the Sun (Johannesburg, Afrika Cultural Centre, 1985). Received an Honourable Mention at the 1986 Noma Award. Also contains the performance text 'Mountain of Volcano' created by Essop Patel, Bhekizizwe Peterson and Benjy Francis from an assemblage of published and unpublished poems. 'Mountain of Volcano' was first presented at the International Book Fair of Radical Black and Third World Books in London, 1985.
The Bullet and the Bronze Lady (Johannesburg: Skotaville, 1987).

ESSAYS
'Towards revolutionary poetry', in *Momentum. On Recent South African Writing*, ed. M. J. Daymond, J. U. Jacobs and Margaret Lenta (Pietermaritzburg: University of Natal Press, 1984) pp. 83–8.
'The historical role of poetry in the South African liberation struggle', *Genève Afrique*, XXVII, 2 (1989), pp. 91–8; also in *Crisis and Conflict. Essays on Southern African Literature*, ed. Geoffrey V. Davies, II (Essen: Verlag Die Blanc Eule, 1990), pp. 247–59.
'Mongane Wally Serote: poet of revolution', *Third World Quarterly*, XII, 1 (January 1990), pp. 187–93.

Mongane Wally Serote

One of South Africa's greatest poets, Mongane Wally Serote was born in Sophiatown in 1944, from which he and his family soon moved to the Johannesburg township of Alexandra, where he attended primary school. After one and a half years at the Sacred Heart College of Leribe, Lesotho, he returned to South Africa and was admitted to Alexandra Secondary School and then went to Morris Isaacson High School in Soweto. After finishing his schooling, he worked as a reporter on one of Johannesburg's popular newspapers and later as copywriter for an advertising firm. He participated in the activities of one of the many theatre groups that sprang up in the early '70s in the wake of the Black Consciousness Movement, and worked in the SASO (South African Students' Organization) Publications Unit. Arrested in June 1969 under the Terrorism Act, Serote spent nine months in solitary confinement before being released without charges. In 1974 he obtained a passport and left for the USA with a Fulbright scholarship. Here he completed a Fine Arts degree at the University of Columbia, participated in the inaugural conference of the African Literature Association of America at the University of Texas at Austin and toured the USA under the auspices of the African Studies Center of Boston University. In 1977 he settled in Gaborone, Botswana, where he collaborated in the activities of the Medu Arts Ensemble and the Pelandaba Cultural Effort (Pelculef). Since 1986, he has been living in exile in the UK, attached to the ANC offices in London.

Known mainly for his poems, which have been widely anthologized, as well as appearing in separate volumes, Serote is also the author of a novel and of several short stories, three of which appeared in 1971 in *The Classic* ('When Rebecca Fell', 'Fogitall' and 'Lets Wander Together'), while 'The Meeting', a story 'filled with smoke from burning tyres', appeared in a recent number of *Arekopaneng Journal*, I, 3 (1989), pp. 9–12.

13

Mongane Wally Serote

The interviews were held in London in July 1986 and September 1988. Parts of an early version of the first interview appeared in Index of Censorship, *XVII, 5 (May 1988), pp. 104–6.*

Could you tell me about your childhood?
I was born in Sophiatown, in 1944. About four years after that we moved to Alexandra, and I went to school near Alexandra and also in Lesotho, Soweto and the US. Eventually I did what they call a Master of Fine Arts in the US. I started writing I think when I was about fourteen. I must say that at that point it wasn't as serious as now. Why I started writing at that age was that I was reading a lot and – I don't know if this is using hindsight or what – but when one reads a lot and one comes from Alexandra you realize that most of the things you read don't have anything to do with the life you lead. At this stage I really felt that I could write about my life as I knew it. I started writing in the form of thrillers, I'm sure because reading for me was based on anything I came across and most of it, besides what we were doing at school, was thrillers and things like that. But then I stopped because at school where I was in Lesotho they told me I was wasting my time . . . Subsequently, for some reason or other, I don't know why, I started writing poetry – if one can call it poetry at that point: I don't know what I was writing, but it was what I thought was poetry.

What exactly were you reading? What were you reading at school and what were you reading at home?
At school we were reading English literature, Dickens and Shakespeare, Lawrence, Thomas Hardy, Wordsworth, Keats . . . In a sense it's not completely true to say what I was reading didn't have anything to do with the way I was living, but in another sense it is true. For instance, if you read *A Tale of*

Two Cities . . . I identify a lot with it, but at the back of your mind throughout is that you are reading about white people and that distances you from it. You share and sympathize with what you read, but you become very conscious that it doesn't describe your dilemma. White South Africans have defined the colour white as a means to exclude all that is not white to the outside of human life. Although we are trapped in this definition as Blacks, we do not accept it. This is the experience I carry when I read literature by Whites who are not South African. At one end, the detail of white life anywhere can be a point of reference for me as a human being. At another, since nothing around me says anything about human beings, but how to fight to become human, at best white normal life can inspire me to fight for freedom, at worst, it can inspire me to vitriolic bitterness and hatred. Afro-American literature or even other African literature expresses what is unique about either's life experience. There is a collective experience of South Africa that nothing has been said about. So other literature helps me to know how I am going to translate or transform people's lives into a book. But then – and I think this is true of all countries – *you* have the responsibility of searching for what it is that makes South Africans South Africans. How this experience contributes to the human experience, and how human experience contributes to it being human.

Could you tell me something more about your family background and your childhood?
Compared to many people in Alexandra, I came from a well-to-do family. My mother was a nurse, my father a mechanic, although I spent more time with my grandmother than with my parents. We were a very large family. Two of us are in exile . . .

You started working in journalism after leaving school, didn't you? Could you tell me something about that experience?
I worked really as a 'stringer'. You see you go in and you say 'I want to write for you', and the editor will say 'You come from Alexandra. I know there's lots of crime in Alexandra. Look round for it, write about it and we'll use it.' So I did that; but it was not what I wanted to do. What I wanted to do was to find out how journalism could be used in the cause of political liberation. So while I wrote about crime, I was writing about South Africa. To start with I used to string for the *Golden City Post* – sports, crimes, socials – and it was all published. Later I tried to do the same thing with the *Rand Daily Mail* – not very successful.

Journalism put me in contact with a wide range of people throughout the country and at that time I began to understand what was happening in South Africa. I mean the first thing that really strikes one about South Africa, if you are doing journalism and doing it in the sections I was doing it in, is that there is very extreme and abject poverty. But when one is aware of this one is also aware that there are also people who are very, very wealthy, and the demarcation is really colour of skin. Being black means being threatened all the time by poverty, by ignorance, by illiteracy, and as you grow, other things begin to become very real for you. You realize that by virtue of being where you are, you are always liable to become a prisoner. The streets that one walks are extremely dangerous: from a very early age it had become normal for us to know that people can get killed in the streets by hooligans, to start with, and also by the police.

176

I think at a certain point all these things combine. On one level they begin to make one doubt oneself as to the significance of being alive at all. On the other you feel you have been wronged – to use a very mild word indeed. And throughout you try to resolve the contradiction: what is the meaning of life? One can deal with it in that sense if one can be abstract, but things in South Africa are not abstract. The police come into the locations, the townships, and you begin to understand that they have absolutely no respect for life and at the same time that they are supposed to be representing law and order. And then of course you hear from your parents about how their lives have been. I'm saying all this to say that it's not possible for me to pinpoint how one becomes a writer and takes writing as seriously as I do and takes what is happening in South Africa as seriously as I do. But amidst all this confusion there is one very significant thing which as one grows older one begins to understand.

The very first thing that one sees is that in these people who are living under those very abject conditions one begins to read pride, one begins to read hope, one begins to read optimism and sheer human creativity for survival, protection of what one loves, etc. The fact of the matter is that from the time the Europeans landed in South Africa our war began: we have a very, very long history of struggle. This is what has consistently defined our life and reality.

Being a writer I realize that to a very large extent I had been dealing with the surface, with superficial issues which registered themselves through the naked eye, the naked ear, not being equipped to deal with the depths of the life that was going on. But I think once one discovers this very deep hope, this very deep optimism, one's life changes. Throughout, with my writing, I've tried to explore all this.

Did you have any access to the work of other South African poets when you started writing?
I think one became aware of works by other writers in South Africa when one began to read *The Classic*, founded by Nat Nakasa, because there was always reference to other writers. One wanted to know what those people had written about and one found that in fact those books were not available, which is one other thing that makes you begin to understand how much of a prisoner you are. And of course we searched very desperately for that work. I remember some people had to leave the country and go to Botswana or Swaziland in search of this literature. Sometimes it was available, sometimes not. But *The Classic* played a very, very important role in our lives. Subsequently one became aware of other literary magazines which one way or the other referred to the writers I've talked about: people like Eskia Mphahlele, Alex La Guma, Kgositsile, Peter Abrahams and others. And then of course one also began to be aware of white writers like, especially, Nadine Gordimer, Jack Cope and many others, some of whose works were available: one read them.

After the events of 1960, especially after Sharpeville, where 69 people were killed by the apartheid regime, the regime really went all out to wipe out our history, by killing people, putting them into long, long terms of imprisonment, making them scuttle into exile, through banning orders, house arrests, banishments and also through banning whatever species of writings had come out of that experience before the '60s. So really we were a generation that had to search very, very desperately indeed for who we were, where we were going, where we came from; which I think at a certain point explains the birth of what came to be called 'the Black Consciousness era'.

How do you view the Black Consciousness Movement today?

It started among students. Initially, it was a movement that didn't take the history of struggle into consideration. But then the organization itself became a vehicle through which the history of struggle was explored. A whole lot of discoveries were made. For instance I remember that the question we kept asking at that time when certain issues were coming up was, if it is 1968 or 1973, and certain leaders of the ANC went into exile in 1960, '61, '62, why is it that we weren't aware of that general question?

I have always asked myself how we arrived at this terminology: 'Black Consciousness'. I remember when we went on a leadership training course and Steve Biko delivered his first paper, it was based on the fact that people were black and that we were conscious of the fact that we should not be ashamed of it, and from that base we could be liberated psychologically. Also he implied that this was conscious rejection of Whites.

The key thing about Black Consciousness and what is happening now is that as an organization the Movement was unable to answer very key questions for our struggle. One, how do you mobilize people so that they become conscious, active fighters for liberation? It's alright to say that you liberate them psychologically, but then what happens? Secondly, the question of armed struggle was very important for us. How was the Movement to embark on this? Thirdly, South Africa is part of the world and in the unfolding process of struggle it must make allies. You are unable to make correct choices until you have allies in the world. Because, if you consistently talk against white people, you have to exclude potential allies. Then there were those black people who were opposed to objectives that we felt even if we hadn't articulated them. What do you do with them? Yet at the same time all these issues had been raised by struggle before us and we didn't have satisfactory answers.

The Movement as a whole experienced very deep and serious crisis, even ideological crisis; on the other hand it was faced with very severe repression and it couldn't have survived. Now the choice was, were we to continue with this or had we achieved what we could? Some of us made the conscious decision that there was no way we could continue it. Especially since when you come out of South Africa you begin to become conscious of the role of the ANC internationally, what it has done. But not only that: you begin to come to grips with policies, positions, ideology – not only about South Africa, but about how we fit into the world. And then all the questions about armed struggle are answered: you realize there has been lots of thought about it, lots of experience, lots of history. For me I felt it was very natural that somebody should begin to take in that process.

I think at a certain level it is important to view Black Consciousness very positively, because, while on the one hand it was polarizing people by colours of skin, it did mean that Blacks could look at themselves as people, not as negatives of other people, and could also assert themselves, especially the young people. It was very important that we do so because we were coming out of a vacuum really where all our leaders were absent. We had to assert ourselves, we had to search for a history of struggle, we had to search for a direction. In that sense Black Consciousness was very positive. It did a whole lot for us to do certain things which other people in other countries take for granted: to understand that one doesn't owe anything to anybody because one is alive; that I am black is not a problem, etc., etc. It was very important that this happened. The problem starts after the young people discover that they have a very, very long history of struggle. For those young people who have acknowledged our history of struggle, acknowledged our leaders, acknowledged our very old and very experienced organization, the ANC, I think there is a point of departure.

Before your involvement with Black Consciousness, you spent several months in prison. Little has ever been said about this period of your life. You were never charged with anything, were you?
No. What happened was this. From about 1965, '64–5, and this has to do with the period of 'silence' people talk about in the '60s, I worked in the underground of the ANC.

I was arrested June 1969 and I was released February 1970. All I can say about that is that I don't wish anybody to experience that. But you see people do experience it, which means it is something we have to face very squarely. During those nine months one was in solitary confinement. One had been told in no uncertain terms that one would see nobody else but the security branch. Those two things are the cruellest things that can be done to a person: to keep somebody in solitary confinement for a full nine months, and to tell that person that in fact he will be there indefinitely and nobody else will see him. Apart from that, there was very, very serious torture. Physical torture was *extremely* intense. I never thought human beings could go to that level, but I saw them go to that level and they are free men now. I still read about them in the newspapers. I'm talking about a long time ago in terms of time, but it's a thing I will never forget, I can't forget.

You said once that your time in America didn't mean much to you. But reading your poetry one feels the presence of Afro-American culture. Was this something you had already encountered in South Africa?
After reading lots of English literature one started probing round in the direction of Afro-American literature. So it's true that by the time I arrived there I had a clear understanding of what was happening among Afro-Americans – as much as one can gain from reading, that is. Ninety per cent of my life in those three years was spent with Afro-Americans, Afro-American authors, Afro-Americans in culture and politics . . . Also I was very active in the Pan-African Student Organization's information office. To a certain extent that's when, in another way, I discovered Africa. I began to question the issue of independence, to wonder what is it to be independent, hearing what these other people – and some of them were in exile – were talking about. It was the time when the Angolan struggle was preoccupying Afro-Americans to a very large extent. So this was another introduction to me, and I had to question the whole concept of Pan-Africanism and the question of independence. And I think it was at that time also that Amilcar Cabral was at his most articulate about all these political issues. So there was this combination of things, while I was trying to search for a political point of reference. The question I needed to find ways and means of answering was: Can Africans oppress Africans?

Were there any particular poets and writers within Afro-American literature – or even American literature in general – with whom you felt affinity?
There was a book called *Ark of Bones* . . . I must have been there for about nine months or so and I'd already made friends with many Afro-American writers: first Sonia Sanchez, then Quincy Troupe, and then Paula Jordan,

Haki, Baraka, etc. They called to say there was a book-launch of *Ark of Bones*. When I got there I found that all of the key Afro-American writers were there. I listened carefully to Angela Davis. When I was in South Africa I had followed this whole question of the Black Panthers very closely. But after lengthy discussions with Angela I came to discover the meaning of what it was and how it came eventually to be defeated. And I came to discover that there are two camps among Blacks and that one had to make a choice. I also had access – to a certain extent, not that much – to the US Communist Party and I began to study what they were doing. Which means I was really beginning to explore for a political reference point. Also I began to look at how all that related to our situation, to have that type of point of reference in looking at our situation, at independence and moderation and Pan-Africanism. I remember a time when I dropped everything that had to do with literature. I had to study and re-study what Cabral was saying, because it was answering most of the questions I had been asking. Now in that sense it is not correct to say I didn't gain anything from America.

But you see I had gone there to study. First of all, my scholarship was for studying writing. By the time I arrived in the States I had begun to look at myself as a writer. Now I was to face a new challenge: here I was at the university, learning how to write. I attended lectures and disagreed a whole lot with what the professors were saying and with what some of the students were saying writing means. I wondered a lot about what they were writing about; and to a large extent began to understand my morals in what I was meeting, and my curiosity was not going to be satisfied by what I was supposed to be studying. The more you read, the more you asked serious questions; the more you read Aimé Césaire in class the more you asked much, much more serious questions . . . The more you got exposed to some of the best Afro-American writers and even white American writers –

Such as, for example?
James Baldwin. I remember once James Baldwin came to our class. I'd read almost all his books and was beginning to question some issues he raised. I respected him a lot. But except when experienced writers came to our lectures, I had the feeling I was wasting my time: the type of discussions I was engaged in were irrelevant. So I switched off from writing and went into filming.

When I went into filming I discovered something else. It's a very difficult thing. You see, as human beings we do have a common culture, but there is something about American culture which is completely unacceptable to me. The commercialization of life. So I entered into another conflict: I didn't want to make the movies they were making. But because I thought film-making was very important I persevered. I'll give you an example: I participated in the making of some pornographic films. Now I'm not moralizing about this. I don't care if people make this kind of film, it's not my business. But I did not want to make pornographic movies. But more than that it was also the fact that I thought if I were going to do anything in this line I wasn't going to do it the way they were doing it.

This was my point of view. I'm not talking about morals, I'm talking about the whole approach to an issue which in my view is very essential to life. A statement you make about something that is very essential to life hopefully must be lasting and contributing to progress in our understanding. As a man, a black man, being exposed to discussing lesbianism and homosexuality, I was at first very angry, and then I discovered I was fearful, why? Everything I thought I knew on the subject of sex was turning upside down.

I had to make a choice. So I said to myself I'll shut my mind and learn the skill and to a certain extent that's what I did. For instance, I made a film for my course which I called 'Letters of the People'. I said, if I have to be subjected to this, perhaps my responsibility is that somebody who comes after me should not be subjected to it. So how do I use what I'm learning now to say that? What I did was to create this character who was trying to do everything possible to keep the link alive and dynamic with where he came from, finding himself where he is. So it was a one-actor film, the background being New York, and exploring all this that I've been talking about. I don't know, technically, whether it was a successful film, but I remember when I took it to my teacher, a German-American woman, we did not see eye to eye. She did not like my film.

As all this was unfolding, I made the decision that this was not where I was staying: I have other priorities that America is not able to meet. When you come from Alexandra, what you learn very well is that you must be able to acquire skills. So I had put a time-table to myself: in five years I must be somewhere where I could acquire skills to deal with the world. The way America provided political consciousness to me was really haphazard and reckless. The way it educated me I felt was very haphazard and reckless. So I left in that state of mind.

In the poem in which you recall your American experience, *Behold Mama, Flowers*, you speak of Skunder Boghossian. Who is he?
He's a painter, an exile from Ethiopia. As I was saying earlier on, in my understanding of independence Ethiopia was independent and Haile Selassie was a great man. And as I was sitting there asking Skunder questions while he was painting or listening to his music, I'd ask him what is Ethiopia and why if Ethiopia is independent is he in exile in America? So he was one of the people who contributed a lot to my consciousness of the continent. To a very large extent the opening of *Behold Mama, Flowers* was written in his flat. I'd left New York and gone to DC to stay with him for a while and we had these *endless* discussions about Africa and the world. He's from the North and I'm from the South, but it seemed to me there was something we were sharing: dissatisfactions about the world, our countries. To me it was a new experience, but for him it was not a new experience that somebody from South Africa should be dissatisfied. To me Skunder was a revelation.

He is responsible for the image of the fragments on the water, isn't he, and then for the image of picking up the pieces of the continent. You find similar images in cultures all over the world, but where did these ones come from specifically?
There is a book called *Song of Mumu*. I met the author, Lindsay Barrett, once or twice at Skunder's house. He was the one who related this story to Skunder. He had actually lived through this process in the sense that he was writing a book, a novel based on this image, and when he was staying with Skunder, short of cutting somebody to pieces, he lived through the motions to find out what makes a person go through that state to do that, how are people who discover this acting . . . Skunder himself at that time, through his painting, was going through all this, because this man had a strange, very strong character, you had no choice but to try to experience what he was talking about. I felt it was an imagery that spoke well about America and about South Africa. To

a very large extent it's an imagery that influenced the whole of *Behold Mama, Flowers*.

The protagonist of *To Every Birth Its Blood* seems almost to be living his experience through music, particularly in the early pages. And music, the use of particular rhythms and repetitions, is strongly present in your poetry. What relationship is there between your writing and music?
It's very difficult to say, but one grew up, was brought up, by music really. It was music that articulated one's dilemma, one's hopes, one's aspirations, and this has always been available, within reach, for us. It is one thing which unlike the written word has crossed the barrier of the generations: music that was composed during the era of Shaka is still available to us. From that point up till now whatever music has been made is available to us. It has been sung on private occasions, by individuals, on public occasions . . . That is one thing that laws could not bar and I think when our lives were stifled it was the only thing we could still define our freedom with. For some reason we have a very long and very strong tradition of music in various forms. Depending on what one does, one becomes sensitized to this. I am very sensitive to music. I have listened to music very, very carefully; not only South African music but music from other parts of the world, and I have been fortunate in the sense that even people who were older than me have always made a point of making music accessible to me. So maybe that has also influenced my writing.

You speak of traditional music. Was this available also in an urban environment? And how about oral culture in general?
I grew up in a very unusual environment. Alexandra is very different from Soweto, very different from townships and locations that have been built in the last twenty years or so, very different. Alexandra had a bit of everything in it. It had a very close relation with the countryside, because there was constant movement between Alexandra and the different rural areas by older people, our parents, their parents. It is my generation and the generation after me that experienced severe urban life. But anybody who grew up in Alexandra my age knows a bit of everything. For instance, it is not surprising for anybody who comes from Alexandra to speak nine languages, because those are the languages which one grows with, because everybody is there. Alexandra is a township which was very un-South African. The majority of the people there of course were Africans. You found Coloureds, you found Indians, you found Chinese people, you found Whites. Everybody was there. Also in terms of background. There were people who had roots deeply in their rural area, but also in Alexandra. Alexandra is like that. So I know a bit of traditional music, a bit of oral poetry, if one can call it that, a bit of everything one was exposed to.

All this through your home life, presumably, not, I imagine, at school?
School is another matter, completely. That is the law coming into our lives. I think one should separate them. I mean, one leads three lives really, when one lives in a place like Alexandra. There is the life at home: where I am with my parents, my brothers, my sisters and other people. And they are aware there is another life they know they cannot share with me because I cannot reveal to them what happens; and that is the street life, a completely different point of reference. And of course through that you also come across how law introduces itself into Alexandra and how you deal with that. So there are those three

broad lives that one leads. All of them in one way or the other, one uses them to keep alive.

The visual arts also seem to have some importance in your work. I'm thinking particularly of *The Night Keeps Winking*, where the art work seems to integrate the poems and vice versa.

I have lived a lot with visual artists wherever I have been, from when I was young up till now. I'm sure it's not something one can ignore. First the lives of those people, secondly, what they create says a lot about our lives and being a writer I could not ignore that. My recent experience with art is with Thami Mnyele, the person who illustrated *The Night Keeps Winking*. We had known each other for a very, very long time, which means I had seen this person and he had seen me develop – I as a writer, he as a visual artist – and there was a time when we were separated from each other for six or seven years and when we met of course we came with our different experiences of where we had been. If he had to illustrate anything I had written, or if I had to write about anything he had created, there were very intense discussions between us, and not only between us but with many other people. When we were in Botswana we belonged to the same group, the Medu Arts Ensemble, and there were lots of very intense discussions about the role art plays in struggle, the role art plays in the life of people.

Thami Mnyele was killed during the raid into Botswana by the Boers in June 1985. Before he got killed, he had begun to explore other areas. He was mainly doing posters, postcards, T-shirts, badges, things like that. A very significant detour in terms of what he had been doing before, which illustrates what I was saying before: that when you grow up in South Africa you deal with what strikes you, your naked eye, your naked ear.

There were other people too, like Dumile Feni, one of South Africa's great painters, whom I've lived with over a long period; there is Gerard Sikoto – I've followed his works over a long period – and many others one has lived very, very closely with as one was creating and one was growing. It's the same way with musicians. One has lived very closely with musicians: they were one's neighbours, they were one's elders, one's elder brother in the terms of the townships, and there were discussions about this. I've had endless discussions with Jonas Gwangwa, one of South African's best musicians. So I'm not surprised one can discover that in my work also.

Have you participated in readings of your poetry in South Africa? I gather this happens quite often, doesn't it?

I've done public poetry readings extensively, in almost all parts of South Africa, from as early as 1969 to about 1974 when I left. It had become a sort of movement. We knew each other as writers, so whenever anything was organized the condition was we should bring others to it. Because of that I think we have known each other very closely, we have influenced each other very closely, we have known our communities very closely and that has influenced our poetry.

You seem to have tended to move towards progressively longer forms, as if you feel you need to articulate your feelings and your thoughts in a wider context. What is the relationship between short poetry and long poetry, and between poetry and the novel, for you? Do you feel differently about these forms?

No, I don't. I think I'd reached a point where with poetry I'd explored it to its limits. For me poetry, in order to articulate what one wants to articulate, one has to prop it up with imagery. But imagery at a certain point doesn't have logic. While if you look at a novel, a novel can have a very technical logic. Poetry has a logic of its own. The other thing is that there's a problem of characters. You can tell an abstract story but at a certain level, at a certain point, the story becomes more 'proper' – for lack of a better word – if it is illustrated through sitting down on a chair, walking the streets, touching your phone, relating to other people, which I found at a certain level poetry could not carry, and I had to move. I had become very, very interested in people, that's why I dealt with the novel. You can become deeply interested in people and still deal with that easily through poetry. I'm not saying it's not possible, but I feel that the novel gives you a much wider scope to do so. But I don't see any contradiction between the two. It's just one way of doing it.

Talking about imagery, would you like to speak about some of the images that recur throughout your work: that of the river running into the sea, moving into the sea; the relationship between the golden city and the dark city, between Johannesburg and Alexandra; the continual presence of mothers, mothers and children, and of different generations, of old and young? Then there is the imagery connected with silence and darkness and time and memory; the visions of birth, or rather of the effort involved in labour: birth pains more than actual birth. Perhaps you'd like to pick up some of those points?
I think what ties all those is that for one reason or other I have been very interested in motion, because within motion so much is implied: change is implied in motion; history; the future. But much more permanent within motion is change. And, although scientifically one understands how motion happens, there is a very strange mystery about motion if one has to use poetic language. I mean, we can explain what 'sunset' is scientifically, but as human beings when we look at this, while we have that scientific knowledge, there are many other things that we observe which make us better people, which illuminate our despair, which make us understand certain things more, depending also on which part of the world you are in when that sunset happens . . . But constant within sunrise and sunset there is a motion. It's a motion that at one level we can say creates a day; but then we think that before it happened to create a day there were other days before that, there are other days after it. But if you put life, life as made by men, women and children, into that context, sunset is really overloaded with experience. But as I said it's motion. So I think constant among all the images I've used has been that thing of trying to understand what we do with motion. Of course I don't approach it scientifically: I'm a writer and I would like to put life into that, not that it just becomes a mechanical thing. Because indeed motion does affect our lives very, very seriously and it has been something that I have tried to explore and deal with. Now whether one talks about the river, the sea, death, whatever, you see that . . . Time itself, children, old people, mothers: there is that motion throughout. Which means one is a historian in that sense; if I'm interested in that I'm really interested in history, in the lives of people; I think that's the way I could put it.

You said when you were talking about life in Alexandra that children there are able to understand many different languages. How have you lived the language question in South Africa and how do you see it today?

It's a very complex question. As I said you can find people who can speak five languages very fluently, including English and Afrikaans. But you also find people who know bits and pieces of language and that is their language. When you are with a person they speak to you in English-Afrikaans-Sotho-Zulu-Tswana, and that's their language: they don't know another language. Of course you still find people who understand a language but can say nothing in it or are unable to write it. This is not general. There will be people who have never heard Afrikaans, though they live in a country which is ruled by the Afrikaners, like the people in the Natal area. You'll find other people who don't know English: the only language they know is Afrikaans. And so even with the different African languages. Given that, what do we do? And there is another very serious factor: the majority of our people are illiterate. That also has to be taken into consideration. So I don't think we have any absolute answers to the question of language. We should see what each one of us is doing as contributing to its resolution. The important thing is that we always have to discuss what we are doing. I would not say, myself, that anybody who is writing in, say, Setswana has a right in terms of resolving our language problem, nor would I say that anyone who is writing in English has a right in solving our language problem. It's much more complex than that. The way I look at it is that, in so far as writing is concerned, we must involve the publishers in this question, we must involve the universities in this question, especially when we are dealing with the question of translations. But also when we deal with the question of literacy: all of us must be involved in resolving this. We haven't started that, precisely because the people who are in power to start it, that is not in their interest, it would frighten them. But in another way we *have* started, because if you look at any theatre production that has come out of South Africa, it will use almost all the languages at the same time, including that as an art form it has much more power of communication than the novel or poetry.

But, as I say, I wouldn't approach the question of language flippantly, because it is also tied up with the whole question of the nation, which is a very large issue.

What was your own first language?
That's very difficult to say in Alexandra. My father speaks Sepedi very well and my mother speaks Setswana very well; there were many people around us who spoke Zulu and more of the other languages. I wouldn't say I speak Sepedi well, nor do I speak Setswana well, or any of the other languages, but I understand them perfectly. I think the language I am more articulate in would be something between English, Afrikaans, Setswana, Sepedi and Zulu: I use them all. Each articulates a life experience associated to its social context better than the other. What I would like to add here is that the unfolding process of liberation itself is contributing to the solution of the problem of language. On the one side the regime was using language to divide people. The fact is that the ANC's policy is to unite people, but it takes into consideration their differences in language. This means that through the process of liberation we will have to recognize the differences among people, the differences in language and encourage the fact that those languages become a means through which people articulate the world they are in and the time the world is in. So we have no choice but to encourage the full fruition and growth of the different languages. Now, if we are dealing with a question of unity, we also have to find what

language unites the people. That's the way I see it, but I don't think one can provide absolute answers. It's an issue that is going to unfold and we are going to learn from the way it unfolds.

SELECTED BIBLIOGRAPHY

POETRY
Yakhal'inkomo (Johannesburg: Renoster Books, 1972).
Tsetlo (Johannesburg: Ad. Donker, 1974).
No Baby Must Weep (Johannesburg: Ad. Donker, 1975).
Behold Mama, Flowers (Johannesburg: Ad. Donker, 1978).
The Night Keeps Winking (Gaberone: Medu Arts Ensemble, 1982).
Selected Poems, ed. Mbulelo Vizikhungo Mzamane (Johannesburg: Ad. Donker, 1982).
A Tough Tale (London: Kliptown Books, 1987).

NOVEL
To Every Birth Its Blood (Johannesburg: Ravan Press, 1981).

ESSAYS
'The Nakasa world', *Contrast*, VIII, 3 (1973), pp. 16–21.
'Preface to poetry anthology "Shaya" ', *Pelculef Newsletter*, I, 1 (1978), pp. 3–6. On poetry by South African exiles in Botswana.
'Shimmers of writing: an exploration', *Marang* (Gaborone) (1978), pp. 69–73.
'Feeling the waters', *First World* (Atlanta), I, 2 (1977), pp. 22–5. Autobiographical sketch.
'Politics and culture: Southern Africa', *Medu Art Ensemble Newsletter*, V, 2 (n.d.), pp. 26–34; *Sechaba* (March 1984), pp. 26–31.
'Power to the people: a glory to creativity', in *Criticism and Ideology. Second African Writers' Conference, Stockholm 1986*, ed. Kirsten Holst Petersen (Uppsala: Scandinavian Institute of African Studies, 1988), pp. 193–7.
'Now we enter history', in *Culture in Another South Africa*, ed. W. Campschreur and J. Divendal (London: Zed Books, 1989).

Tsitsi Dangarembga

The 'nervous conditions' of Tsitsi Dangarembga's first novel are those of two generations of women living in Rhodesia in the '60s: Tambudzai, the young but lucidly analytical narrator, and her mother, aunts and cousin. The story opens with a death, or rather with Tambudzai's reactions to it. But her account, she says, is 'not after all about death, but about my escape and Lucia's; about my mother's and Maiguru's entrapment; and about Nyasha's rebellion – Nyasha, far-minded and isolated, my uncle's daughter, whose rebellion may not in the end have been successful'.

Born in Zimbabwe (then Rhodesia) in February 1959, Tsitsi Dangaremgba spent her early years – from age two to six – in Britain, where she began her schooling. She later attended a mission school at Mutare and then an American convent. She began reading medicine at Cambridge in 1977, but returned to Zimbabwe in 1980, just before independence, and worked in an advertising agency. She then read psychology at the University of Zimbabwe and enrolled at the Drama Group, for which she wrote three plays. After receiving the Commonwealth Writers' Award in August 1989, she left for Berlin where she is studying filming.

14

Tsitsi Dangarembga

The interview took place in London (4 September 1989).

Among other things, your novel *Nervous Conditions* is about how a young girl can develop into somebody who can write her own 'account' of things, her own story of 'how it all began'. But how did it all begin for Tsitsi Dangarembga? I'm taking it, as I think one should, that Tambudzai and Tsitsi are two different people . . .

I'm not really sure . . . I think I've always been a person with creative or artistic leanings. I remember when I was very young and very plump I was convinced I was going to be a ballerina! We lived in England at that time. Then I went into a phase of telling my young brother horror stories all the time, till my mother told me to stop. When I went to secondary school I found myself writing letters to my brain . . . I was quite isolated and I think that was when I actually began to put my feelings onto paper. I'd spend quite a bit of time doing this, which disturbed the other girls no end of course. Then when I came to Cambridge in 1977 I was very homesick and missed my family tremendously and I began writing a lot of poetry. I didn't take it seriously: it was just something that I did that I found interesting. I was studying medicine, but eventually I decided to give it up and return to Rhodesia. It was just before independence, early in 1980. I think by that time I had decided that I was going to give up my scientific leanings and do something creative. Then I found a job in an advertising agency as a copywriter and I found that quite stimulating creatively. It was also useful in terms of proceeding from the idea to the finished copy and then the finished product. But I didn't have enough time to express my own feelings, so I thought I should leave that kind of job. That's when I decided to go back to university, this time to the University of Zimbabwe. I was studying Psychology. You could say that *that's* where it all began!

To return to what I suppose we'd better call your pre-history then, you say you went to school in England, but when did you leave Rhodesia?
Well, I began school here in Britain when I was about five or six, but I only did Grade One. When I went back to Rhodesia I went into Grade Two. Then I went to school in Mutare, first of all a mission school and then a private convent, an American convent but certainly very European oriented: we didn't learn much about anything indigenous at all.

What about literature – in general?
Well, my mother had studied English at Master's level and we had all these books, all the classics, Dickens, Shakespeare, Edgar Allan Poe, everything . . . And there wasn't much else to read. It was actually quite funny because my father would go up to Salisbury – now Harare – quite regularly for meetings and that sort of thing, and he would bring back all the other stuff, the Enid Blytons and so on. So here was father bringing me these books and here were mother's books and I was reading all of them at the same time, so I think I had quite a mixed background and it was probably good that I wasn't entirely seduced by the children's literature. When I went to school we did the English classics: *Wuthering Heights* and *Romeo and Juliet*, this kind of thing. Then I stopped taking literature seriously because I went on to do sciences – maths, physics, biology and chemistry – for my A-levels. I've always enjoyed reading, so obviously I carried on, but there was no structure to it, I'd just go into the library and if I found something I would read it. It was very much the same at Cambridge as well, basically just reading whatever was available. I found it rather difficult when I went back to Zimbabwe because it was difficult to buy decent books to read what with the foreign currency problems and that kind of thing. So I can't really put a structure on how my interaction with literature has really resulted in my own literary experiences.

When were you born?
On 14 February 1959.

So Tambudzai is slightly older than you are – she was thirteen in 1968, wasn't she? There are various strands from your life that link up with her story. Presumably you're creating alternative lives to your own, but with a certain amount of interweaving.
Well, I think the point is that one has to write about things one feels strongly about, otherwise it doesn't work. And the things that I *can* feel strongly about, or at least that I did at that early stage – I was only twenty-five when I wrote the book – were things that I had observed and had had direct experience with. I also felt that these things were larger than any one person's own tragedies or so forth, but actually had a wider implication and origin and therefore were things that needed to be told. So I would say that at the moment my writing really does come from things that are quite concrete, that I've had quite a lot of first-hand experience of. But I'm hoping that will change. I'd like to start writing real fantasies.

In your book at one point your characters draw a distinction between fairy tale and romantic stories on one side and reality, history, on the other. But in the end even history, or the kind of history Nyasha is reading, is inadequate.
One of the problems that most Zimbabwean people of my generation have is

that we really don't have a tangible history that we can relate to. And I think this is where the inadequacy arose in terms of Nyasha's ability to relate to the history she was taught. There is this great big void. And it's not only with the history in fact, it's also with the myth. So I think what happened with Nyasha is that this history was distant enough for her not to become one hundred per cent involved in it. What I would like to say is for example that I come here now and I read about, say, this divorce in the Royal Family and my reaction is that I didn't know people still worshipped royalty! So I think this is the distance Nyasha was looking at myth from. Perhaps Tambudzai, given the kind of background that she had, was more at home with what could be termed myth or romance or fairy tales with all the stories that her grandmother told her about her actual family and her ancestors, which to Nyasha would have sounded like a myth. She would have had no experience of those kinds of hardships: people travelling hundreds of miles on ox-carts and running around in loin cloths and this kind of thing. So I think that's actually the tragic thing that has happened in terms of Zimbabwean history and I think that is another reason why Nyasha suffers. Because at the end of the day it's like this Jungian idea of embracing the shadow, isn't it? I mean, where you have fact you have fiction as well and sometimes the interface between the two is difficult. For example, people always ask me 'Is this novel autobiographical?' and I just say 'Well, it's a novel', so it's the same kind of problem.

This seems to connect with the general theme of remembering and forgetting that runs through your story: the danger of forgetting and the protagonist's certainty that she won't forget. Her very writing is a remembering – a very constructive kind of remembering, not just telling the story or stories, but thinking about them and interpreting them. Then there is the Grandmother's telling of Babamukuru's story as a kind of success story with a moral behind it, and it seems to me that one could almost read your novel as a kind of rewriting of that story.
Well, the way it ends at the moment, yes. But then I think also Nyasha was really intended to balance that idea out.

When I said 'rewriting' I meant a *critical* rewriting! Perhaps the departure point is the same, to some extent, but then it most definitely does not develop into a success story.
I would agree with you there entirely. I personally do not have a fund of our cultural tradition or oral history to draw from, but I really did feel that if I am able to put down the little I know then it's a start. People perhaps who know more will realize that maybe it's something worth doing and it can be done and will continue.

I think this problem of forgetting – remembering and forgetting – is really important. What is interesting is that Nyasha as an individual does not have anything to forget: she simply doesn't know. She is the one who is worried about it. I think it comes back to the Jungian idea of archetypes of soul. She obviously feels some great big gap inside her and that she ought to remember it because this is her heritage. And she really doesn't come to the consciousness that even the reasons for this gap are so far out of her own control that she doesn't have to tear herself into pieces to have to try and rectify the situation. Tambudzai on the other hand I think is quite valid in saying that she can't forget because she has that kind of experience Nyasha is so worried about forgetting because it's not there for her to remember. Tambudzai is so sure that this is the framework of her very being that there is no way that she would be able to forget it. It is, as she says, a question of remembering and from what you remember picking out what is going to be useful in the future as you progress. In a way you could think of Nyasha's attachment to what has been as romantic – those clay pots for instance, while Tambudzai knew that nobody made clay pots any more: it just wasn't worth the effort when you have these ten-gallon tins instead. So it's really interesting. I hadn't thought of that aspect myself. You could in a way perceive Nyasha as a very romantic character, for all that she insists that she is entirely factual and logical and rational.

Even her rebellion is a romantic rebellion I suppose: she is burning herself out as Tambudzai says, whereas Tambudzai is preserving her energy . . . Going back to the oral-writing theme, there seems to be a kind of dialogue between orality and writing in your book. There is this feeling of retelling something that has already been told, and then there is the storytelling flavour when the narrator addresses an unspecified 'you'. But at the same time it's very clearly stated right from the beginning that this is a written account. Now you were talking about putting down the 'little' you know of the oral tradition. What exactly is your personal relation with the oral tradition?
The most that I can remember is an elder cousin of mine telling me stories, folktales, when I was very young. What is very interesting is that in those folktales – as I think everywhere in the world – there are places where the audience has to reply and you are actually drawn into it. And I feel that that's a very successful way of telling a story or making a point. So when I was writing *Nervous Conditions* that was very intentional: I did my best to draw the reader into the story as well. One of the things that I felt was that something like *Nervous Conditions* was relatively new in African literature, and in order for people not to be dismayed by that I thought I'd have to use a strategy that would bring the reader into the story rather than just have the reader on the surface. I also find it very much easier to write in that way. I really do imagine that there is somebody there. I am actually talking directly to this amorphous audience when I'm writing. I find that that helps.

You say an 'amorphous' audience, so you haven't got a particular audience in mind, I gather?
I feel that perhaps later on I would be able to do that, but at the moment all I am convinced of is that I have a story to tell. That's my starting point: I want to tell it and I want to make sure that any passer-by could stop and listen to this story. Maybe later on I'll think about targeting and more careful structure and so on.

On at least two occasions in the novel you point to the therapeutic quality of storytelling. For instance when Tambudzai comforts Nyasha by speaking to her, on and on, telling her the story that you've already told. And then there's the occasion where as Tambudzai talks to the schoolteacher she feels herself 'recoalesce'. That made me wonder if the 'you' the narrator is talking to might also – as well as being the reader – be another self: your story also has a lot to do with split selves.
That's something I've been thinking about recently as well. I actually find the process of storytelling has helped me as an individual because I feel I have this story that's made up of all these parts that I know are a whole but they're

disorganized. So sitting down and putting it into a framework, I can also be the reader. I can go back and read it and enjoy it and find some order in all these complexities that prompted me to sit down and write it in the first place. So, yes, definitely. There was some writer who said 'I don't write to save the world, I write to save myself' or something to that effect. I really believe that's the only valid reason for writing!

You talk about order and disorder, 'chaos', 'havoc'. With Tambudzai you are presenting an example of a person who wants to see order and to be able to make order in life, and who doesn't think about the things that risk bringing havoc to her life. On the other hand there is Nyasha, with all her misconnections and the havoc she creates. Tambudzai feels attracted to her and frightened of her at the same time. There are several references to gluing things together. But it seems to me that there is something in this split-apart condition that Tambudzai comes to see as perhaps also very positive.
It's interesting that you should say that. One very sensitive man who read the book in Zimbabwe told me that he was actually worried about Tambudzai, because she seemed to be going in the same direction as Nyasha! So I think it comes back to this idea that we were talking about before. What has Tambudzai got that can enable her to perhaps appreciate some of these chaotic aspects of Nyasha without being drawn into it and becoming chaotic herself? And I think my answer to that would be that she has this very solid background. She knows exactly where she's come from. She may be leaving it, but it's there for her. I don't know whether Nyasha ever thought there was really ever anything admirable in Tambudzai's orderliness and so forth . . . But she is a very naïve adolescent and maybe she'll grow out of it!

Is she growing out of it? I mean, is she coming into your next novel – I gather you're working on one?
Yes, I think she would. But at the moment I think I would pursue this idea of 'how does Tambudzai come through?' I think that's a very intriguing idea. Because on the face of it, as the story ends, really one could not see how she could come through. I think there we really have a very serious social dilemma. What with fifteen years of war, the last eight or so very serious, that had great impact on everybody's lives, and now with independence and socialism and going back to our roots, very few youngsters have anything really solid to look back on. One could perhaps be pessimistic about it. But I hope that it won't turn out to be a general tragedy, although you never know: I look at the rest of Africa, Nigeria for example . . .

Will your new novel be a kind of sequel to this one, taking up on some of the themes, if not on the actual characters?
Well, that's the intention. I find that with my experience, being a woman and an African woman and having had the kind of background that I have had, it's difficult to make any points of any sort outside the family framework. This is the clay that I am used to working with. So it very well could pick up on several of the characters.

You studied medicine, and medicine, both traditional and modern, also comes into your novel, in quite a subtle way, together with the feeling, it seems, that there's a need for something else. At the same time, on one of the occasions

when traditional medicine is called for, Babamukuru contrasts this with a suggestion of a 'solution' in the sense of an orthodox Christian solution which seems just as superstitious and probably just as useless as the other.

Again, this split is represented here at a group level. But I think that there are a lot of people in Zimbabwe at the moment who are experiencing this at a very individual level. I think in this particular novel the solution Babamukuru came up with seems to be totally useless, but at the personal level it's all very well to talk about throwing out these superstitions that we've had, but having thrown them out what will you do? Will you go back to those superstitions that you had before? And will they be as effective now that you have these alternatives in your head? And can human beings live without superstitions of some sort? I mean even these extremely rational societies like socialist societies are all a myth as well, aren't they? So I think probably the question that was being asked there is OK, we need another set of norms and norms can even be called myths, but what are they? What shores are we going to go to?

So really it's a call to rethink all these norms and values and customs – both traditional and Western – and find something in them which might be valid in the end. After all, Tambudzai eventually sees that the wedding has been a success, but on the other hand, so was her decision not to go to it.

Yes, I think also the fact that the wedding was a success makes an important point in that again it's a question of embracing the shadow. We may think we value rationality very highly, but at the end of the day we simply are not terribly rational beings, and so if irrational systems can help us to cope with the fact that we are irrational beings I feel that's OK. That is the whole question here. It's a question of survival, not so much how to become extremely rational like Nyasha, but what particular sets of behaviour are we going to use on this particular situation, so that at the end of the day we can say we have lived a productive day? That's basically what it is, and if it's a wedding, well, fine, if it's a cleansing ceremony, well, that's also OK.

When did you first encounter African literature? It was fairly late, wasn't it?

Well, it wasn't terribly late. I remember the first thing I ever read was *A Grain of Wheat*, and I read that quite early because it was something my parents had. And then contrasted with that was Wilbur Smith! I can remember being extremely impressed by it as a teenager, at thirteen, fourteen or fifteen. I didn't have a clue what it actually meant, but I could just feel that this was a powerful piece of writing. It's one of those books that I have not gone back to because I don't want to have to rethink my opinion of it. I think then, because of the nature of the home that I lived in, I didn't really make any distinctions in terms of who has written this and why. It was just literature and it was there and I thought it was good. It was when I actually came back from Cambridge that I began to feel the need for an African literature that I could read and identify with. I'd had a rather negative experience at Cambridge. I had hoped that going to a place, a university that is known to be a cultural centre of some sort, I would be able to give expression to the other aspects of myself that did not find expression in my scientific subjects. This was not possible, because the cultural activities, though plentiful, did not relate to anything that seemed to be important to me. So it was when I came back from there that I began a quest as it were for the kinds of literature that I could really relate to, that could teach me something about myself and why I was and where I was and so forth. In fact it wasn't African literature that I came to first. It was the Afro-American women writers, I found them very helpful.

Such as, for example?
Toni Morrison, who is really incredible. Then I read Alice Walker and Maya Angelou, and of course there are several others I can't remember right now . . . basically all the Afro-American women writers that people ought to read. And then of course there was Chinua Achebe and more Ngũgĩ wa Thiong'o. And I also became involved in a very different kind of literature through drama. We had a marvellous person called Robert MacLaren who'd come to the university to start a Drama Department. I had not been introduced to community theatre before and it was just wonderful.

Another very significant experience was in fact the 1980 independence celebrations. I heard the most beautiful poem I'd ever heard being recited, and of course it was in Shona. It brought back to me that we have an oral language here. It isn't written, it's oral, and when it is reproduced in the medium in which it is meant to be, it is absolutely astounding. But it was also a painful experience: to think we'd lost so much of it. I sometimes feel that we need a programme, almost immediately, of sending out tape recorders and cassettes to any point possible and just asking people, old people in particular, to come in and just talk. It's all going. I think about the Tavangwena story of Chief Tavangwena who refused to leave his land in the mountains just before independence and one of the reasons was that this area is holy and it has a lot of significance in our culture. He died some years ago and it's all gone. It's the same with Sekuru Nehanda and Mbuya Kaguvi, the spirit mediums who were involved in the first Chimurenga in the late nineteenth century I think it was . . . It's terribly, terribly sad. I found it very painful that this wealth of literature existed but it hadn't been written down, and so one simply doesn't have access to it and it's being lost. It was good to have people like Achebe and Ngũgĩ wa Thiong'o. They were the people I think who really pointed me in the direction of African literature as such as opposed to Afro-American literature. There are others who I fail to understand, for example Soyinka: I love to see his plays performed, but I have a lot of difficulty understanding them. And of course there's all the literature coming out of South Africa at the moment. It's very interesting because here you have the two extremes. You have the Nadine Gordimers and you have the Mphahleles. Of course Doris Lessing, *The Grass is Singing* and the *Children of Violence* series. That again was actually a very positive influence upon me. I particularly liked her writing in the *Children of Violence* series: so down-to-earth and real! It made me think that this is the material that I have. It just relates to ordinary people that live ordinary lives, but, if Doris Lessing thinks it's important enough to record and the world agrees with her, then maybe I can use that same kind of material as well to make the points that I think should be made.

When did you come across her?
It was when I went back to Zimbabwe, in 1980.

You mentioned the wealth of oral literature in Shona. What exactly is your language background?
Well, my family brought me to England at the age of two, and of course I had begun to talk at that stage, but my language wasn't fully developed,

and so, being here and not living with our parents, my brother and I then spoke English as a matter of course and forgot most of the Shona that we had learnt.

You didn't live with your parents?
No, they were busy studying and accommodation was difficult and so forth. Anyway, when we went back – when I was about six – we learnt Shona again. It wasn't all that difficult. I think in terms of language development the difference between six and seven is absolutely enormous, so I didn't have much of a problem learning Shona again, whereas my brother had terrible trouble, because he was a year and a half older than me. So I would say that basically my first language actually is English, in terms of my familiarity with it, and my second language is Shona. And then of course all through the education English is the language you use. Sometimes I worry about Shona: how long it's going to survive. No matter where you go – you could go out to the most remote rural areas – you'll usually find people using English words in their speech. There are very few people who can speak good Shona and even fewer who can write it. Maybe we've caught it just in time with the Government's policies of traditional culture and so forth, so maybe it's not as sad as it seems.

You wrote your novel in 1985, didn't you? But I see that you had already written a play. Was that at your time at the University of Zimbabwe?
Actually it was before MacLaren. Again, I had the same problem at the University of Zimbabwe as I had had in Cambridge, although the problem wasn't colour, the problem was general. There were simply no plays with roles for black women, or at least we didn't have access to them at the time. The writers in Zimbabwe were also basically men at the time. And so I really didn't see that the situation would be remedied unless some woman sat down and wrote something, so that's what I did! I would actually date my serious writing from that time, about 1983-4, with my enrolment in the drama group and writing things for it.

So *She No Longer Weeps* isn't your only play?
Well, I actually produced two which were performed on campus, although I left before I had finished 'The Third One' and got it ready for performance, which was quite sad. I find it very difficult to write a play unless I know it's going to be performed.

What was *She No Longer Weeps* actually about?
It's a typical tale of a young student who falls pregnant and her family and boyfriend reject her and of how she pulls herself together and makes good, but also looking at the cost to her in personal terms of having had to go through with all that and succeed in spite of it. This was definitely written for an audience, as opposed to the stories, yes.

And what was your other play called?
That was called *The Lost of the Soil*, and it was about a group of young Zimbabwean exiles in London before independence and basically how they deal with their different conditions of alienation. Then there was also a white woman character whose parents had been missionaries and her father had been killed by freedom fighters. She had become quite alienated by all these experi-

ences and the question was, was she also one of the 'lost of the soil' or was she *not* of the soil?

Have your plays been published?
She No Longer Weeps has; it was published by the College Press in Zimbabwe in 1987. *The Lost of the Soil* was meant to have been published but it never was. In fact that was the first one, and I really wasn't serious, I didn't think I was achieving anything in that direction at all, I don't even have a copy of it!

Did you have problems getting your novel published?
I think perhaps by normal standards no. What happened was that I submitted the manuscript to a Zimbabwean publishing house and they dilly-dallied over it, so eventually I asked if I could have it back and then they said they didn't think they were going to publish it anyway. So I wondered, but I think by this time having written these plays and a couple of short stories and this novel I had begun to think of writing seriously and this was the test: was it worth putting my energy into creative pursuits altogether or should I carry on with my academic career? I wasn't willing to give up because I knew what I really wanted to do, I just didn't know whether it was possible or not. I asked myself whether this decision from this publishing house really reflected the fact that I could not write, or did it reflect perhaps the fact that I was writing about things that they were not ready to read about? So I decided to send the manuscript to a women's publishing house. I'd read Alice Walker – *The Color Purple* – in a Women's Press edition at the time and enjoyed her, so I thought I'd try the Women's Press. I think about eight months after sending it to them I had to come here on business and I popped round to the office and asked if they'd read it and they said 'No, we get so many manuscripts, but we *will* read it' and they did! So I suppose I didn't have that many difficulties, now that I know what usually happens!

Do you think the reason you weren't able to get it published in Zimbabwe had anything to do with the fact that there are not many women writers there? Or am I wrong? Perhaps there are plenty of women writers, only we don't get to hear about them outside Zimbabwe?
I think there are quite a number of women writers now. A lot of them write in either Shona or Ndebele, so this would not be for an international audience. I don't think that should be a criterion, and in fact I think there were more delicate issues at stake.

Have you related to any other stories of children or adolescents, of young people growing up?
There was *The Catcher in the Rye*, the *Diary of Ann Frank* . . . Yes, actually I have, definitely. There was *To Kill a Mocking Bird*.

Do you feel you relate to other African books about childhood?
Not really, I think it's just that if at the age of twenty-six somebody has a story to tell it's likely to be about growing up! Also, I'm always conscious at the back of my mind that there is very little that a woman in Zimbabwe can pick up – in Zimbabwe today – and say yes, I know, that's me. And that is something that really is quite a strong motivation quite frankly. Because I know I felt that gap so dreadfully. There was a time when I was working in a publishing house and

they were just beginning to rewrite the history. I was editing this Grade Seven text and I can remember saying to my editor that, if I had read that particular version of history when I had been at school, I would have been a much more integrated person. I am very conscious of that gap and of anything that I feel I or anybody else can do – I think the problem is also there with men and I think it may even be worse, because when they write they're not really going to talk about the day-to-day tensions and trouble, there's usually some grand cause that they're serving or deciding not to go to or to go to, and so I think that apart from Mungoshi – and there are some other writers – there are very few people in Zimbabwe that have really started to fill that gap for example of *The Catcher in the Rye*. Having said all this, I must add Camara Laye's *The African Child* was marvellous.

When did you first come across Mungoshi, when you came back from Cambridge?
Yes, I didn't even know he existed before! It is so sad, it really is.

Well, of course, some of these books were banned, weren't they?
This is what I mean: that was the system we were living under. Even the history was written in such a way that a child who did not want to accept that had to reject it and have nothing.

Which is Nyasha's problem.
Exactly.

SELECTED BIBLIOGRAPHY

THEATRE
She No Longer Weeps (Harare: College Press Zimbabwe, 1987).

NOVEL
Nervous Conditions (London: The Women's Press, 1988).

Musaemura Bonas Zimunya

Like his kingfisher persona, Zimunya 'skims from shadow to light / in and out of sunfare' as he sings the beauties and passions of Zimbabwe. But he also sings of its poverty and suffering, the deaths brought on by the war for independence and by intertribal fighting, and the physical and spiritual alienation of the 'city lights' of Harare and its 'Delivery Lane', the haunt of prostitutes and of the desperate, scavenging 'mangy dogs' who seem, increasingly, to symbolize humanity.

Born in Mutare, in the 'topographically dramatic' Eastern Highlands that have inspired the insistent physical dimension of his poetic explorations, Zimunya is a central figure in contemporary Zimbabwean literature. Engaged not only in creating and publishing his own poetry, but in documenting and making known the works of his compatriots, he is co-editor with M. Kadhani of *And Now the Poets Speak* (Gweru: Mambo Press, 1981), an anthology inspired by the liberation struggle. After studying at Chikore Secondary School and Goromonzi High School, Zimunya attended what was then the University of Rhodesia, but was expelled in 1973 for 'disturbing the peace'. During his exile in Britain he read History and English at the University of Kent at Canterbury, studied for an MA in Modern Literature and wrote a dissertation on the development of fiction in his country which was subsequently published as *Those Years of Drought and Hunger*. Senior Lecturer in English at the University of Zimbabwe, he has been Secretary General of the Zimbabwe Writers' Union. Together with Peter Porter and Kofi Anyidoho, he co-edited *The Fate of Vultures: New Poetry of Africa* (Oxford: Heinemann International, 1989).

15

Musaemura Bonas Zimunya

The interview took place at Montpellier (France), during the conference on Southern African literatures organized by the CERPANA (Centre d'Etudes et de Recherches sur les Pays d'Afrique Noire Anglophones), May 1987.

Could you talk to me a little about your own background, your beginnings, how you came to start writing?
What I recall is reading English poetry in Form One and Two about 1967–8. I thoroughly enjoyed the work of the English poets, particularly of Wordsworth and Browning. Then by coincidence we were taught by a very good teacher who was very much of a nationalist and had studied in India – then a beacon of anti-colonial struggle – at a time when African literature was starting to develop. He taught us the poems of Négritude, Senghor, and we used to wonder endlessly about this beautiful poetry. Then we started to read *Things Fall Apart, No Longer at Ease, A Grain of Wheat* and we enjoyed them tremendously. He seemed to receive or buy up every new African book that came out. I would say that's how I began. Gradually I moved away from writing poetry about the beauty of the country, which was what a lot of people enjoyed, what ruled the poetry. And then at that time also there was a very good magazine published by Whites, *Two Tone*, which published black poetry as well as white poetry. It made no attempt to bring the two together ideologically, it was a kind of omnibus where everybody wrote together whatever their differences. It was a fascinating experiment for a country like Rhodesia, because in every other field Blacks were not accepted. I would say that my poetry grew with publishing in that magazine and reading what else was published there: white writings, black writings.

Now, Zimbabwean literature as a whole had a slightly different development. I'm only one of many players. In 1956 the first novel in Shona (*Feso*) was published, in '58 the first big poem (*Soko Risina Musoro*). Those first two books, the epic novel and the first epic poem, were subsequently banned by the Rhodesian government on account of what was said to be 'subversive' content. Then a lot of books were published in the African languages on topics that were considered to be 'safe'. Books about going from the country to the city, how the city had crooks and prostitutes and thugs and so on, with the moral that you were better off in the country and coincidentally – and ironically – making the point the Whites were making: that the Black doesn't belong to the city, he belongs to the country, that's his rightful place. A lot of that literature was published in Ndebele and Shona.

Part of the problem was the Rhodesian Literature Bureau. Its business was to sift manuscripts and get rid of all politically sensitive material so that as a result a lot of the young writers went for these very, very simple themes about how an innocent young man who goes to the city gets corrupted and therefore gets punished in one way or another. Then there was a new movement in the publication of literature in English by black people starting with the publication of *On Trial For My Country* by Samkange. It was a historical novel and he followed this up by other historical novels like *The Year of the Uprising*. Now, *On Trial For My Country* deals with how Cecil Rhodes cheated Lobengula, gained rights to exploit gold in the country and gain political control. And then it also shows how the Blacks were victims of a very intricate trick of the colonial settlers, the missionaries, miners and politicians. Samkange followed this up with another book called *The Mourned One*, published in 1975. *The Mourned One* deals with the story of a twin brother who was saved from death in his childhood because in those days it was considered evil or taboo to have twins. A trial takes place in 1935, so you can work backwards to when his 'mourned one' was born, very early in the days of the white settlers. *The Mourned One* ends with this young boy saved from death by being brought to a mission, being brought up there, studying there, getting educated – the mission actually exists – until he graduates, he joins the working force, goes to Bulawayo, and then finds he doesn't like it and moves to the east to the mission where, having had a few drinks, he finds himself in a room with a white lady missionary who cries 'Rape!' So he's tried, in fact the whole story is about his trial for a rape that didn't take place. And he is actually sentenced to death for committing it. It comes from a true story. Soon afterwards Samkange published a new book called *The Year of the Uprising*. He went back to the theme of the wars of resistance, to 1896.

On Trial For My Country came out in '66. The next book was in 1972, *The Coming of the Dry Season* by Mungoshi, very beautiful short stories that you want to read and read again, there's such tenderness there. The subjects are of Africa in transition, you find the legacy of the indigenous novel, and then there are simple stories about the vulnerability of young boys. One story I will never forget for its sheer power – it reminds me of *Moby Dick* – is a story about boys hunting birds. They shoot a crow after they fail to shoot any more meaningful birds. They have a go at this crow, but the crow won't come to the ground, it perches onto another tree and, when they shoot it, it continues to fly stumblingly, while they don't stop chasing after it. It's bloodied but it doesn't actually die or stop flying until they catch it. Eventually they catch it, they try to crush it, but it doesn't die. They end up in tears, nauseated by this. It's short, the sort of thing you find in dreams a lot. Mungoshi writes like that, about the vulnerable. He also writes about boys looking for work and not getting work; of boys going up a lift for fun and being told by someone official that being black boys they shouldn't be going up there and they sit down waiting for sunset because they haven't got a job. It is pessimistic writing because it doesn't look to anywhere for hope.

Then came *Waiting For the Rain* (1975). The plot takes place over two days. The hero, a man with the ironic name of Lucifer, comes back from the city to say farewell to his family because he's going abroad with missionary sponsorship. But when he gets home it's to find that the family is caught up by superstition and everybody gets together to give him a farewell ceremony which is full of magic and drums and witchcraft. It's all very nightmarish to him because he thinks it's bunk. Eventually he is given some magic potions and sticks and he crushes them and says 'No, I will not take these at all' and he leaves home. And he even questions whether the colour of his skin is relevant, whether he wasn't born where he was born by sheer accident, whether he doesn't belong anywhere else . . . In terms of our struggle for liberation there are a few hints. The old man, Lucifer's grandfather, comes of the stock that fought in the 1896 war. He talks excitedly about how they killed the Whites: they had blood, the Whites! Unfortunately, though, nobody can live up to that now. There are a few characters in the book, but they all move like funny, funny characters who are too clever for the liberation struggle: some of them talk hypocritically about the struggle when in fact they are serving the Rhodesian regime.

Then you have the work of Dambudzo Marechera, *The House of Hunger*, which a lot of people have read. His work demands a lot of attention, it's the sort of work that you associate with mainstream European literature. He insists that he doesn't write for anyone. Once a writer says that, he doesn't write for the audience at home. In fact he's free to be himself and there's nothing very wrong with that. But you'll find the problem that his readers have a little difficulty to relate to him, because some of the things that he's doing with the material are not familiar to the African reader. He confuses and bewilders a lot of readers and I don't think that's a virtue at all. Take Soyinka for example. Although his works can be very abstract, a lot of his material is very accessible. You can see what he is doing on stage and in his books.

In *House of Hunger* you have an extension of the pessimism of Mungoshi's *Waiting For the Rain*. You can extend the logic of drought to hunger, *House of Hunger*. In the book there's actually no terrain, no landscape to speak of at all. He deals more with the symbolism of living in a city, a dog-eats-dog situation, where love between mother and father just doesn't exist, they just screw each other for fun and when it doesn't suit them the husband goes his way and the wife goes her way. In one of the incidents of the story the mother is screwed under the eyes of her own children. When one of them attempts to protest against this intruder who came in through the window, he's given a backhander and the man resumes his sex. That is the sort of thing that happens in *The House of Hunger*. One girl delivers at the head of the stream, she was thrown out of school because she was pregnant, and she washes her baby in the water of this stream and, we are told, 'there was blood everywhere'. Sex diseases, VD, fights and madness, violence and blood abound. The narrator himself is a student, thrown out of university, like Marechera himself – we were together at university in 1973, when we were thrown out and I actually served a prison sentence.

What was that for?
It was for 'disturbing the peace' because we rioted against the university and against the Government. Together with seven others, he was thrown out of the

university before we were arrested, but the rest of us were arrested in sympathy. He wasn't the only one, there were quite a few, including men who are now ministers! But then with Marechera you find that he moves away from Zimbabwe with his second book, *Black Sunlight*. It's a surrealistic, existentialist novel where the plot is an anti-plot and the characters are anti-characters and the whole idea of the novel is anti-novel, very modernistic in that sense. You don't go to read Marechera for pleasure, you read him I suppose for fascination with the anguish of the human mind. But in his book *Mindblast*, published in 1983, a collection of poems, short stories, journalese and dramatic sketches, he comes home to a rude shock. He finds that all that he had been saying in *Black Sunlight* is true: dog-eat-dog, independence doesn't really matter. Everyone's hard, they'd like a posh house, a posh car, a posh position in the new order and in the process they don't mind putting their foot on a little frog or a little millipede along the way. He has this vision of the corruption of power throughout this work.

There's also a book called *The Non-Believer's Journey* by Stanley Nyamfukudza that is very important and which ties up with the whole business of pessimism from Mungoshi to Marechera, because the main characters in the stories are moving away from Zimbabwe. In Nyamfukudza the main character is actually *in* Zimbabwe during the war. He goes to the rural areas for a funeral and to give fees to his parents during the war. He enjoys the life of an anarchist in the city, staying up at the nightclub till very late in the morning, dancing with women he had no inclination to screw, although they looked ready, and all that sort of thing. Eventually he gets home. The war is on and it's a very big struggle for his parents to cope with the liberation war. But unfortunately for him the guerrillas come and enquire what he is doing. He tells them, but they're not impressed because he should have joined the war, he might be a traitor. He shouts at them and reminds them that it's none of their business. A big fight ensues and they shoot him. Now this guy insisted on non-commitment, freedom of conscience. In a situation like that he has no hope whatsoever. So you have a continuation of the line of pessimism in this fight with the guerrilla fighter. Then there's a story called *Jikinya* by a writer called Geoffrey Ndhlala. It's a very interesting story because it belongs to the romantic tradition. It's a book that deals with the pre-colonial era, a peaceful, loving community, a sort of Eden or Paradise, nostalgia for an innocent past. The book is about an innocent past that is rudely shattered by an explorer who finds that a little white girl is living among the primitive people. How this little white girl came here is not known to him. This innocent community had brought this child up from being a little, little baby whom they'd found after a war beyond their borders. One of the men was a hunter and it was he who found this baby, beyond the border, and brought it home where the child is raised after a big conflict with some people saying 'We have no business to keep this child, a white child!' Yet she grows up among the Blacks just like any of their own people.

It's a myth you find in several different cultures . . .
Yes, there are myths like that in Zimbabwe, but also real stories. After the war of 1893–6 many stories were told of abandoned or captured white children. That story strikes a very different theme because it shows how colonialism is destructive of a whole people, a whole way of life, a whole way of looking at human beings and the world.

Thereafter we had independence, and with independence there came a need to recapture the war. The whole thrust of the liberation struggle was not captured at all. All the books I have been talking about were published abroad. The only books that were published in Rhodesia were in Shona or Ndebele. But I think one of the problems with 1980 is that it's a very artificial boundary in human sensibility. People do not change because of 1980, they change over years and there were not many books that came out to recapture this struggle in heroic terms. There have been a few, there have been two as a matter of fact, apart from *Mindblast*. One is called *Crossroads* by a writer called Spencer Tizora and another called *Contact* by Mutasa. Those books actually belong to the war. *Contact* deals with the heroism of a guerrilla fighter who comes home and then gradually finds that his society is becoming corrupt. In *Crossroads* you have a very interesting Black/White situation. There's a white woman on the other side and a black boy on this side, then you have white soldiers, black soldiers, the whole lot. It attempts to bring out the humanity of the Whites, although I think in artistic terms it actually collapses. Then there's another called *A Fighter For Freedom* which is even more disastrous in literary terms and I would actually rather it was never studied because it doesn't do much credit to Zimbabwean writing: it's very badly written in terms of structure, and the writing itself, the art itself. It was written by a man who is now High Commissioner in Kenya.

How about Zimbabwean poetry?
In 1978 a book came out called *Zimbabwean Poetry* which was a great event because it brought together a whole lot of previously written black poetry showing how there was actually a definite historical sensibility in process, whereas with white poetry you could take poems from 1950 and 1978 and there wouldn't be very much difference at all, because the ideas are the same. In 1978 the only changed situation might be the war, but, according to white writers, the safari goes on . . . Then in 1979 a book of poetry came out by D. E. Borrell and myself called *A Patch of Blue Sky and Zimbabwe Ruins* – 'A Patch of Blue Sky' is by D. E. Borrell and 'Zimbabwe Ruins' is by me. It was an interesting publication because it showed exactly what I've just been saying: white poets write as though the world is comfortable, or, if it isn't comfortable, they can cope with it. They don't actually see that there is something afoot, whereas black poetry has always been anxious about this new world, this brave new world, and about how, eventually, behind the anxiety is the conflict. It comes through eventually, even if a bit late, in the black protest poetry in Zimbabwe. Really, therefore, you find that that collection gives you all these contradictions. First of all there was a collection done by the Poetry Society of Rhodesia, a white organization, which makes you say 'Why did the Whites bring together black and white poets when they are radically different? What could be gained by that?' To maintain the sort of family relationship? That could be true. Nobody ever saw the white novelists, nobody ever knew what they thought, they wrote what they felt like and what they wrote and felt like was the *spleen* of racism. The white poets were different, they appear as more human in their relationship with black poets. They didn't even bother to censor what the black poets were writing or to *censure* them! I still don't understand why they didn't do that.

In 1981 *And Now the Poets Speak*, a book edited by myself and Mudeneri Kadhani, was published by Mambo Press in Zimbabwe. A very interesting book, because it brings out the more radical material that wasn't published in the '70s. Thereafter you talk of individual publications like my own *Thought-tracks, Kingfisher and Jikinya* and *Country Dawns and City Lights*. Jikinya is a woman's name, a legendary name in popular music, she's a dancer, a beautiful woman who breaks the hearts of the men . . . A new writer called Chenjerai Hove, the author of *Up in Arms*, is the one author who speaks very authentically about the war. He is also the author of *Red Hills of Home* which is very interesting for the vagueness with which he treats subjects that are very, very serious, like the sufferings of black people even after independence. He's so vague that it frustrates and infuriates a lot of people who prefer poetry and literature to be more precise about these things. But other developments after independence show a very vibrant situation.

A lot of things have happened in Zimbabwe that other African countries envy: a lot of publishers are interested in Zimbabwean writers *in* Zimbabwe, then there is the biennial Zimbabwe International Book Fair, and the Zimbabwe Writers' Union, which is very powerful. There was a very big confrontation with the Ministry of Youth over *Workshop Negative*, a production by Amakhosi, a Bulawayo-based theatre group. I am Secretary General of the Writers' Union. From now on if the ministries want to censure art they're going to have to be very careful. Our staunch support for Amakhosi (the production group, a sort of cooperative of workers' theatre groups in Bulawayo) was quite unprecedented. We insisted that authors should not be intimidated, that authors should be understood – particularly this author who represented the problems of not a few individuals in society – and that he was looking at *types*, not at individual ministers or party politicians or factory workers. He was looking at a *type* that is prevalent in Zimbabwe at the moment: a person owning a factory when he has come out of an oppressive situation and turning out to be an oppressor himself. The play touched on the raw nerve of post-independence Zimbabwe (it was refused permission to tour Zambia). I would say that it can be taken as a watershed. It marks an irreparable rift between bureaucracy and art. Bureaucracy will come, it will appease, it will pretend to patronize, it will give money, but there's no doubt about the fact that there is a rift now between bureaucracy and the arts. Whether this will lead to tensions is beside the point. We as artists are keen to make our views, our freedom, the necessity of our freedom a matter of urgency in post-independence Zimbabwe in a manner that they have not been, because unfortunately we are a very relaxed folk in Zimbabwe; we haven't got the excitement of other African nations at all. But I would say that the situation is very optimistic for the artists themselves. The trouble is that our literature is not very well known, so it's underrated.

But something else that should be looked into in Zimbabwean literature is the popular magazines. The short story goes back to about 1930 with the publication of these stories in the popular magazines. They were owned by men from South Africa and were published up to the days of Federation (1955). There was a flourishing of culture around the time of Federation. Some of our best journalists matured then, in fact it was the golden age of Zimbabwean journalism. After that came UDI [Unilateral Declaration of Independence] and there was a splintering and a scattering of people and the world is never the same after that. It's like in South Africa. Serote was telling me that you have a literary flourish and then there is a crisis and that crisis has actually stemmed the whole flourish of the tide and everything has to begin again. So you find in

South Africa itself you have a whole series of beginnings. Outside people may have different views, they see a development, a pattern building up, but inside there's a series of fractures. So you had that in our development. In fact the short story remained something you read in the popular magazines and not in a book and it always tended to reflect the taste of the sales manager, i.e. it must be a story about love, broken hearts and so forth.

In English or also in Shona and Ndebele?
Actually Shona didn't have any short stories at all. The Shona short story is a dead factor. The *tale* survives, the *fable* survives, but that is different. But hitherto there are no Shona short stories. I have written some; I'm actually doing a sequence or cycle, but it hasn't been published yet and we can't talk about that. But there's no tradition in Shona or Ndebele.

But in English there most certainly is.
Of course, of course. It's very strange: the Rhodesian Literature Bureau encouraged publication of Shona or Ndebele, not English. No black person who wrote in English was published through the Literature Bureau, none. But a lot of short stories were published in local magazines. That explains why people had to publish abroad: Mungoshi, Marechera, etc. The Bureau didn't touch English poetry either. It is the largest literary agency in the country. Most aspiring authors, the first thing they think of is to send their manuscripts to the Literature Bureau. They have piles and piles and piles of scripts. There's a whole library of manuscripts, unread, going back to the '80s. I walked in one day and was shown around. The Bureau is central to the history of Zimbabwean literature. Now they are interested in short stories. A lot of the officers of the Bureau come of the generation of the '50s. They worked as translators when the Bureau was started and they had very little education, they are way behind the times, but some of them are still around, since 1955, with the education they acquired then. Of course they did so much work, to give the devil his due. And the Shona novel has got a tradition of very good writing, to say the least, the only problem was that it was restricted in the themes it could actually treat.

You write in English; what is your relationship to Shona?
Well, actually, when I speak our traditional languages I'm very, very much at home and I don't use English at all, except when I don't find the equivalent word. When I go home or to the rural areas and speak this language, the older people find it crazy that I should still speak the language this way, after all that has happened. To me, I think this is the biggest flattery I've ever had. Once you've mastered a language it's good to speak it well and if you love language you speak it well.

Your schooling was also largely in Shona, wasn't it?
Shona, Shona, Shona from when I was in Sub-A, which was the colonial first grade. The first book I read was in Shona and I didn't start to read in English until my second year. Our first year book was a picture book, and I didn't have a copy of it because my parents were very poor and I didn't have the money to buy my English picture book. Eventually my mother took things in hand. My father drank a lot and he actually died at a beer drinkhouse. That's neither here nor there because I owe him a lot for the artistic dimension. He was an *mbira* player.

Could you talk about your own poetry, your own production, now? How did you come to write poetry? You said earlier that you liked the poetry of Wordsworth and Browning, would you like to pick up from there?
I'll tell you what I liked about Wordsworth and Browning. I come from Mutare. Mutare is beautiful, absolutely beautiful. I live under the foothills of the Vhumba mountains which together with the Inyanga mountains form the Eastern Highlands. In fact one of my poems says:

I live in the highlands / encompassed by great green ridges / where is my home, / in the heart of the storms of the world?

It's a very beautiful poem, though I don't like the way it ends when I look back now, because it ends with a little Wordsworthian hut! The poetry of Wordsworth and Browning made me wish to record the beauty of nature, of the mountains where I come from. I don't think I'll ever be able to do that again. It's a stunningly beautiful place, it suits itself to nature poetry, particularly in the spring and summer. The reason why Robert Browning appealed to me – I actually got a little crazy at one point and even started imitating him – was the dramatic nature of his poetry. Like the one to Fra Lippo Lippi. It was mainly because my father was a very dramatic person himself, very dramatic. Although he didn't ever act in a play, he was always improvising some little drama for his audience, even in old age – he was quite old you see because he had two wives and our eldest sister was four or five years younger than the last daughter of the other wife! And the conflict between the two wives naturally made its way down to the children and we had to struggle in many ways, even if today our family is more interesting in terms of achievement than many others, perhaps because we had that extra nudge. Our mother was always treated as the family doormat. So what appealed to me in Browning was his dramatic quality.

Then what happened was that as we were reading Ngũgĩ and Achebe and Senghor it suddenly occurred to me – Senghor didn't see African landscape for its own beauty only – suddenly it occurred to me that there was something wrong in this land that I was praising! I couldn't go on just eulogizing when I knew very well that the farmland actually looked more beautiful then, because it was inhabited by *one* farmer, hectares and hectares and hectares! And there we were, *crowded* in one little hectare, and I was saying the land was beautiful! I remember a friend being taken in by the police and I will never forget that, my anger, my frustration, my bitterness, they were all there, how could I go on just praising the beauty of the country? Suddenly it didn't make sense. That's how I moved away.

So it was really a combination of what was actually happening around you and what you were reading, which helped to increase your awareness?
Awareness is something that takes a very long time for some people. We were happy writing beautiful poetry and I would think 'I'm going to be a poet!' I was writing in English, but when I got to Salisbury (Harare) the English people weren't seeing me as a human being at all! Then in 1970 I won a prize for poetry, the first black person to win a prize for poetry! I was nineteen and the school provided funds for me to travel to collect the prize. When I was there I was fêted, I ate all sorts of things that I wasn't used to and I attended lectures coinciding with the prize-giving. But on my way back, on the train, somebody asked 'Where are you coming from?' and I said 'From a prize-giving, I won a

poetry prize.' When I told him I wrote English poems he said 'Do you think you'll ever make money out of English poetry? Go and write in your own language!' I told him he was ignorant, 'There are people like Achebe, people like Ngũgĩ!' I didn't take him seriously, but this guy shocked me. Afterwards things like this turn in your mind in their own way and make you question yourself, and I did question myself. I wrote poetry in Shona and submitted it to the Literature Bureau, but the Literature Bureau told me 'Thank you very much for submitting your manuscript. We found it very, very promising and we intend to use some of your work, but we would like to warn you against subjects of a politically and religiously offensive nature.' So I stopped writing Shona poetry!

Was there much difference – in terms of content – between your Shona poetry and your English poetry?
There was. I suppose that when I started to write in Shona it coincided with my awareness that it wasn't enough to write about the beautiful landscape, it wasn't enough to write a praise poem, the most common type of poem then. People would write praise poems about *anything*, about a spoon, porridge, meat!

When you say 'praise poems' are you talking in general about a eulogistic sort of poetry or about the praise poem tradition in the oral culture?
Well, it comes from a Shona tradition. But what they did was, instead of just saying 'I've had a few drinks and I'm feeling groggy', they would sit down and actually compose a praise poem about the beer, the colour of it, the honeyed look of it, even the container in which the beer is served. At some point it was absolutely farcically ridiculous that a whole literature should be hijacked by a fascination of this nature, of no apparent use in general. It provided immediate excitement: like at school where boys are excited to read a poem about beer or about love, they want to know more about them. But the beer is personified in the poem. The Shona are very adept at that, they personify everything in poetry. So I moved away from that sort of poem and towards another kind of poetry. I wrote a poem about 'Blindness'. I didn't mention Africa or anything. I just mentioned 'land' a few times. I was just talking about being blind. In fact the poem came out of the fascination with blindness that I had since I was young: I actually had regular dreams about being blind and groping about, until I wrote about it. Somebody said the poem was very political – I used the word 'land', 'the land' – and when I looked at it again it clearly read political, but I hadn't been aware of that. Then there were other poems that I hadn't submitted because one always feared that these publishers could betray one. So I moved away from writing poetry in Shona. Originally I had had all sorts of ideas for things I would write in Shona, things I would write in English.

Was it easier for you to express yourself in English rather than Shona because English was less susceptible to censorship?
It was. In fact you will find that that is the history of Zimbabwean literature. Most of the serious work was written in English. For one thing, because it could be published abroad and there was no way the Censorship Board could stop publication of things abroad. As a matter of fact, *The Coming of the Dry Season* was banned in 1975 under the Rhodesian regime, but it had already

been published, some people already had copies and it was available abroad. So that the whole development of Shona and Ndebele literature, poetry, novels, drama, was dictated by the publishing forces.

Presumably with independence all this must have changed?
Oh yes, the good thing about independence is that even publishers are not bothered about publishing things that may look very critical, like *Mindblast*, which is one of the most critical works about Zimbabwe you can find, but it's on sale and is probably the most popular of Marechera's works in Zimbabwe.

Has the writing in the Zimbabwean languages increased since independence?
I wouldn't actually say so. Ndebele and Shona literature grew at such a pace after the '60s, particularly Shona literature, that it's very, very big. I know that other African countries have problems in this area, like Kenya, for instance. That's why it's difficult for people in Zimbabwe to bother about what Ngũgĩ says about language, because we never had the problems Kenyans have. The literature was there, the question was simply how much of what literature and not so much that we should write in our own language. I am actually writing in my own language now, but you don't even think about it, you just write! It doesn't arouse any excitement or debate in Zimbabwe at all. As a kid, the first novel that I read was a Zimbabwe novel. The first play that I saw enacted was an adaptation of a Shona novel. I was doing Standard One at the time. Then, when we were doing Standard Four we had a reader in class of an African story and it was very, very popular. Further than that, all the way up, in Shona. As well as Dickens, in the abridged series, and so on. Zimbabwean literature in the indigenous languages is *big business*. I wrote JC exams in my mother language, we studied the grammar of the language and took exams on it: O-levels, A-levels. I did some of it at university before we got thrown out. For as long as the University of Zimbabwe has been around there's always been teaching of the local languages.

In the writing in English, would you say there is much relation with the traditional oral literature?
Oh yes. Think of *Waiting For the Rain*. This whole business of going to the city and being punished and being corrupted which we find in the indigenous literature comes from the moral tales, the fables of the Shona people or the Ndebele people. The fable always has an instructive message at the end.

Does the influence come through also in the form of the writing as well as in the story and moral?
The characterization for example, the behaviour of the characters and the mould of the characters may easily conform to a fable. You'll also find that the style of the narratives themselves – from the point of view of the narrator, for example – conform to the idea of the oral fable-maker and his audience, the intimacy, the rapport. Then also you have songs. And you have *improbability* as the structural feature of some of these stories, an inheritance from the fable where human beings speak with animals and animals speak with human beings. Then you have the role of superstition as part of the fantastic effects or improbability effects in the stories. So you do indeed have the oral tradition transmuted into the writing. In *Waiting For the Rain* you have a lot more. The effects of that story are from a heavily oral society. The language the people use

is rich and indicative of orature. Then you have the sessions of poetry and music that interspace the action.

Sometimes it is said of African writing that there is a tendency to look too much towards the past, neglecting the problems of the present. Is this sort of criticism put forward in Zimbabwe too?
I think this is where scholars will find Zimbabwean literature very interesting because, far from looking backwards, Mungoshi, Nyamfukudza and Marechera himself – those are the most important writers one can speak of at the moment – actually look into the future. The main character in *Waiting For the Rain* rejects even the colour of his skin: 'I was born here by accident, I could have been born elsewhere,' he says. In the meantime, the whole weight of the book is showing how the large majority of his family depend for sustenance on a past, a spiritual past, an ancestral past. I wouldn't say that whatever elements of orature remain in our writing are detrimental. Marechera himself uses devices and forms that are associated with orature, except that he does unexpected things with them.

Which itself is part of the tradition.
Yes, you can't run away from your past completely, unless you think of his book *Black Sunlight*. That has nothing to do with the past. There are no ghouls arising from the ancestral past, there are no stories or fables at all. It's a modern state, a human estate which is corrupt, whether it's African or white – he actually leaves the setting unidentified, anonymous.

Is there much connection between Zimbabwean literature and other Southern African literatures? What you said about the beauty of nature in your poetry made me think of Malawian poetry.
'Sunset Comes to Sapitwa', 'Dawn' . . . I haven't read many other Malawian poets except Felix Mnthali – who was born in Zimbabwe, by the way – and Jack Mapanje, who strikes me as being a very different kind of poet though. I can't see Jack Mapanje as the praise singer to Mount Mulanje. Mnthali was born in Zimbabwe and then went on to Malawi after about two or three years' schooling. He writes the sort of poetry some of which I would love to have written, although in some instances it's just too beautiful and also he gets so involved in it that there's a clash of tone and symbols. That may be neither here nor there except its spirit is more exciting, until you come to those poems which tell you that all his spirit is a tragedy called Malawi and not only Malawi but a tragedy called life, like in the poem 'Butterfly', which is one of the most powerful poems I have ever read. It's a prophetic voice. The persona is in a desert, looking for an answer to life. After all his searches the only thing he comes to is a butterfly, a very beautiful butterfly, and he goes backwards in his search as he's looking at the butterfly. This is the middle section of the poem. And then he says 'When I go on another search in another world for what I have been looking for I'll find another butterfly like this.' A very haunting idea.
It's interesting to compare Malawi, Zimbabwe, Mozambique and Angola. I don't know what Angolans and Mozambicans did, but, with the exception of Pepetela, they are not so much lovers of nature at all. Where it exists in their works nature subserves the human with such relentlessly tragic or problematic or sad imagery. By the time you've been through *Mayombe* you've gone through the jungles of Angola. And not only that, you've gone through the

jungles of human character, its beauties and its ugliness, what it holds in store, its love, love-making, its joys and its tragedies. Ondine is a character I find very fascinating, although in the end she seems to be an incomplete symbol. She's the erotic power behind the power of liberation.

Zimbabwe is somewhat different both from Mozambique and Angola, because the Mozambicans and the Angolans were very close to the proletariat. They were moved by the pain of workers on contract to South Africa, to the mines and plantations not very far from Angola. Their psyche was much more responsive to that tradition of going away to work, which you don't find very much in Zimbabwean literature. I wrote about nature and for a long time I saw things representing the peasant more than the workers. For a long, long time.

Who do you feel most affinity to among the African poets?
For a long time I've liked Okara, his mysticism. He has a facility for blurring things that look very obvious. Then when you look through what he's actually blurred there's something there which could not be expressed in any other way. I know mysticism is debunked, but as a technique it can be more powerful than a lot of things that are mythified. I have doubts about the rest. I like Okot p'Bitek's experiments in popular poetry and I have tried to do some of that in *Country Dawns and City Lights*, which is my latest book of poems, although I found the structure of *Song of Lawino* monotonous. It may work well as a play, but as a poem to be read, by the time you've come to the end there are things that have been said over and over again. Senghor I still admire a great deal for the originality of his style, which I haven't found anyone able to imitate, perhaps because he writes in French. Diop – that's another who wrote with the heart of a proletarian that I find very admirable.

Is your knowledge and appreciation of Francophone writing the result of your schooling, or more particularly of the literature teacher you told me about?
I suppose *he* was great. He introduced us to *The African Child*: we read it in class, although it's not one of the stories I would make my child read. The most telling part was the part I didn't understand, when the boy had to depart and go to the mission school. That was probably the most important part, everything had been leading up to it. But when he read it at school I didn't understand it all. Things had been happening, there was a snake, but so what? But now, looking back, I can see that things were building up towards the child's being wrenched from a world. Then we read *Mission to Kala*. And then of course Senghor, 'New York'! At first I was struck by the 'golden legs', and then he goes on to show the two sides of New York, Manhattan and the negro ghetto Harlem, and he transfers images of pleasure and happiness from Manhattan to Harlem. Nowadays you'll find that a lot of students do know about these Francophone writers. We teach Mongo Beti, Sembene Ousmane, Mbella Sonne Dipoko and the Négritude poets, Aimé Césaire. Now we've actually moved to the Caribbean and Afro-American writers.

Earlier you mentioned an epic novel and an epic poem in the '50s, could you tell me about them?
They are classics now, the two classic works of Shona literature, and both are about being dispossessed, about being landless, about having nothing to eat, about being forced to survive on the scabs of your wounds (a Shona idiom for living in misery). *Feso* is the first novel published in Shona in the country. It is

an epic set in the height of one of the oldest empires in the country, called the Mwenemutapa. The story is about a king's beautiful daughter and about the conflict between two kings, how one of them would not rest until he had the daughter of the other king. In the end it becomes an allegory of the relationship between black people and white people. *Feso* wasn't noticed by the Rhodesian authorities for a long, long time until an excerpt was recited at a political rally at the height of nationalism in the mid-'60s. Suddenly the authorities realized there was something wrong with the book, so they withdrew it and banned it altogether. It wasn't until 1980 that it was unbanned and permitted to be read in schools. That was the first epic novel. Its author was Solomon Mutswairo, by the way. He is currently lecturing in African languages at the university. He and Herbert Chitepo, another hero of the liberation war who was killed in '75 in Lusaka, are considered the forefathers of Shona literature.

Herbert Chitepo wrote a book called *Soko Risina Musoro*, 'The Tale Without a Head'. It was the first written epic poem to come out of Zimbabwe – accessible epic poetry. I would put it alongside the old Greek epics: straightforward, but yet very complex. It's the story of a wayfarer who arrives in a kingdom and finds that there is a great amount of commotion, the people are walking in some direction and he asks what the excitement is all about. They ask him, 'Are you new in these lands, don't you know what has smitten these lands, don't you know what we don't have?' – and so it goes on. He's quite amused by his respondent who thinks he's an ignoramus, and he panders along. It's rather picturesque. He's led eventually to the king's court, where all the people are gathered and there is a lot of oratory. One after the other the king's councillors are talking about how the king should do the most decent thing available to kings who have failed and simply abdicate. In the land there's no rain, you see. To whom has it ever happened, which king presided over a drought-stricken people? And he goes on in that vein. Eventually what happens is simply that the king comes up and says 'It is not my fault alone, it is the fault of you and I that the country is in this state. We can only do our best and our best is to pray before our ancestors, that is all I tell you now, let us kneel down and pray.' And that is what they do.

It's very dramatic, the poem is full of such satire about the chiefs of the tale. The chiefs were the first victims of our wars of resistance. They were the most direct customers of the imperial powers and as such they had not much option but to succumb, otherwise they were in trouble. So the poem satirizes them. And then it also satirizes the people for being lost and bewildered and without any sense of direction. It was after *Feso* was banned, it was also considered that this book could be dangerous too. They didn't understand literature really, but they realized it could be dangerous. What on earth was he talking about? He doesn't refer to the Whites, he doesn't refer to colonialism, he just says 'There's no land, there's no land!' Those are the two epics.

They haven't been translated into English?
They have, both of them. The first was published by Donald Herdeck, Three Continents Press, in a book called *Zimbabwe*.

Have they had much influence on other Zimbabwean writing?
Well, *Feso* would have had a very powerful influence on all future writing, but it was put out of circulation, and now writers can write better anyway. Now nobody wants to write like *Feso* because it's old-fashioned. There was a book

that came out after *Feso* that didn't deal with the Whites, but with the Ndebele and the Shona. It's a Shona book. The man who is sent to steal a beauty from the tyrannical other king in *Feso* is developed now into a warrior, an orphaned warrior, who grew up and was unbeatable: when he learnt to use arrows he became a sort of William Tell of the Shona. This goes on until he gets taken in a raid to Matabeleland. Here his prowess gets to be noticed and in fact he gets married there and decides to flee back to his homeland and does so under all sorts of odds. It's like a fairy-tale, improbability and all! But it doesn't deal with the crucial issues. It isn't intelligent enough to allegorize this young man's fate as a universal Zimbabwean suffering fate. It's just a tale and the Ndebele/Shona conflict becomes a sort of historical throw-back at a time when it doesn't really bother anybody.

When did *Feso* and *Soko* begin to circulate again?
In 1980. But of course they've become more interesting to the new generation. For us, some of us now, *Feso* is forgotten about, but not *The Tale Without a Head*. I really would like to write something like that. *Feso* was good at the time and it remains with its own integrity a very outstanding work for a first-time Shona novel ever, a seminal work that came before all the others. But *The Tale Without a Head* is beautiful, absolutely beautiful, and it's not very long, not more than about twenty pages. In terms of power, in terms of integrity, in terms of something seen, a vision with its own completeness, it has not been emulated anywhere in Zimbabwean literature. Its title has been bothering a lot of Zimbabwean teachers, even to this day. They don't know what it means, can you believe that? These are the people who grew up on the diet of country-to-city / country-to-country / city-to-country diet of plots and themes and they can't actually wean themselves away from it. So that it is not strange they should find they can't read the book. When I go to it I humble myself before this first-time poetic epic, short, precise, with characters who look as though they're coming out of a Greek play, although there's something so modernistic about it because there are no soft options, no easy choices, no easy narrative, no concession to quick understanding. You have to understand the background and the symbols and the direction of the allegory. And very strangely, the idea of drought and hunger which was picked up *years* later by Mungoshi and Marechera is there.

And yet Mungoshi and Marechera were writing before 1980, so they wouldn't have had any contact with it, would they?
Mungoshi may have read it, because the author went to school in the same place as Mungoshi. I didn't read it myself until 1978, and that was abroad.

But, apart from the possibility of direct influence, it's interesting to see the same themes, the same problems, coming through.
There's this thing about the spirit of the place and the spirit of the time. We have a very powerful story going back to the nineteenth century. There was a nine-teenth-century prophet called Chaminuka, who was there before Rhodes was given the territory and was killed before Rhodes came to live in the land. Before he died – he died under some very unhappy circumstances – he was a medium, people say he could disappear: he would sit on the rocks and invoke mist, but at the time his opponents wanted to kill him it didn't work. They say he could parry assegais, swords, with his bare hands and he was a rich man. Lobengula,

the Ndebele ruler, was fascinated by this man and he invited him – the one thing about the pre-independence chiefs and kings was that they insisted on respecting the spirits of the place. This man represented the spirits of Zimbabwe. Even during the war his name was invoked and there are so many songs about him, even now; he's like a saint I suppose in our traditional belief. He was actually killed by the Ndebele and this is how it happened. Lobengula's soldiers said 'You can't keep this man for too long, he's too powerful, let's kill him.' They tried to kill him with their swords but without success, so in the end they said 'OK, bring a child, a little child, give him a sword and he will kill him.' And actually he was killed by a child, a little boy. But before he died he said, 'Whatever you do, know you this, that although you've killed me, this land of yours – meaning Matebeleland – shall know no peace, shall have no rain, and there shall come people of a white skin who will have no knees – our old people called the Whites 'people with no knees' because they wore trousers – and they shall bring into the land a big iron millipede that will send smoke into the sky and there will be no rest for your people.'

So this question of drought is not only real in the sense that every now and then we have drought in Zimbabwe – one has to take that into account – but the question of this prophecy lingers on. I remember singing a song about this prophecy.

Did he make any reference to a possible redemption? Did he stop at the drought or did he allude to a possible future rain?
Well, he said, 'As long as these Whites are here your land and mine shall know no peace, no rain.'

So he left it open. I asked that because it's quite similar to the story about Mugo wa Kibiro, the Gĩkũyũ prophet.
Yes, it's all over Africa! But I'm saying this in connection with the frequency of the drought theme. Apart from the fact that every four or five years there is lack of rain, we have this myth. I think it's a myth: the Whites are gone, but in the years between independence and now we've still had drought! This old prophet is worshipped. There are places you go and there is music playing – the *mbira* – and they are praising this man. They will tell you 'There is something wrong with this Government, that's why there is no rain!' They won't be very precise about what is wrong, but they understand the basic symbol.

SELECTED BIBLIOGRAPHY

POETRY
(With D. E. Borrell), *A Patch of Blue Sky and Zimbabwe Ruins* (Harare: Poetry Society of Rhodesia, 1979).
Kingfisher, Jikinya and Other Poems (Harare: Longman, 1982).
Thought-Tracks (Harlow: Longman, 1982). Honourable Mention in the Noma Award of 1983.
Country Dawns and City Lights (Harare: Longman, 1985). Honourable Mention in the 1986 Noma Award.

CRITICISM
Those Years of Drought and Hunger. The Birth of African Fiction in English in Zimbabwe (Gweru: Mambo Press, 1982)

Index

INDEX

INDEX

Pirandello, Luigi, 37; *Six Characters in Search of an Author*, 37
Plaatje, Sol T., 150
Plato, 77
Poe, Edgar Allan, 190
Porter, Peter, 200
Powys, T.F., 96
publishers: BLAC Publication House, 165; College Press, Zimbabwe, 197; Ethiope, 92; Fagbamigbe, 92; Fourth Dimension, 92; Ghana Publishing Corporation, 42; Heinemann (African Writers Series), 94; Longman, 14, 66–7; Mambo Press, 205; Onibonoje, 92; Ravan Press, 151, 161; Rhodesian Literature Bureau, 202, 207, 209; Secker and Warburg, 69; Woeli, 16; Women's Press, 197

Randall, Peter, 161
Rawlings, Jerry, 14
Rhodes, Cecil, 202, 214
Rifaat, Alifa, 56; *A View from the Minaret*, 56
Rotimi, Ola, 38, 72
Rousseau, Jean Jacques, 60; *Confessions*, 60
Ruganda, John, 114
Rushdie, Salman, 74, 102; *Satanic Verses*, 74

Samkange, Stanlake, 202; *The Mourned One*, 202; *On Trial For My Country*, 202; *The Year of the Uprising*, 202
Sanchez, Sonia, 179
Sangster, Ellen Geer, 8
Sarbah, Mensah, 22
Sarbah, John Mensah, 22; *Fanti Customary Constitutions*, 22
SASO, 156, 174
Seal, Bobby, 152
Sekyi, Kobina, 22; *The Blinkards*, 22, 36–7
Selassie, Haile, 181
Senghor, Léopold Sédar, 201, 208; 'New York', 212
Sepamla, Sipho, 151, 164
Serote, Wally Mongane, 3, 4, 5, 151, 172, 174–86, 206; *Behold Mama, Flowers*, 181–2, 186; 'Fogitall', 174; 'Lets Wander Together', 174; *Letters of the People*, 181; 'The Meeting', 174; *The Night Keeps Winking*, 183, 186; *To Every Birth Its Blood*, 151, 182, 186; 'When Rebecca Fell', 174
Serumaga, Robert, 114
Setsoafia, Bidi, 21
Shagari, Shehu, 97
Shaka, 140, 141, 182
Shakespeare, William, 2, 33, 36, 39, 40, 52, 82, 114, 115, 118, 138, 175, 190; *Hamlet*, 37, 101; *Henry V*, 118; *Macbeth*, 37, 117; *Merchant of Venice*, 33; *Othello*, 89; *Romeo and Juliet*, 190
Shaw, George Bernard, 36, 37, 63; *Androcles and the Lion*, 117
Shelley, Percy Bysshe, 60, 67, 138
Sheridan, Richard, 36; *School for Scandal*, 117
Sikoto, Gerard, 183
Small, Adam, 164
Smallburger, Mavis, 172
Smith, Wilbur, 194
Solarin, Tai, 93
Soyinka, Wole, 2, 4, 5, 37, 38, 40, 43, 58, 68, 69–70, 74, 83, 88, 89, 90–108, 119, 120, 137; *Aké*, 96, 108; *Blues for a Prodigal*, 90, 97–8; 'Climates of Art', 104; *Culture in Transition*, 90; *A Dance of the Forests*, 37, 108; *Death and the King's Horseman*, 97, 108; *The Interpreters*, 102, 108; *Isara*, 90, 106–7, 108; *The Invention*, 106; *The Lion and the Jewel*, 37, 90, 108; *The Man Died*, 68, 90, 96, 108; *Mandela's Earth*, 104–6; *Ogun Obibimañ*, 103, 106, 108; *Poems of Black Africa* (see under anthologies); *The Road*, 83, 108; *Season of Anomy*, 102, 108; shot-gun sketches, 4, 97; *A Shuttle in the Crypt*,

100, 108; *The Swamp Dwellers*, 90, 108; *Unlimited Liability Company*, 90, 98
Splendid Sunday, 149
Stewart, MacNeil, 23
Suliman, Ramadaan, 165
Sundjata, 87
Sutherland, Efua, 8, 24, 35–6, 37, 38, 39, 40, 41; *Edufa*, 37; *The Marriage of Anansewa*, 42

Tavangwena, 195
television productions, 40–1
Tennyson, Alfred, 23, 99
theatre groups and companies: Abibigromma (Ghana), 32; Adzido (Britain), 58; African Brothers International (Ghana), 34; Afrika Cultural Centre (South Africa), 165–6; Azim Trio (The Two Bobs), (Ghana), 35; Amakhosi (Zimbabwe), 206; Anokye Players (Ghana), 39; Arts Centre (Ghana), 39; Arts Council Concert Party (Ghana), 35; Drama Group (Univ. of Zimbabwe), 188; Free Travelling Theatre (Univ. of Makerere) (Uganda), 114; Free Travelling Theatre (Univ. of Nairobi) (Kenya), 114–15; Freelance Players (Ghana), 38; Ghana Drama Studio, 38; Ghanaian Cultural Centre, 39; Guerrilla Theatre Unit (Nigeria), 90, 98; Kakaiku Concert Party (Ghana), 35; Kusum Agromma (Ghana), 41; Legon Road Theatre (Legon 7) (Ghana), 32, 39; Medupe Cultural Group (South Africa), 151; Medu Arts Ensemble (Botswana), 174, 183; Osagyefo Players (Ghana), 18; Pelculef (Botswana), 174; Wazalendo Players (Britain), 111
Themba, Can, 158, 161; *The Will to Die*, 161; *The World of Can Themba*, 158, 161
Thomas, Dylan, 149
Thompson, Tunde, 92
Tizora, Spencer, 205; *Crossroads*, 205
Tlali, Miriam, 151; *Amandla*, 151
Troupe, Quincy, 179
Tutuola, Amos, 56, 63, 88, 96; *The Palmwine Drinkard*, 56
Twain, Mark, 77

Uncle Tom's Cabin, 49
Under African Skies, 58

Vilakazi, B.W., 136
Vorster, J.B., 163, 170

Walker, Alice, 195, 196; *The Color Purple*, 197
Wanguĩ wa Goro, 131, 134, 135
Were, Wasambo, 113
Wesley, Charles, 23
Whitman, Walt, 70; *Leaves of Grass*, 70
Wordsworth, William, 1, 60, 118, 138, 175, 201, 208; 'Daffodils', 24; 'Upon Westminster Bridge', 161
Wortenberg, Joris, 40; *The Corpse's Comedy*, 40; *Osofu Moko* (Le Tartuffe), 40; *Osofu Dadze*, 40
Wright, Richard, *Black Boy*, *Native Son*, 119
writer's associations: Association of Nigerian Authors, 58, 70; Congress of South African Writers (COSAW), 146, 155–6; Creative Writers' Association (Ghana), 8; National Association of Writers (Ghana), 8; Poetry Society of Rhodesia, 205; Union of Writers of African Peoples, 90; Writers' Forum (South Africa), 155; Zimbabwe Writers' Union, 200, 206

Yeats, William Butler, 67
Yevtushenko, E., 169

Zimunya, Musaemura Bonas, 5, 6, 200–15; *And Now the Poets Speak* (see under anthologies); *Country Dawns and City Lights*, 206, 215; *The Fate of Vultures* (see under anthologies); *Kingfisher, Zikinya and Other Poems*, 206, 215; *Those Years of Drought and Hunger*, 200, 215; *Thought-Tracks*, 206, 215; *Zimbabwe Ruins*, 205, 215

Studies in
African Literature
NEW SERIES

HEINEMANN Portsmouth (N.H.)
JAMES CURREY London